The Academic Man

Foundations of Higher Education
David S. Webster, Series Editor

The Academic Man, Logan Wilson,
with a new introduction by Philip G. Altbach

Centers of Learning, Joseph Ben-David,
with a new introduction by Philip G. Altbach

The Distinctive College, Burton R. Clark,
with a new introduction by the author

The Future of the Humanities, Walter Kaufmann,
with a new introduction by Saul Goldwasser

The Higher Learning in America, Robert Maynard Hutchins,
with a new introduction by Harry S. Ashmore

The Ideal of the University, Robert Paul Wolff,
with a new introduction by the author

The Impact of College on Students,
Kenneth A. Feldman and Theodore M. Newcomb,
with a new introduction by Kenneth A. Feldman

Making the Grade, Howard S. Becker, Blanche Geer,
and Everett C. Hughes, with a new introduction by Howard S. Becker

Mission of the University, Jose Ortega y Gasset,
with a new introduction by Clark Kerr

The Organization of Academic Work, Peter M. Blau,
with a new introduction by the author

Rebellion in the University, Seymour Martin Lipset,
with a new introduction by the author

Reforming of General Education, Daniel Bell,
with a new introduction by the author

The Rise of the Meritocracy, Michael Young,
with a new introduction by the author

Universities, Abraham Flexner,
with a new introduction by Clark Kerr

Logan Wilson

With a new introduction
by Philip G. Altbach

The Academic Man

A Study in the Sociology of a Profession

Transaction Publishers
New Brunswick (U.S.A.) and London (U.K.)

New material this edition copyright © 1995 by Transaction Publishers, New Brunswick, New Jersey 08903. Originally published in 1942 by Oxford University Press.

Library of Congress Catalog Number: 94-41612
ISBN: 1-56000-810-5
Printed in the United States of America

Library of Congress Cataloging-in-Publication Data

Wilson, Logan, 1907–
    The academic man : a study in the sociology of a profession / Logan Wilson ; with a new introduction by Philip G. Altbach.
        p. cm.
    Originally published : London : Oxford University Press, 1942.
    Includes bibliographical references and index.
    ISBN 1-56000-810-5
    1. College teachers—United States.   2. Universities and colleges—United States—Social conditions.   3. United States—Social conditions—1933–1945.   I. Title.
LB1778.2.W55   1995
378.1'2—dc20   94-41612
                                                                CIP

CONTENTS

INTRODUCTION TO THE TRANSACTION EDITION ix
PREFACE   xxvii
I. INTRODUCTION   3

PART ONE: THE ACADEMIC HIERARCHY

II. PROFESSIONAL RECRUIT   15
III. STUDENT AND APPRENTICE   33
IV. STAFF MEMBER   53
V. PROFESSOR ADMINISTRANT   71

PART TWO: ACADEMIC STATUS

VI. STATUS APPRAISAL   97
VII. PROFESSIONAL STATUS   113
VIII. SOCIO-ECONOMIC STATUS   134

PART THREE: ACADEMIC PROCESSES AND FUNCTIONS

IX. PRESTIGE AND COMPETITION   157
X. PRESTIGE AND THE TEACHING FUNCTION   175
XI. PRESTIGE AND THE RESEARCH FUNCTION 195

PART FOUR: CONCLUSIONS

XII. CONCLUSIONS   217
APPENDICES   228
INDEX   243

LIST OF TABLES

TABLE   PAGE

I. Relative Demands of Different Types of Service upon Time and Energy of the Academic Staff   105

II. Average Number of Published Studies of Each Type during the Five-Year Period by Members of the Faculties Who Were Connected with the University during the Entire Period   108

III. Cases Relating to Academic Freedom and Tenure between 1928 and 1935   129

IV. Average Annual Salaries Paid for Instruction by Ranks in a Sample of 99 American Colleges and Universities   143

V. Average Annual Income of College Faculty Members at Land-Grant Institutions and Certain Other Professional Groups, 1929-33   145

VI. Regression Weighting of Items of Importance in Staff Competence   159

VII. A Comparison of the Physical Resources of the Thirty Leading Graduate Centers   165

VIII. Bases of Teacher Rating Used by Administrators   180

IX. Frequency Ratings for Ten Living American Economists   189

INTRODUCTION TO THE TRANSACTION EDITION

THE AMERICAN ACADEMIC PROFESSION: PERSISTENT THEMES, ESCALATING CONCERN

IN 1942, Logan Wilson, then head of the Department of Sociology at Tulane University, published his pioneering book on the American academic profession, *The Academic Man*. Very likely the first full-scale social science-based study of this topic, *The Academic Man* has provided a benchmark. Indeed, Wilson himself used it as the base line for his 1979 volume, *American Academics: Then and Now,* and he refers back to his 1942 volume frequently.[1] Much has happened in American higher education since *The Academic Man* was published—massive expansion, the turmoil of the 1960s, greater focus on research in the top-tier institutions, and, of course, the fiscal problems of the past decade and a half. Higher education's "golden age," as Clark Kerr put it, has come and gone. Yet Logan Wilson's book is just as relevant today as when he wrote it. The issues he identified then remain central to any consideration of the American professoriate. His book proves that a historical perspective is useful in understanding the present, and that there is considerable continuity in higher education. A careful reading of *The Academic Man,* perhaps supplemented by David D. Henry's *Challenges Past, Challenges Present: An Analysis of American Higher Education Since 1930* will provide the necessary long-term perspective to understand today's problems.[2]

Logan Wilson had a long and distinguished career in higher education. His bachelor's degree was earned at Sam Houston State College in Texas in 1926; he obtained his doctorate in sociology at Harvard in 1939; and he taught at ten different universities in the United States and abroad. He served as a teacher and administrator at Tulane University, as provost of the University of North Carolina system, as president of the University of Texas at Austin, and later as chancellor of the University of Texas system from 1953 to 1961. For a decade, he was president of the American Council on Education, heading this important organization during the campus turmoil of the 1960s. Logan Wilson is probably best remembered for his two volumes on the American academic profession.

It is interesting that his two volumes on the academic profession were written at the beginning and toward the end of his career. The two books are similar in tone, and his 1979 volume, written after a long career as an academic administrator and as a Washington higher education spokesperson, shows none of the disdain for academics that is characteristic of the writings of many senior administrators. Wilson expresses a deep respect for the professoriate, and sees the centrality of the academic profession for the mission of the university. He understands that professors are a rather special breed, marching sometimes to different drummers.

His two books provide an analysis of the academic profession, rather than a critique of it. They provide a much better basis for understanding a profession that is not only central to the educational enterprise but also provides much of the research and cultural criticism for society as a whole. His books provide a useful counterpoise for such poorly documented and exaggerated attacks as Charles Sykes's *Profscam*[3] and a number of others. Wilson also has a more balanced view of the role of the university in American society than, for example, does Page Smith, who argues that the university has lost its soul because it places too much stress on research.[4] Logan Wilson sees the American university as a central institution and one that is basically sound. He is also able to see the university in a broader historical context.

CAVEATS

It is useful to point to some of the problems in Logan Wilson's analysis of the academic profession. The most glaring is in the title of the book—*The Academic Man*. There is hardly a mention of gender in the volume, although Wilson does point out that in 1942 approximately a quarter of the profession was female. He very briefly acknowledges this omission in his 1979 update, and he proceeds to discuss in a brief section the well-known realities of the situation of women in the academic profession. Gender is, nonetheless, largely ignored in Wilson's work. This is especially surprising in *The Academic Man* because such a significant proportion of the profession was female at the time. Women achieved a somewhat higher proportion in the profession during the 1920s, and their numbers gradually declined through the 1930s. This trend continued after World War II, and only began to reverse itself after the 1960s, with the impetus of the feminist movement and the advent of affirmative action policies in higher education. Only recently has the proportion of women in the professoriate reached the proportions evident in the first two decades of the twentieth century. It is significant, of course, that the involvement of women in the profession was achieved in the 1920s without the benefit of legal arrangements such as affirmative action.

Although Wilson discusses the social class origins of the academic profession, and points out that the academic profession comes largely from middle-class backgrounds, he does not devote much attention to the ethnic and religious makeup of the profession. It is now well known, for example, that there was active discrimination against Jews in the academy prior to World War II. We find no discussion of barriers to participation by a number of groups during the period that he is discussing.

It is possible that Wilson's lack of analysis of gender is related to another problem with his book. Like a number of analysts of American higher education, Wilson is mainly concerned with the top tier of institutions, and of the academic profession. His observations ring true for the top tier of academic institutions, the research universities and prestigious liberal arts colleges, and in these institutions, the proportion of women is lower than in American postsecondary education in general. We learn little about the conditions of the profession in the large number of "normal schools"—institutions devoted to teacher training at the undergraduate level—that were a significant part of the higher education system until the 1950s. These institutions have now largely become "comprehensive universities" and have branched out from a focus on teacher training to general higher education. In his overemphasis on the research universities, Wilson is joined by such contemporary analysts as Henry Rosovsky.[5] Even Charles Sykes and other current critics are more concerned about conditions in the top fifth of the academy than with higher education as a whole. Academics in most of the higher education system spend much time in the classroom and have few opportunities for international travel and other research-related activities. In all of these analyses, there is virtually no discussion of the community of colleges, now constituting a quarter of American postsecondary education, but in the 1940s somewhat less prominent although nonetheless quite important. Perhaps a better title for Wilson's book would have been *The Academic Man in the Top Quarter of American Higher Education*. In Wilson's defense, it should be pointed out that the academic system was smaller and less diverse at the time he wrote his book.

Thus, *The Academic Man* does not tell the whole story of the academic profession—it has a bias toward the elite segment of the postsecondary system, although it is the case that in 1942 this segment comprised a larger segment of higher education than it does today. Logan Wilson makes it clear in his book that he is concerned with both teaching and research, and so it is logical that he would concentrate on that portion of the profession that is involved in these activities.

THE CONTEXT

The American academic system in 1942 had taken the basic configuration that it has today. The system was shaped during the period from 1880 to 1940, with the rise of the research universities, the growth of the great land grant public universities, the development of the community college, and the beginning of a commitment to mass higher education.[6] The basic pattern of the system in 1942 was not significantly different from that of 1995. However, there were some important variations. For example, American postsecondary education now enrolls more than 12 million students. In 1937, enrollments stood at 1,350,905, and the proportion of the age group attending colleges or universities, currently around half of the relevant age group, was considerably smaller in 1942. America was making the move to mass and later to universal access to higher education (usually defined as attendance by at least half the relevant age cohort), but these developments were in their early stages. The "missing element" was the large number of comprehensive colleges and universities in the public sector, which are currently the heart of the academic system and have absorbed the massive enrollment increases of the past several decades. In addition, the intervening period saw the proliferation of community colleges, which have moved to a more vocationally oriented curriculum as well as providing an "open door" for students who could not otherwise obtain a postsecondary education.

There were, in addition, fewer "non-traditional" students—those over the standard 18-22-year-old age group. The student population was more homogenous. African Americans were largely concentrated in the traditionally black institutions, and the proportion of other ethnic and racial minorities was significantly lower. Jewish students were still subject to admission quotas in some institutions, especially in the prestige sector, and there were the vestiges of discrimination against Catholics persisted in some parts of the academic system. While Wilson only discusses the social class background of the academic profession (largely middle class), the academic profession too was much more homogenous than it is today—whiter, somewhat more male, and much less diverse in terms of ethnicity and religious background.

Not only was American higher education a smaller enterprise than it is today, it was also less complex. There were approximately 1,600 colleges and universities, compared to more than double that number today. Individual academic institutions were smaller—very few had enrollments of more than 10,000 students on a single campus. There were no multicampus systems, although there were some branch campuses. The private sector was a significantly larger part of the total academic system than it is today.

Graduate education, one of the main foci of Wilson's book, was even more limited in scope. In 1939, only ninety institutions offered the Ph.D. degree, and only 3,088 doctorates were awarded nationwide. Four-fifths of these were awarded by a mere thirty institutions and more than two-fifths by the ten leading universities. The vast majority of doctorates were awarded by the member institutions of the Association of American Universities, the organization of the top universities, and a much higher proportion than today were given by private universities.

At the time that Logan Wilson wrote *The Academic Man*, the United States was still feeling the effects of the Great Depression. The worst was over, and by 1940 the United

States was involved in supplying the Allies in Europe and in preliminary preparations for war. But the economy did not really improve until after America's entry into the war following Pearl Harbor at the end of 1941. Enrollments modestly fell during the depths of the Depression in the early 1930s, but soon began rising even while the nation faced extreme economic hardship. Faculty salaries declined. Few professors were hired, and at many schools academic staff agreed to share salary cuts rather than see colleagues fired. Tuition could not be increased because students could not afford to pay more for education. Public institutions were faced with even more serious fiscal constraints than have been experienced in the 1990s. There was relatively little support for research, and academics had to be more innovative about securing funds and conducting small-scale research.

While all of the contemporary elements of the academic system were in place in 1942, the system was smaller, somewhat more limited in scope, and was less generously funded. Logan Wilson was one of the first to argue for the centrality of the higher education enterprise and its importance for American society. He saw the potential for higher education's contribution not only to the American economy, but also as a vehicle for social mobility.

The Academic Job Market

Wilson points out that the academic job market was relatively informal. The "old boys" network ruled, and Wilson notes that contacts among senior scholars at the top institutions were the main sources of information about academic jobs. There were fewer top-tier and middle-ranking universities in 1942 and, at lower ranked schools, a larger proportion than now did not possess a doctorate. Wilson's description of the operation of the market a half century ago is virtually the same as the situation later portrayed by Theodore Caplow and Reece McGee in their classic study of the profession, *The Academic Marketplace,* published in 1958.[7] Very little had changed in two or three decades. Markets were highly segmented, with little mobility among the tiers of the academic system. Jobs, according to Wilson, were seldom obtained through a "cold" application. Rather, contacts were made at scientific meetings, and generally contacts were "brokered" by third parties, usually senior scholars. Vacancies were often not publicly advertised. Institutional prestige mattered much, as it continues to do today, and Wilson points out that even a mediocre person from a major university might well have a better chance at a good academic job than a truly brilliant person from a less central place. He notes that most young scholars were looked after by senior mentors, and few had to fend for themselves in a difficult and, in many ways, partially closed marketplace. The academic job market during this period resembles a medieval guild, with apprentices being looked after by masters. Many of Wilson's insights continue to be valid today, although other elements have entered into the equation and emphases may have shifted.

It was only in the 1960s that the academic marketplace significantly changed. The expansion of American higher education that began in the late 1950s and continued unabated until the mid-1970s tremendously increased the size of the professoriate and, for a period, what had been largely a buyer's market became one favoring the seller. Young scholars had their choice of jobs and salaries increased to reflect new market realities. This boom proved to be short-lived, however, and many of Logan Wilson's comments concerning unemployment among degree holders mirror the realities of the 1980s and 1990s. Other changes also took place in the market. The impact of legal requirements relating to affirmative action have brought many new elements to the academic job market, including the need to advertise for positions, monitor such issues as the gender and race of applicants, and to be able to prove the selection process was entirely free of bias, and that special efforts were made to obtain and select candidates from "protected" groups in the society.

Even with the end of the period of rapid expansion of higher education, the job market has become immensely larger and more complex. More than 30,000 doctorates are produced annually in the United States, and by a larger number of institutions at all levels of the academic system. While it is still the case that relatively few Ph.Ds from second-tier universities are able to obtain positions in leading institutions, there is a much more downward mobility in the market. The contemporary phenomenon of part-time and "gypsy" faculty migrating from one temporary job to another is not discussed in *The Academic Man*. Perhaps this tendency was not as pronounced in the 1940s as it is in the 1990s, or maybe Wilson simply chose not to deal with it. The academic market in 1942 was certainly not robust. Wilson indicates that a significant number of new Ph.Ds could not find jobs in their fields, and that doctoral unemployment was by no means unknown.

CONDITIONS OF THE PROFESSORIATE

The "academic man" portrayed by Logan Wilson in 1942 was hardly living in the lap of luxury.[8] Wilson believes that academics are, in general, underpaid for the work that they do when compared to similarly trained professionals. The salary of a full professor in 1942 was, for example, $4,302, hardly a munificent amount even in those days. An assistant professor in a southern university was paid about $2,300, while a full professor at Harvard earned an average salary of $9,700. Wilson points out, as have other commentators, that academics are concerned about prestige and status and that perhaps this accounts for their relatively low salaries. He points out that academic salaries were depressed by the fact that there were many low-paid instructors (perhaps the equivalent of today's part-time faculty), and by the large proportion of "women workers" (this is virtually the only mention made of women academics in the entire book!). Wilson cites data to show that most professors do extra work, most of it related to academe, in order to earn additional income, and most indicate that their salaries are too low to support themselves and their families adequately. Wilson felt that the practice of individual bargaining for salary and the lack of collective bargaining in higher education are additional factors in depressing academic salaries. In his 1979 book, Wilson also decries the relatively low salaries of academics, and cites statistics to show that for decades academic salaries have lagged behind inflation. He notes that severe problems occurred in the inflationary 1970s. He would no doubt have been dismayed by the further deterioration of the salaries during the 1980s!

Even in the 1940s, academics were not especially productive when it came to publications. Wilson cites several surveys to argue that most scholars publish relatively little. An inquiry from the American Historical Association notes that only a quarter of Ph.Ds in history are consistent producers. Another study of mathematicians noted that 46 percent published no papers following graduation; only about 10 percent were very productive in terms of published papers. On the other hand, a detailed study of the faculty at the University of Chicago, at the time one of the largest producers of Ph.Ds in the country and generally considered the second most prestigious university in the nation, found that 70 percent of the total faculty were making consistent scholarly contributions in the 1924–1929 period. The average number of publications by each Chicago professor over a five-year period was 10.8, including books, articles, reviews, and so forth. One can see that, overall, the American professoriate was not especially productive in terms of publications. At the same time, scholars and scientists at the top institutions published a great deal more than did their colleagues lower in the academic pecking order.

The figures cited by Wilson concerning the time spent by faculty in teaching and other academic activities differ little from the results of more recent studies. There is a consistency across the decades—although some recent studies claim that teaching loads in the top-tier institutions have declined during the boom years of the 1960s and have not markedly increased since then. But these institutions account for only a small proportion of American academe. Professors in the 1940s spent more time on their academic duties than the average for other workers in the economy. They spent the largest proportion of their time on teaching, and saw themselves mainly as teachers. While statistics are not cited for academics in the various tiers of the academic system, research seemed to be mainly a function of the top institutions—just as it is today. From the incomplete data cited in this book, it would seem that academics today work somewhat harder than did their compeers a half century ago.

While the academic "marketplace" has had its ups and downs, the basic roles of the academic have not changed much. Wilson devotes considerable attention to what he calls the "professor administrant." By this he means that faculty throughout the academic system have multiple roles, including the administration of academic programs and departments. He discusses at some length the roles of department chair, dean, and other administrative posts typically held by faculty members. In 1942, the professionalized administrative cadre that characterize today's colleges and universities had by and large not yet appeared, and faculty members had a greater responsibility for day to day administration. At the same time, although Wilson does not discuss it much, most academic institutions took *in loco parentis* more seriously. Faculty, especially at the less prestigious schools, were involved with regulating the lives of students and, to some extent, with extracurricular activities in a way that largely disappeared with the student revolts of the 1960s.[9]

At the same time, most colleges and universities were much less complex institutions than is the case today. They were, as noted, generally smaller, and many of the functions now required of an academic institution had not yet evolved. The immensely complex web of accountability, especially in the public institutions, was largely absent. Few reports were required by federal or state bureaucracies. In fact, there was little federal support for higher education in the period prior to World War II. The immensely bureaucratic state higher education systems that emerged following the 1950s were also absent—campuses dealt directly with state government authorities. Private institutions were just that—private—and they controlled their destinies without much external control (or much assistance either).

The complex governance and faculty senate structures that characterize the contemporary university were largely absent. Governance was carried out in meetings of the general faculty. Departments were generally smaller, and internal administration easier. At the same time, it is generally agreed that at lower-tier schools there was a considerable degree of control by the president, and sometimes the trustees, with faculty subject to administrative authority.

While Logan Wilson specifically excluded a careful discussion of academic freedom in his book—a decision that seems surprising in a comprehensive study of the academic profession—he does note that teachers who engender academic freedom cases tend to have "deviant" personal characteristics as well as institutional behavior; they are, he argues, "difficult" people whose personal traits combine with academic unorthodoxy to create problem cases. He reports that the AAUP's Committee on Academic Freedom and Tenure handled about seventy-five cases annually during the 1930s, and it is likely that this is only the tip of an unreported iceberg. Wilson devotes no discussion at all to the growth in faculty radicalism and its consequences on campus during the 1930s, when a small but significant number of professors were attracted to leftist causes. He comments that faculty members were generally more concerned about salary and conditions on campus than with academic freedom.

RESEARCH ON THE ACADEMIC PROFESSION

Logan Wilson pioneered the sociological study of the academic profession, and in this respect he made a significant contribution to our understanding of American higher education. He not only provides insights concerning the professoriate but he also adds to our understanding of the history of colleges and universities at an important juncture. Wilson's 1942 book stands virtually alone as a full-scale study of the profession. Further, in the thirty-seven years between the publication of his two books on the professoriate, there was not a great deal of research carried out. The professoriate only became more frequently studied after the 1960s.[10] Social scientists study virtually every other social group in society, but they have been reluctant to study themselves. It is only recently that academics have been seen as an important group in the population. With more than 400,000 full-time academics in the United States, the professoriate is a large and increasingly differentiated population. Furthermore, the professoriate is a very influential group, not only as educators of the future elites, but also as researchers and analysts of the society and culture. Academics contribute to the op-ed pages of influential newspapers and are vocal in the nation's cultural debates.[11]

While it is beyond the scope of this discussion to analyze the now quite substantial literature on the academic profession, it can be said to fall into two broad categories. There is a significant body of research studies dealing with virtually all aspects of the professoriate. There is also a much smaller, but highly influential literature mainly concerned with criticizing the profession. These books, written largely from a conservative perspective, have attracted a fairly wide readership. Unfortunately, many of the generalizations made in these studies are not truthful assessments of the profession.[12] These books have not helped the image of American higher education or of the academic profession in a difficult period.

A much larger body of literature concerning the academic profession is based on social science studies. These studies cover a broad range of topics relating to the profession—from political attitudes, to working conditions, to views about teaching and evaluation. Economists have looked at the remuneration of the professoriate.[13] Other social scientists have examined the attitudes of the professoriate on a range of topics, including political views, perspectives on teaching and learning, and attitudes concerning social issues. These attitude surveys seem to have started in earnest only in the 1960s. *The Academic Man* provides us with no hints concerning what the professoriate thinks, although there were a few studies done concerning professorial views in the pre-World War II period.

Sociologists have looked at the characteristics of the profession in terms of social class, gender, ethnicity, and other factors. This literature indicates that not only is the professoriate much larger than it was when Logan Wilson wrote his book, but it is also more diverse and differentiated. The proportion of women is somewhat higher than it was in the 1940s, and the number of racial minorities has greatly increased. The profession today presents a much less Protestant, upper middle-class profile than it did in 1942. Nonetheless, the professoriate remains predominantly a male, white, and middle-class group.

One can gain additional insights about the academic profession, and especially about public perceptions of professors, through novels. There are a surprising number of novels that feature professors. Novels about professors existed in the 1940s, but it seems that the genre has greatly expanded in the postwar period. Numerous American novelists have written about professors; among them are Mary McCarthy, Saul Bellow, John Updike, and Joyce Carol

Oates. While the portrayal of academics is often not especially favorable in novels, fiction tells us a good deal about
the image of the academic profession.

The literature on the academic profession is large and
varied. Logan Wilson would have greater difficulty writing
The Academic Man today than he had in 1941 because he
would have to take into account a much larger amount of
data. In 1941, Wilson was able to obtain and reflect on much
of the relevant literature. Today, this would be a very considerable task. Yet, there are many holes in the existing research: we know very little about entire segments of the
profession (community college teachers, for example); research on teaching styles and attitudes toward teaching is
quite limited; our understanding of some subsegments of
the profession (African-American faculty, for example) is
minimal; and we know very little, in detail, about the culture of academic life in various academic disciplines.

CONCLUSION

The Academic Man is a book that is central to understanding American higher education from several perspectives.
It is one of the first detailed analyses dealing specifically
with the professoriate. Logan Wilson was preceded by
Thorstein Veblen, whose analysis of the university, published in 1918, had some choice observations on the professoriate.[14] Wilson's is certainly the first book to compile
the available social science literature in order to understand the professoriate. Thus, Logan Wilson provided the
basis for later research on the academic profession, defining some of the key variables for analyzing the topic.

This book provides a sociological portrait of a profession at an important juncture in the development of the
American university. Wilson's research was done just prior
to the turmoil of the Second World War and before the
great expansion of the postwar period. The profession
portrayed in *The Academic Man* is perhaps the last vestige

of the "old regime" in American higher education—a time when the academic system was relatively small, when academics were regarded with great esteem by society but were nonetheless significantly underpaid and remained somewhat at the margins of society. The price of postwar expansion—and the consequent movement of higher education to the center of American society—has been accountability, bureaucratization, and, to some degree, the loss of community on campus.[15] *The Academic Man* also is an important historical document because it provides an original analysis of American higher education at a specific point in time. Perhaps most crucial, *The Academic Man* helps us to understand the issues facing the academic profession today. It provides both a historical and a sociological perspective.

Philip G. Altbach

Chestnut Hill, Massachusetts
February 1995

NOTES

1. Logan Wilson, *The Academic Man,* (New York, Oxford University Press, 1942. Logan Wilson, *American Academics: Then and Now,* New York, Oxford University Press, 1979.

2. David D. Henry, *Challenges Past, Challenges Present: An Analysis of American Higher Education since 1930,* San Francisco, Jossey Bass, 1975.

3. Charles J. Sykes, *Profscam: Professors and the Demise of Higher Education,* New York, Regenery, 1988. See also Richard M. Huber, *How Professors Play the Cat Guarding the Cream,* Fairfax, Va., George Mason University Press, 1992, and George H. Douglas, *Education without Impact: How Our Universities Fail the Young,* New York, Birch Lane Press, 1992.

4. Page Smith, *Killing the Spirit: Higher Education in America,* New York, Viking, 1990.

5. Henry Rosovsky, *The University: An Owner's Manual,* New York, Norton, 1990.

6. For a discussion of the development of the American postsecondary system in the twentieth century, see Laurence Veysey, *The Emergence of the American University,* Chicago, University of Chicago Press, 1965, and Steven Brint and Jerome Karabel, *The Diverted Dream: Community College and the Promise of Educational Opportunity in America, 1900–1985,* New York, Oxford University Press, 1989.

7. Theodore Caplow and Reece McGee, *The Academic Marketplace,* New York, Basic Books, 1958.

8. For a discussion of the current situation of faculty, see Philip G. Altbach, "Challenge and Change: The American Professoriate," in P. G. Altbach, R. O. Berdahl, and P. Gumport, eds., *Higher Education in American Society,* Buffalo, N. Y., Prometheus Books, 1994, pp. 225–48.

9. For a further discussion of student culture and the role of the faculty, see Helen Lefkowitz Horowitz, *Campus Life: Undergraduate Cultures from the Beginning of the 18th Century to the Present,* Chicago, University of Chicago Press, 1987.

10. For an analysis of the literature on the professoriate, see Martin Finkelstein, *The Academic Profession: A Synthesis of Social Science Inquiry since World War Two,* Columbus, Ohio State University Press, 1984.

11. For a further discussion of this theme, see Philip G. Altbach, "The Politics of Students and Faculty," in Burton Clark and T. N. Postlethwaite, eds., *International Encyclopedia of Higher Education,* Oxford, England, Pergamon, 1993, pp. 1438–45.

12. See note 3 for examples of recent critiques.

13. The most comprehensive data concerning the economic status of the professoriate is collected by the American Association of University Professors and published annually in its journal, *Academe.*

14. Thorstein Veblen, *The Higher Learning: A Memorandum on the Conduct of Universities by Businessmen,* New York, B. W. Huebsch, 1918.

15. A similar landmark volume which provides a snapshot of American higher education at the beginning of the 1960s is Christopher Jencks and David Riesman's *Academic Revolution,* Garden City, N. Y., Doubleday, 1968.

PREFACE

THIS BOOK about the academic man is written in a spirit neither of praise nor of pique. Rather, it is intended as an objective description and analysis of a special occupational culture. As a participant in this culture, I was initially curious to see what light a sociological treatment of structure and function might throw upon personnel problems of the academic profession. If, on the whole, less attention seems to be given to the satisfactions than to the dissatisfactions of a university career, it should be remembered that problems of social organization appear in the latter nexus. Throughout the work I have tried to maintain a detached point of view, and my presentation of the subject is expository rather than argumentative.

Since no single investigator could gather all of the material used in this inquiry, I have drawn freely upon a wide range of sources. I am indebted directly and indirectly to many persons, and wherever reference is made to published data, credit is given. It is impossible here to express thanks to the innumerable academicians who have helped in checking and extending first-hand observations in a variety of institutions.

I do want to note my special obligation, however, to a number of men. For certain germinal ideas of this study, acknowledgment is due Willard Waller, of Columbia University. For criticisms and suggestions during various stages of the inquiry, I wish to thank the following: P. A. Sorokin, C. C. Zimmerman, Talcott Parsons, and Gordon Allport, of Harvard University; Robert K. Merton, of Columbia University; and Read Bain, of Miami University. For reading the manuscript and suggesting revisions, I am indebted to Hans Gerth, of the University of

Wisconsin; Carl S. Joslyn, Harold C. Hand, and C. W. E. Hintz, of the University of Maryland; Kingsley Davis, of Pennsylvania State College; and Paul W. Ward, Chairman of Committee T of the American Association of University Professors.

For permission to quote copyright materials I am grateful to the following publishers: American Book Co., The Antioch Press, D. Appleton-Century Co., Harvard University Press, McGraw-Hill Book Co., The Macmillan Co., Oxford University Press, The Science Press, University of North Carolina Press, and W. W. Norton Co. Permission to reproduce printed matter was also granted by the American Council on Education, Brown University, Teachers College, Columbia University, and the University of Chicago Alumni Committee. In addition, I wish to express appreciation for permission to quote from the following periodicals: *American Historical Review, The Atlantic* (and Professor Carl J. Friedrich), *Popular Science Monthly, School and Society,* and *The Scientific Monthly.* Finally, I am indebted to *The Journal of Higher Education* and the *Journal of Social Philosophy* for permission to incorporate large parts of my own articles originally appearing in these publications, and to the *A. A. U. P. Bulletin* for the same privilege, as well as for making extensive citations from its various issues.

L. W.

New Orleans
January 1942

INTRODUCTION: THE ACADEMIC MAN

I. INTRODUCTION

EVERY society considering itself civilized has a special class of persons with an institutionalized concern in that part of culture known as the higher learning. Members of the class *homo academicus* flatter themselves upon differing from the common run of men by having their ideas and attitudes less directly and exclusively derived from simple sensory impression. Laymen in turn acknowledge this differentiation. Yet they do not always take it as a mark of superiority, as is evidenced by the depreciatory tone used to characterize certain types of problems as being of 'purely academic interest.' Regardless of the truth or falsity of identifying the academic mind with impracticality, the special folkways and mores of the profession afford an inviting subject for sociological inquiry.

THE ACADEMICIAN AS AN OBJECT OF INQUIRY

Since this book is about the academic man, it is pertinent to state here the sense in which the designation will be used. What the phrase means is best seen in terms of a functional definition. Broadly stated, the basic functions of academicians everywhere are the conservation, dissemination, and innovation of knowledge. So varied and complex are these tasks, however, that the English language has no precise generic word for the functionary. In the line of professional duty, academicians may be engaged in everything from lecturing to mothers' clubs to peering into the outer limits of the universe. Latinists, economists, and physicists share university

3

berths with professors of advertising, manual training, and folk dancing.

Specialists in every field participate in both teaching and research. The words 'teacher' and 'professor' connote the diffusion of learning, while neglecting other kinds of endeavor.[1] The word 'scientist' implies cultural discovery or invention, but under-emphasizes conservation and dissemination. Using any existing appellation does some violence to the fact that the functionary seldom operates exclusively in any one role. As we are obliged to refer to materials using common designations in a rather loose sense, we shall refrain from furthering confusion by the coinage of still another term. Instead, with distinctions noted wherever necessary, the academician will be variously referred to as a scholar, teacher, educator, researcher, and scientist. Although medievalists and professors of dairy husbandry are as far apart in their main intellectual interests as bankers and brain surgeons, both of the former have a common locus as employees of the university.

It is with the occupational culture of the university world rather than the specific technological functions of its members that we are primarily concerned. Much has been written about various phases of the higher learning in this country— so much in fact that it may appear supererogatory to say more. Lay novelists and essayists as well as professors, deans, and presidents have all had their word. In addition to informal commentaries there are the more formal reports of numerous investigating committees, special interest groups, and statistical agencies. Despite a plethora of miscellaneous matter, there is as yet no single work giving a broad but unified view of the academic profession in its institutional setting. Nowhere is there available an over-all treatment such as cultural anthropologists give of primitive associations, or such as sociolo-

[1] As has been noted by several facetious members of the profession, a professor in this country may be many things besides a member of a college or university faculty. He may be a secondary school teacher, an instructor in a barbering college or a business school, a quack 'psychologist,' a circus barker, or even a piano player in a house of prostitution.

gists have set forth for a few occupational groupings in our own society.

Indeed, on the basis of present sociological literature the future historian would have less difficulty in ascertaining the social behavior of the railroader, the taxi-dancer, or the professional thief than he would that of the contemporary university professor. Of more immediate import—especially for prospective or young academicians—is the fact that only through the retrospect of actual life experience or by reference to widely scattered sources can one obtain a comprehensive knowledge of the occupational culture of the academic man, together with a candid delineation of the satisfactions and dissatisfactions of a university career.

The Academic Man is a work designed to meet this need by providing an objective basis for understanding professional life as it exists within the social organization of the contemporary American university. It should prove of interest to persons deliberating entry into any branch of the profession, to administrators who may have forgotten how institutional problems appear from the staff perspective, and to general readers who may be curious about what goes on behind the scenes of university organization. Faculty members themselves should find unfamiliar and useful data bearing on familiar problems, as well as a sociological insight into situations that remain obscure when seen merely on the common-sense level.

The Purpose of This Study

The purpose of this book is to bring together related material from a wide variety of sources, systematize it according to a logical scheme, and present an ordered view of the complex roles and processes in which the academician participates. This study is neither a historical treatise nor a cross-sectional investigation of any particular university. Rather, it is a description and analysis of behavior patterns found in almost all leading American universities today.

Specific problems appear as intermediate or end products of an inquiry into one sector of a general field. This field, the sociology of the professions, has emerged so recently that the present work had to proceed without benefit of methodological models in dealing with the whole structure of one of our major professions. With certain modifications, the scheme of analysis might be used in studying any occupation having the status of a profession.

Let us get clearly in mind at the start that we are not concerned with the entire teaching profession, or even with the occupational culture of all persons employed in the higher learning. Institutions of higher education differ widely in aims, facilities, procedures, levels of accomplishment, and in other respects. There is no exact pattern to which they all conform. Since university environments in which academicians work vary extensively, according to the kind of knowledge they profess to advance and the type of men they purport to produce, we shall confine ourselves to the mode of organization found in the central or major universities. By central or major universities is meant such centers of research and advanced study as Harvard, Chicago, Columbia, Yale, California, Wisconsin, and others that rank high in the universe of learning.[2] Only for the sake of comparison and contrast is reference made to situations found in lesser universities and in other types of institutions of higher learning. Major universities have been selected for a number of reasons. In the first place, these institutions wield the most influence in setting the pattern of higher learning; in the second place, it is only in such centers that there is sufficient uniformity to yield the kind of generalizations in which we are interested.

The organization of the university, which is largely the organization of the occupation, is treated as a social system in which every part exists in an interdependent relation to

[2] The distinguishing characteristics of the major university are mentioned in various chapters of this study. For a list of the thirty leading graduate centers in this country, see Table VII and Appendix I.

every other part. Hence there is a delineation of the formal and informal organization of the university, the influences it brings to bear upon recruits and employees, and the reactions of personalities to certain derived problems. Emphasis is placed upon factors within this social system, and these are treated in terms of a typological academic man. Consistent with the use of the typological or ideal type concept, extreme cases and crucial situations are often utilized, since averages tend to blur distinctive features of the social phenomena described.

Problems of the Academic Profession

Since one cannot observe social facts in the same way that one observes birds or other concrete entities, there must be some frame of reference or point of view to guide the selection of materials. Concrete reality being inexhaustible, one must choose a method for selecting and analyzing data. Because the general reader is not interested in methodological concerns, however, they will be made as unobtrusive as possible, on the assumption that they should be implicit rather than explicit. Or, as someone has put it, the scaffolding of a building, indispensable in process, should be removed when the structure is finished.

Here we shall merely state some of the focal points of inquiry. What are the more significant problems that confront participants in the occupational culture of the academic world? What are the various statuses and functions of such individuals? How is the academic career affected by the social processes of the contemporary American university? Considering the amount of curiosity about such questions, it is astonishing that we have so little systematic knowledge about those social institutions having intellectual activity as their primary function.

Society at large has an interest in the end-products of science and scholarship, but its concern is indirect and impersonal. Those persons within the academic profession, or who may be contemplating membership, have a direct and personal relation to the higher learning. Possible recruits for the profession want to know about the responsibilities and privileges of an academic career. What are the qualifications demanded? How are individuals recruited? Does the supply exceed the demand? [3]

Once he has appraised his own interests and qualifications with as much care as possible, the student deciding upon academic work as a life career needs to pick his field of specialization and choose his college or university with much more foresight than does the person who goes into higher education primarily for non-professional training. Few young people are aware in advance of the general nature of the conditioning process, or where the best training may be obtained. What is the prestige value in ulterior terms of a degree from a given institution? What does it offer in the way of placement possibilities later? One finds scant mention of such intensely practical questions in the ordinary vocational guidance brochure, and educators are apparently averse to having other departments of academic endeavor rated in the same way that medical schools are. Answers are obtained largely through informal channels whose accuracy is often very dubious.

At the end of a long and rather arduous period of conditioning, the fledgling Ph.D. today no longer enjoys the bargaining power that mere possession of the degree once betokened, and as competition becomes keener, the matter of placement grows more critical. Where may employment be expected, and how is it secured? Since the young doctor of philosophy usually has had some teaching experience, he has an idea of what will be required of him as an instructor, but what knowledge does he have of normal career expectancies? When may he anticipate becoming an assistant professor, an associate professor, a full professor, and under what conditions? Although all employees of the university share many

[3] Cf. Harold C. Hand's chapter, 'Problems Confronting the Student Who Is Contemplating Education as a Life Career' (by the Stanford University Education Faculty), in *The Challenge of Education*, N. Y., McGraw-Hill, 1937.

common problems of tenure and status, each level of the hierarchy has its peculiar features. In order to avoid false starts and unnecessary mistakes, the novice needs advance knowledge.

Many of his perplexities center about the matter of status. How will his services be evaluated? Should he concentrate his best energies upon teaching or upon research? Will he be called upon to play antipodal roles? Unlike the average doctor or lawyer, the academician is an employee. The novice soon discovers that this fact has all sorts of implications for his status as an intellectual worker. He hears much said about academic freedom, and yet he may at times wonder to what extent his opinions really are free, and upon what effective organizations he may depend to support his status as a professional.

No matter how zealous the beginner's devotion to the higher learning as a calling, he cannot be indifferent to the socio-economic status of the profession. What are the salaries in various brackets within the profession? How do professors live? How do their modes of life affect their own and their families' personalities? The young man with a career decision before him requires objective data in order to choose wisely. He should know what kind of regimen he will be subjected to, the personal qualities demanded, and the sort of prestige commanded by average and by unusual success within a given field of specialization.

Aside from acquiring a necessary or desirable technical competence, the young academician must become acquainted with the university as a social system. How are its objectives phrased for staff members? Partially in lieu of the pecuniary rewards of commercial enterprise, the university system holds out for him a great many other varieties of prestige symbols. Notwithstanding these returns, the absence of high monetary rewards should not be mistaken for an absence of competition. Divergent types of colleges and universities compete on different levels, and the individual should seek the kind of competition for which he is best suited.

In many institutions, staff functions are phrased primarily with reference to teaching and personal functions. In other places, the highest prestige values are reserved for researchers. Everywhere there are techniques for 'getting on' that have indirect as well as direct relations to merit. What are these techniques? Do they lend themselves to a Machiavellian analysis?

ACADEMIC STATUSES AND ROLES

If our objective were merely to gather materials for a work in vocational guidance, then common-sense answers to these questions would be sufficient. A major purpose of this study, however, is to inquire into the institutional as well as the individual aspects of the social organization of academic life. Fortunately, the sociological concepts of role and status enable us to look at problems from both points of view.

As those acquainted with the terminology of social science are aware, an individual's total status is the position he occupies in society. Status is determined by all sorts of reciprocal relations, so that one's self or social personality is the net result of these relations. Certain statuses are ascribed on the basis of sex, age, class position, et cetera, and entail definite or vague rights and duties. Other statuses, such as being a professor, Rotarian, Republican, are primarily achieved, but they also involve rights and duties. Role is the acting out of status, or the dynamic side of social position.[4]

Within the college or university, as in any other social system, these statuses or social positions supply the principal facets composing the occupational whole. Such statuses as we are to deal with are social positions created formally or informally by the social organization of higher learning, and

[4] The concepts of role and status have been developed in the works of such social scientists as R. E. Park, G. H. Mead, E. W. Burgess, and Ralph Linton.

when occupied by concrete persons they become individual roles. The acting out of statuses is seen dynamically in the functional aspects of organization.

The social organization in which individuals participate must be regarded, therefore, from the point of view of function (what it does) as well as of structure (what it is). A university with a large number of well-supported professorships cannot function effectively merely because it has a sound plan of social architecture. Its structure must be activated by competent persons who make it a 'going concern,' as the economists would say. Structure and function, moreover, stand in a mutual relation. Just as a well-organized university can get nowhere with a weak staff, so do able academicians find themselves handicapped by membership in a poorly organized and articulated institution.

And so we come to the conclusion of our introductory remarks on the academician as a subject of inquiry. In Part i we shall follow a hypothetical staff member through the various levels of the academic hierarchy as he ascends the occupational ladder. Part ii deals with the more important problems of status—status evaluation, socio-economic status, and professional status. The social processes and functions found in academic endeavor are set forth in Part iii. Conclusions are given in Part iv.

We shall see that each special relation between structure and function provides a nucleus about which expected problems cluster as we proceed, and shall note how the integration of these relations into a pattern gives them significance. There are other ways in which the subject might be organized, but this general scheme has the merit of being both simple and workable. Since our field of interest and method of approach should be clear at this stage, let us now turn to the first social situation in which the academician finds himself.

PART I

THE ACADEMIC HIERARCHY

II. PROFESSIONAL RECRUIT

Entering university work as a life career is very much like entering matrimony: everybody agrees that it is an important event but so many intangibles are involved that nobody knows exactly how it happens. The candidate must choose and be chosen, and despite the indeterministic beliefs of a democratic society, chance and the pressure of circumstances are just as decisive as sentiment and rational choice.

In any case, the status in which the prospective academician initially finds himself is the result of many variables. Whether the observer takes the 'superiority' position that social selection causes superior individuals to be drawn upward, or the 'privilege' view that members of an envied occupation are there as a result of good fortune rather than any marked biological endowments, there is no gainsaying that occupations ranking high in prestige and desirability usually impose rigid requirements. These are particularly exacting in the case of the major professions, so that many aspirants are debarred by lack of ability, social background, or financial resources.

Though standards of training and licensure admit a good many of the unfit as well as discouraging much potential talent, imperfections in the recruiting process do not nullify its main utility. Since this process is a very elaborate one in the academic profession, we want to know how it determines the status of occupational recruits. The class position of persons entering the professions is usually high enough to give them the economic independence needed for the exercise of choice; hence it is of interest from this perspective to know why large numbers of them should launch upon the academic career.

Where individual choice can be exercised, the general prestige of an occupation becomes an important factor in selection. That the academic profession ranks high in this respect is indicated by a number of investigations of the prestige values assigned various occupations by college students, business and professional men, and even C.C.C. workers. In no instance was the college professor given a rank lower than fourth, and the academic profession was consistently surpassed only by the medical profession. Such speech-reactions are not an infallible index to drawing power (as is evidenced by the high position invariably given the ministry), but they are indicative of the positive attractions of a university career.

Possibilities of Negative Selection

Regardless of positive selection for employment in the higher learning, it is very likely that a number of negative elements enter the sifting process. Many individuals still lack vocational orientation upon completing a general education, and simply go on into the graduate school as the next obvious step at hand. A liberal education is of direct occupational utility only in teaching or research, and hence continuation in graduate school often means a life commitment to academic work.

Dilatory inclinations or avoidance motivations also influence choice. Confronted with such facts or impressions as the clergy's diminished drawing power, the unsavory nature of politics, the routine of civil service, the large capital outlay or low starting salaries in business, the greater necessity for self-financed training and placement contacts in medicine, law, engineering, and other professions, a college graduate may elect academic work as an alternative. Further, the higher learning complex undoubtedly contributes to a certain type of temporarily unemployed, the 'learned unemployed,' who are unwilling to take whatever jobs may be directly available upon graduation, and who continue their college work on a higher level for this reason.

A recent inquiry conducted by the Carnegie Foundation [1] has shown that formal education is a rather faulty sifting mechanism, and especially so for those who become teachers in secondary schools. It was found that 'about 25 per cent of the pupils who were in college for at least two years after leaving high school had lower high-school test scores than over half of those who left high school to go to work'; furthermore, prospective teachers, the traditional 'beneficiaries of special care and attention,' were in fact 'below all other group averages [for college students] except those of the business, art, agriculture, and secretarial candidates.'

It is important to add that the implications of this conclusion for college teaching, a predominantly male occupation, are altered by the fact that 'among the prospective teachers graduating from arts colleges and technical schools the male contingent alone ranks high . . . higher than any other large occupational group, except, in the second test, engineers' (op. cit., pp. 38-9). These results suggest that superior individuals are recruited for college and university positions.

Notwithstanding, the notion persists in certain quarters that the academic profession is not on an equal plane with other major professions in its power to attract the ablest men. There is the widely quoted remark of the academician-literary critic, Stuart Sherman: 'The very best men do not enter upon graduate study at all; the next best drop out after a year's experiment, the mediocre men at the end of two years; the most unfit survive and become doctors of philosophy, who go forth and reproduce their "kind".' A similar, but more seriously held opinion was advanced by the late Professor W. E. Dodd:

And here come the problems: the ambitious young folk enter business, for that leads to what modern society calls

[1] William S. Learned and Ben D. Wood, *The Student and His Knowledge*, N. Y., Carnegie Foundation for the Advancement of Teaching, 1938.

success, the handling of vast sums of money or evidences of money. The second class or even the third class of young folk enter upon the professions, perhaps the lesser lights upon the profession of teaching. Business dulls and deadens the minds of the capable; the professions lead into high specializations (medicine, law) or into a slow broadening of the mind of the less intellectual (preaching and teaching and writing). What we have then is to take in the main the poorest material and make of it the thinking element of the country.[2]

Various university people comment from time to time upon the desirability of attracting abler recruits into the profession, and A.A.U.P. arguments for security of tenure and higher salaries are often rationalized in this way.

Professors may be more candidly self-critical than lawyers, doctors, and engineers, or it may be that the complexity of their standards engenders an unwarranted sense of inadequacy. The actual situation concerning the composition of recruits varies from one department and university to another, but at Harvard, to cite only one leading graduate center, it has been found that a disproportionately high number of honors graduates go into graduate work. Of still wider validity are the findings of the Committee on Personnel of the Social Science Research Council, that 32.5 per cent of 1,765 first-year graduate students had been graduated from college with high honors or their equivalent.

Social Origins of Professional Recruits

We can thus dismiss the notion that academic recruits are of inferior intellectual caliber. The impression that they are more of an intellectual than a social elite, however, may be a more logical inference. Unquestionably the emphasis upon course marks as a basis of selection places more premium upon scholarly aptitude than upon general cultural attainments. With such a criterion, the membership of the group inevitably

[2] From Marcus W. Jernegan, 'Productivity of Doctors of Philosophy in History,' *American Historical Review*, XXXIII, 1927, p. 19.

includes large numbers of persons who have undergone an abrupt rise in the class structure. That university and college work do provide a comparatively open channel for social as well as occupational ascent is borne out by at least one comprehensive inquiry.

A circularization of 4,667 members of the American Association of University Professors [3] revealed the following social origins of academicians, according to the occupational status of their fathers (distribution in terms of percentages): businessmen, 26.6; farmers, 24.7; manual workers, 12.1; clergymen, 10.6; teachers, 5.1; physicians, 5.1; lawyers, 4.1; professors, 3.9; chemists and engineers, 3.0; public officials, 1.9; editors and writers, 1.2; artists and musicians, 1.0. Although comparable figures are not available, it is a matter of common observation that in many other occupations, notably the medical profession, where doctors are often the sons of doctors, there is more social inheritance of occupation, and less recruiting from below middle class ranks.

The social composition of the academic group, together with its economic status, as will be seen later, makes for strongly democratic-minded faculties, typically plebeian cultural interests outside the field of specialization, and a generally philistine style of life. If one were looking for comparisons in other societies, American academicians would have more points in common socially with the new quasi-proletarian intelligentsia of the U.S.S.R. than with the aristocratically inclined university staffs of pre-Nazi Germany.

In making the ascent from lower class origins, academic recruits are more likely to acquire the intellectual than the social graces. Except in the humanities, the regimen of becoming a professor may indeed so groove the social personality that it is left undeveloped culturally and artistically outside the field of specialization. It may be that young men are recruited in disproportionate numbers from the 'greasy grinds' who have

[3] B. W. Kunkel, 'A Survey of College Teachers,' *Bulletin of the A.A.U.P.*, xxiv, 1938, p. 262.

eschewed or been denied full participation in such socializing forms of undergraduate life as fraternities and clubs, athletic activities, and other extra-curricular affairs.

Social and family background are not to be minimized as factors in eventual occupational placement, but they are of less importance than in those professions where personal factors have a major role. Since graduate work is from the economic point of view a more accessible channel for vertical mobility than are most other types of professional training, it is logical to assume (but difficult to prove) that mental superiority is more often coupled with proletarian characteristics among scientists and scholars than is the case in other professions. It appears, then, that individual instances of faulty speech, boorish manners, bad dress, and general uncouthness are primarily the results of a system of selection that stresses what a man knows rather than how he appears.

While personality inadequacies may constitute no source of embarrassment to those persons who have elevated their status, professional members who are acutely sensitive about the general social prestige of the academic group readily become desirous of introducing non-intellectual criteria of selectivity. These criteria would be similar to those already in effect in many medical schools, which have quotas and specious 'psychological tests' designed to diminish recruits from certain social classes and ethnic groups, or to eliminate those possessing undesirable personality traits, regardless of their social origin. Whether it is possible to increase the number of social fraternity pins without at the same time decreasing the number of Phi Beta Kappa keys that embellish graduate student vests is a matter which these policy makers have not considered very seriously.

INDUCEMENTS TO ENTRY

At any rate, the sentiment that the selective process is defective cannot be ascribed to a few malcontents. This 'defect' is sometimes attributed to the lack of inducements which the academic career offers. Enthusiasms are diminished by prospect of the grind for the Ph.D. A. Lawrence Lowell expresses the view held by many educators that what is needed is not so much subsidies for training as 'a great prize to be won by facing an obstacle,' that less encouragement should be given to good but docile scholars with 'little energy, independence, or ambition,' and that there is a danger at present of attracting an industrious mediocrity.

The whole question of student subsidy and staff remuneration is a complicated one. In a society where success is commonly measured by affluence, there may be little inducement for the able, aggressive individual with high standard of living requirements to enter a profession in which the range of remuneration from the highest to the lowest brackets is not wide. The lack of financial incentive, however, is offset by reasonably secure tenure, public esteem (sometimes overplayed as a sop for low pay), pleasant work and surroundings, sufficient leisure for the pursuit of personal interests, and so on. Even though the average young recruit had the knowledge to calculate all such mundane considerations as requisite training, monetary returns, the opportunity for advancement, and the probable demands upon him, it is doubtful that his selection would be lacking in irrational elements. Often he has in mind a real or fictitious 'model' based upon some person he has known or upon a composite type embodying all the favored attributes of success in an idealized career. Seldom does the aspirant consider realistically his own probable achievement.

He is likely to have false ideas or to lack precise information concerning even such a matter as earnings. The academic recruit may have decided against medicine as a career, for example, because of a mistaken belief that doctors go through an initial starvation period. Again, if he accepts the modest remuneration of university work as an unavoidable concomitant of pure research, he may be unaware that its closest approximation is much better paid in government service. Further, he may believe the myth that professors are less well paid than plumbers, when actually professorial incomes almost triple those in the skilled trades.

INSTITUTIONAL ASPECTS OF SELECTION

The composition and the status of recruits to the academic profession are influenced by complementary factors. Organized higher learning elects the man of thought rather than the man of action, just as this temperamental type is more likely to choose teaching and research because he is fitted for these pursuits. Highly intellectualized work favors the verbal-minded rather than the motor-minded. Thus, in its stress upon scholastic achievement for eligibility, the academic profession imposes a condition that keeps it from getting a cross-section of those who attend college.

To encourage able persons to enter a vocation where average and even top salaries are relatively low, more inducement must be offered at the start. Whereas law and medicine offer few scholarships, fellowships, or other financial aids during the period of training, a prospective scholarly or scientific career does. This policy is often justified on the basis that recipients are in training for a form of public service where low income must be offset by other desiderata in order to attract talent.

Fellowships were originally designed to encourage the most talented to carry on graduate study, and at the same time were considered distinctions of honor. They were nominally conceived to have no bearing on inter-university competition or registration statistics. In many instances, however, subsidization resolves itself down to nothing more than the hiring of young men to pursue graduate studies. Each spring impecunious undergraduates look over bulletin boards and graduate school catalogues to weigh the comparative values of scholarships and fellowships.

Undoubtedly these remunerative 'baits' do lend a competitive aspect both to the choice of a career and to the selection of the particular institution where training will be secured, and at the very outset may inculcate an opportunistic attitude which is inimical to the spirit of disinterested inquiry. But the competitive feature may not be without its positive values, for it is the better universities and those with the strong departments that have most incentives of this type to offer.[4]

Besides, the situation is not merely a matter of economic inducement, for it represents a philosophy of higher education. If the premium is to be on mental ability and trained capacity rather than private financial means, some provision of this sort has to be made. Such a provision is the only device whereby the high-cost universities can meet the competition of the low-cost institutions without drawing their clientele entirely from wealthier classes. Because graduate training makes heavy demands upon professional recruits and leaves little time for self-support except at a dangerous drain upon energy, the 'poor but bright' students must be subsidized.

The granting of scholarships and fellowships is now a widespread practice in nearly all American colleges and universities. In 1936 there was available a total of 66,708 scholarships, worth nearly nine million dollars, and 5,797 fellowships worth more than two and a half million dollars.[5] More than 400 institutions offered such aids, ranging in annual value from less than

---

[4] Also, as is mentioned in *Depression, Recovery and Higher Education* (a report for the A.A.U.P. edited by Malcolm M. Willey; N. Y., McGraw-Hill, 1937), 'The selection by the student of an institution for graduate study is heavily conditioned by its reputation. This doctrine of "the best," regardless of its lack of validity, has a compelling influence. The institutions with the dominating reputations are primarily eastern, endowed universities' (p. 246).

In addition, see the various ratings of graduate schools, such as E. R. Embree, 'In Order of Their Eminence,' *Atlantic Monthly*, 155, pp. 652-64.

[5] Most of the scholarships are for undergraduates, but practically all fellowships are for graduate students. For detailed figures, see E. B. Ratcliffe, *Scholarships and Fellowships Available at Institutions of Higher Education*, U. S. Office of Education, 1936.

$50 to more than $1,500. Usually a scholarship or fellowship is assumed to be awarded for scholarly achievement or intellectual promise, yet such is not always the case, for the terms are often used (especially 'scholarship') for loans, grants-in-aid, or even miscellaneous employment, rather than as betokening recognition of superior ability and achievement.

Indeed, abuses have become so numerous that there has grown up what is known as the 'scholarship racket.' The most flagrant practices occur on the undergraduate level, however, where a small total outlay for recruiting produces more appreciable numerical results. For example, it is estimated that Ohio colleges alone spent $150,000 in 1934-5 in overt attempts to boost enrollment figures.

It is interesting to observe with reference to student aids that the practice is not confined to America. A similar system prevails throughout continental Europe, and even in England, where higher education has traditionally been of the cultural type designed to prepare youths for careers as gentlemen. As is stated in a volume edited by Kotschnig and Prys: 'It has been calculated, on the basis of official returns, that nearly *one-half* of the total number of students in British universities have obtained assistance in one or another of these ways, on account of the promise they show, either before entering a university career, or at some points in its course.' [6]

UNANTICIPATED EFFECTS OF SUBSIDIZATION

While the system of offering scholarships, fellowships, and other aids is undoubtedly a boon to students of limited means, it not only promotes competition among universities, but also generates considerable pressure upon the recipients. Since awards are made almost exclusively on the basis of scholastic marks, the 'grind' tends to stereotype the graduate student.

[6] Walter M. Kotschnig and E. Prys, *The University in a Changing World*, London, Humphrey Milford, 1932, p. 106.

That this type of competition is more likely to foster opportunism than independent thought is an inadvertent outcome. A seriousness of attitude and of application are unquestionably necessary for scholarly inquiry, yet whether there is not an optimum before they become distorted into rivalry for prizes or a deadening solemnity which stifles imagination and the joy of learning is another matter.

This oppressive spirit seems to be pervading even the undergraduate level in certain American universities, and has gone much farther in Europe. The following statement has been made of the Germany university:

> The anxious question must also be repeated in reference to the students. One can hardly reproach them to-day with not working industriously. The pressure of severe economic necessity weighs too heavily upon them, and very few are tempted to fritter away their time of study. The students passionately repudiate representations of student life which would give the impression that university days are still a time of carefree enjoyment . . . Time is scarce, and so is psychic energy, for 'diversions' which do not definitely belong to the prescribed course of study. For many students it is still essential to earn while studying. The transformation of the student type which has taken place in the last fifteen years is, however, not in every respect gratifying. For with the apparent freedom and unconcern about definite material ends, those imponderable treasures of academic freedom are also lost which used to determine the atmosphere and individual colouring of German university life. On this side too the university is threatened with the fate of dropping to the level of a school for professional education.[7]

Viewing the academic world from the professional side, it is important to note that these much-sought scholarships, fellowships, and other aids often involve a type of professional apprenticeship. Whereas the beginning physician serves his internship and the young lawyer begins his connection at a very

[7] Ibid. pp. 69-70.

low salary, the future professor often interrupts his student career by teaching in an academy, a high school, or a small college; or else he may become a student assistant whose spare time is at the disposal of the department in which he is majoring. The employment is ordinarily part-time and involves reading papers, correcting examinations, taking care of office tasks and routine research, arranging and caring for apparatus and museum collections, teaching freshman and sophomore courses, assisting in more advanced courses, or acting generally as intellectual valet to the professors in charge.

Extensive data are not available for the percentage of graduate students throughout the country engaged in this way, but random information indicates that it must be high. At Cornell 40 per cent of the graduate students are doing part-time work of this sort, and at Harvard 44 per cent engage in such work. The nearest approach to this percentage of subsidization in other fields of advanced professional study is perhaps represented by engineering, where nearly one-third of all graduate students are on subsidized appointments.

Aside from the financial assistance of such aids to the student (often amounting to total upkeep), they also serve university uses, and may easily become a source of cheap but highly trained labor. There are a number of well-known universities, for example, having a system of intellectual peonage in the form of teaching fellowships valued at $500. These entail half the teaching load (computed in course hours) carried by regular staff members, in whose cases salaries range from $2,000 to $7,500. Is this a form of exploitation? In any event, the remuneration is disproportionate by the usual standards and the position primarily serves the cause of the university administration rather than that of individual scholarship.

Indeed, it is not to be overlooked that the increased need for numerous assistants in the laboratory sciences is one direct cause for increased aids. To give but one illustration, at the University of Chicago the ratio of fellows and assistants to full professors is as follows: physical sciences, 2.2; biological sciences, 1.8; social sciences, 0.8; humanities, 0.7.[8]

The uses of these forms of apprenticeship are patent in the case of the university, but there is a cleavage of opinion about their value or function from the point of view of all concerned. The question continually appears in the proceedings of the Association of American Universities, some authorities maintaining that they result in poor teaching for undergraduates—others holding that the assistants are actually more enthusiastic and less jaded in dealing with freshmen and sophomores than are the professors. Others insist that the in-service training the assistant gets is just as useful to him in advancing his learning as the courses he takes, and others are in dispute over whether or not the experience gained more than offsets the energy drain and time diversion from regular course work.

That the worst feature is the premature injection of ulterior motives may be presumed. The idea that the system calls forth opportunists of mediocre ability is very dubious; still, the need for 'opportunity rather than extraneous stimulus'[9] can hardly be questioned, and there is certainly no gainsaying that on the whole there is both an institutional and an individual utility in such forms of financial assistance. Able but impecunious individuals whose talents would otherwise remain latent or lost elsewhere are salvaged for the higher learning. Meantime, however, the dysfunctions of the whole process have been widely ignored and generally disavowed.

A normative standard of selectivity is found in certain of the higher-paid fellowships and scholarships which require an intensive examination of all applicants and offer substantial remuneration to those who are successful. Representative of

[8] From Floyd Reeves, and others, *The University Faculty* (The University of Chicago Survey, Vol. III), Chicago, University of Chicago Press, 1933. See also the *Conference and Proceedings of the Association of American Universities* for the years 1931 and 1936.

[9] See J. McKeen Cattell's discussion in *University Control*, N. Y., Science Press, 1913, p. 41. This work is several decades old, but much that he had to say then is still timely.

this ideal type is the method of selecting fellows for first-year graduate study devised by the Social Science Research Council.[10] The applicants themselves have been required to submit the following information:

(a) An explanation of the type of research for which they wished to prepare themselves for graduate study; (b) a statement showing why they were interested in a research career; (c) a statement of what they regarded as their qualifications for such a career; (d) a chronological record of schools and colleges attended; (e) a record of positions held; (f) a list of prizes, fellowships, and honors awarded (page 2).

Five persons selected by the candidate as knowing his work best were then asked to rate him on an A, B, C, D scale ('A' representing 'clearly and unmistakably in the top 5% of all college seniors not over twenty-five years of age with whom you have come in contact,' down to 'D' for those below average) in six categories. The six categories were: (1) intellectual equipment, (2) originality, (3) ability to organize and interpret data, (4) zeal for investigations, (5) social characteristics, and (6) physical vitality. It was stated that the first four qualities seem to 'belong together,' while the last two 'appear as independent of each other and the rest.'

Selection of students for the graduate school can be no more discriminating, nonetheless, than the supply permits, and minimum entrance credentials are typically none too high. Although the Ph.D. degree grants a form of monopoly to do college or university teaching, this is a privilege not exclusively in the control of the academic profession to the same extent that monopolization of standards for the medical diploma is in the hands of the American Medical Association.

Also, the fact should not be lost sight of that individuals exercise selectivity in choosing the institution as well as in choosing the profession. In selecting a graduate school, the

[10] Carl C. Brigham, *Examining Fellowship Applicants*, A Report to the S.S.R.C., Bulletin No. 23, Princeton, Princeton University Press, 1935.

student is more likely to use objective judgment than is the case when he chooses a college for undergraduate work. The migration of graduate students has never been so great in this country as in pre-Nazi Germany (where distances between universities were less), but the very extensity of migration furnishes a specific index to extra-geographic factors in selection. On the average, 24.4 per cent of all college and university students in the United States go outside their residential states to attend college—ranging from 9.6 per cent in California to 78.9 per cent in New Jersey—and the percentage is much higher for graduate students.[11]

According to my own computations, of 102 Ph.D.'s from Harvard in 1938, only 19 had taken the bachelor's degree there, and a total of 196 colleges was represented among the 1,055 graduate students. In 1937 at the University of California, 21 of 54 Ph.D.'s had taken their undergraduate degree in the same institution. The graduate schools of Harvard, Columbia, Chicago, Michigan, and other leading universities are essentially national institutions in their drawing power. Although minor universities have this capacity in certain strong departments, on the whole their service areas are distinctly regional.

Other things being equal, it is to the student's advantage to attend one of the major universities, where, as Willard Waller has said, 'He can rub elbows with the great and serve his apprenticeship under "big men" in his respective field.' Regardless of the candidate's own merit, some of the prestige of the institution accrues to him merely by virtue of his attendance, since he profits by the 'halo effect.' Actually, the training he gets is more often than not superior to that afforded by lesser universities where student competition sets a slower pace and research facilities are more limited. However small the actual difference may be between major and minor universities, it is greatly accentuated when the candidate enters into competition for professional placement.

[11] Data from George Zook's *Residence and Migration of University and College Students*, Office of Education Bulletin, No. 11, 1926.

EFFECTS OF SUPPLY AND DEMAND UPON SELECTION PROCESSES

In concluding our remarks on the professional recruit, the influence of economic 'laws' of supply and demand on status should be noted. There is a growing opinion that on advanced levels, the saturation point of employability in higher education is already close at hand. When such a stage is reached it is doubtful that automatically limiting factors will operate effectively, and a further doubt is being expressed in some quarters that it is wise educational policy to wait for the socially disturbing and wasteful consequences of natural checks to become operative. President Conant has recently stated that it might be well for graduate schools to adopt some *numerus clausus* similar to that practiced in medical schools in an effort to balance supply and demand. In his report of 1934, the Dean of the Graduate School of Yale suggested that enrollments should be limited to about half the present number through a more rigid initial selection.

Walter M. Kotschnig has studied the problem on an international scale,[12] and has shown that there is no simple solution. The demand for intellectual labor is elastic, and even more so in response to general economic conditions than is the demand for those occupations dealing in 'necessities.' Kotschnig has pointed out the utility of distinguishing between unemployment and underemployment with reference to overcrowding and normal demand. 'Supply' equals those just entering a profession, plus the reserve army of those unable to make a living in their profession under normal economic conditions. 'Demand' is estimated by experts roughly at 3 per cent of the number of gainfully employed persons with academic training.

To be sure, possible increases in demand may be brought about through population growth, changes in age composition

[12] See his *Unemployment in the Learned Professions*, London, Oxford University Press, 1937.

of the population, a better appreciation for professional services, a rise in national income, the elevation of professional standards, shifts or enlargements in cultural values, and so on. Overcrowding is not merely a matter of definition or quibbling, as is proved by the vast amount of professional unemployment and maladjustment in Germany and Austria, where such conditions became factors in social upheaval. Not only does the unemployment of professionally trained persons depreciate the general social prestige of the affected occupations, but also the presence of large numbers of such individuals creates a prime source of instability in the whole social order.

Because of the dangers inherent in overcrowding and in an indiscriminate selective mechanism, various forms of restriction have been proposed. Rigid examinations may discourage the less able from seeking entry into a profession, but often they only add to individual difficulties by merely prolonging and adding to the expense of training, so that general examinations coming late in the educational process are seldom highly effective as eliminative procedures. Raising fees and lengthening the time requirement penalizes those of limited means, and such measures are thus contrary to the merit system in placing a premium upon wealth or the initial class position of recruits.

Aside from examinations and other forms of limitation in the selection of graduate students, a strict *numerus clausus* such as is applied in certain of the *Ecoles* of France may aim at the production of an intellectual elite in the end, but be completely democratic in administration. Democratic ideology is on the whole antithetical to such a scheme, and in America it is only when a profession is in almost complete control of a centralized organization (e.g. the American Medical Association) that it can enforce such practices, and even then they have to be rationalized into apparent harmony with prevailing sentiments for equality of opportunity. Nonetheless, educators are going to find it increasingly imperative either to expand the market for academic work or else change the qualifications for entry into the profession.

The average student is not immediately concerned with such broad questions when he enters the graduate school, for the implications for his status as a recruit are not brought home to him until three or four years later when he seeks placement. He then may realize, however, the significance of institutional disjunctions bearing upon the status of recruits to the academic profession.

III. STUDENT AND APPRENTICE

RECRUITS to the academic profession are drawn annually from some 1,600 institutions of higher education in the United States. The vast majority of the 150,000 or so students taking the baccalaureate degree do not pursue their formal education further, but one in seven goes on to take the first advanced degree, and one in fifty goes on to the Ph.D. Advanced training may be secured in all sorts of places; however, in 1939 the Ph.D. was actually conferred in only ninety institutions. Still more indicative of the concentration of advanced graduate work is the fact that of the 3,088 doctor's degrees conferred in that year, more than four-fifths were granted by thirty institutions, more than three-fifths by fifteen, and more than two-fifths by ten leading universities.[1]

Although our prospective academician ordinarily begins his status as an advanced student and apprentice in some fairly well-known university, he may have been recruited from an obscure college in the hinterland. As an undergraduate he was associated largely with young persons who were concerned most intensely with the trappings of higher learning, and he too may have shared this attitude. The graduate school, he soon discovers, is not so tolerant of the lackadaisical.

Graduate-study centers share with the college the functions of conservation, dissemination, and innovation, yet with much greater stress upon cultural innovation or invention than is

[1] For detailed statistical data, see *Doctoral Dissertations Accepted by American Universities*, 1939-1940, N. Y., H. W. Wilson Co., 1940; *Statistics of Higher Education*, 1935-36, Bul. No. 2, U. S. Dept. of the Interior; Walter C. John, *Graduate Study in Universities and Colleges in the United States*, Bul. No. 23, 1934, U. S. Dept. of the Interior.

true of the college. Cultural innovation is a less necessary and at the same time a more difficult societal function than the other two. Undergraduates are called upon primarily to assimilate the higher learning, and it is only upon upper levels that students are expected to reflect very critically upon culture, or to contribute individually to its advancement. Since it is neither expedient nor possible to carry the masses on to such levels, graduate-study centers need not be so numerous as those where undergraduate work is pursued.

Not a few of the persons trained in the graduate school go into non-academic pursuits, and rival institutions (such as the Carnegie and Rockefeller foundations) share with it the function of pure research. In its triad of major responsibilities to the social order, the graduate school is based upon two assumptions: first, the advancement of learning is most effectively done by intensively conditioning a select group; and second, this conditioning is best achieved through a stress upon research methods and objectives.

With reference to professed objectives, a number of interesting contradictions arise. Whatever may be its wider nominal purposes, the graduate school is a place where professors are engaged in the process of turning out other prospective professors. The largest number of those in training will become teachers rather than researchers.

In practice there is much merging between the graduate school and the college, and in few institutions is the separation rigid or complete. The same persons may offer instruction in both divisions, and proceed in their teaching as if all of their students expected some day to become professors. Indeed, so centripetal is the scholarly ideal, that the self-styled 'elite' among the votaries of higher education require an occasional reminder that the university serves a clientele of diverse bourgeois, parvenu, and aristocratic demands.

Rigmarole of the Conditioning Process

It has already been noted that those undergraduates failing to show at least average scholastic aptitude are not likely to be admitted to the graduate school. Those who have not ranked even higher are usually weeded out during the first year in the better universities. In order to get a more realistic and less generalized idea of the conditioning process, let us follow a typological recruit through the whole system and watch its operation.

On a higher level the student finds much the same mode of acquisition and assimilation of learning experienced earlier, but the requirements are more complicated. More original work is expected and examinations call for a higher order of ability and application. Where the alphabetical system of marking is used, nothing lower than 'B' is customarily given credit, and so lacking is the prevalent undergraduate indifference toward top grades that anything less than an 'A' is regarded as somewhat discreditable. A number of outstanding universities have fewer grade categories; these less differentiated systems render evaluation more imprecise, but at the same time less artificial, and serve to diminish the invidious comparisons of scholastic status.

High requirements and numerous safeguards, as one might suspect, do not always have their intended effects. According to a study made by the University of Minnesota, less than 50 per cent of the students in leading graduate schools ever get either the M.A. or the Ph.D., although 90 per cent of the work done is rated as satisfactory by instructors. Hence it appears that elimination of the unfit is centered elsewhere than in nominal requirements. In some institutions the practice is to get rid of a man without placing upon him the onus of an outright 'flunk.' He gets 'B' or 'B—' marks, and perhaps an M.A. degree as a consolation prize, while the institution makes no effort to place him vocationally, or else in indirect ways discourages his continued attendance.

The mediocre quality of many Ph.D.'s attests the fact, moreover, that by persistent plodding the poorer students often master the elaborate rigmarole of credits, examinations, theses, and other measures designed to sift them out. Such failures of the system are due primarily to neglect in application rather than to the system itself, for faculties in general are more ingenious in devising and piling up new requirements than in rigidly enforcing those already at hand. As one frank observer, Norman Foerster, has said:

For the scientific passion of the faculty, which implied high standards attainable by the few, was undermined by its humanitarian passion, which implied low standards accessible to the many . . . A few might be weeded out, the rest must be allowed to set the standards for passing . . . Thinking of particular students rather than students in general, professors displayed a sympathy which, at times admirable in itself, unquestionably had the effect of depressing standards. Mr. A. is a likable, hardworking person who has greatly improved; he may have the benefit of the doubt, even if there is no doubt. Miss B., though a weak student, is financially pressed and wears unsightly shoes; she has done her best, will never do better, and might as well be passed. Mr. C., gaunt and worried, has unluckily a wife and child but little else; if he does not get through, he and his will be stranded. Miss D., also gaunt and worried, sore beset with want of funds and brain power, is actually in danger of losing her mind; a pass may save her. And so it goes. In each case a service is rendered to human beings with whom the instructor has been rather closely associated for a year or two. This was not graduate education, but personal charity overriding professional duty.[2]

Few professors would have difficulty in duplicating from their own experience cases similar to those mentioned, yet it may be said that they represent distinctly marginal types and

[2] From *The American State University*, Chapel Hill, University of North Carolina Press, 1937, pp. 110-11.

exceptions to the general rule that both competitive and objective standards of the graduate school are of a high order.

In the larger universities, mere numbers of students necessitate a definite paraphernalia of careful accrediting, which in catalogues becomes an elaborate rigmarole to sanctify and fortify the highest degree. (Kotschnig has noted, 'The Germans, who in their thoroughness reached a sorry perfection in this system, coined a special word for it—*Berechtigungswesen*.') Examination and repeated quizzing are extremely important for the candidate's final academic status as a professional. To affect the common undergraduate indifference toward marks would be not only foolish but also fatal. Wishes for recognition are thus from the very start tied to a competitive system of scholarship, since the percentage of top marks is by definition limited.

RITUALIZED HURDLES AND MILEPOSTS

If the anthropologist were not an academic man himself it might occur to him that those who are professionally initiated into the mysteries of the higher learning undergo modes of treatment that are analogous analytically to the initiation rites the primitive youth submits to in becoming a member of the adult circle. The academic recruit is not physically scarified, yet the various critical events in his conditioning undoubtedly leave indelible marks upon his psyche; he is not circumcised or subincised. but his youthfully buoyant ego is likely to be pared away or punctured; he does not fast in the wilderness waiting for a vision, but much mental anguish is experienced before the 'inspiration' for a satisfactory dissertation idea comes to him. Culturally viewed, each of the 'ordeals' in his conditioning is a crisis situation which functions as a status-changing ceremony.

A competitive system enforces quantitative requirements and erects hurdles for the prospective academician to surmount; in the training necessary to overcome them he is brought closer to professional norms. From another point of view, to be sure, these hurdles may be regarded merely as stages in a process of growth, or as demarcations in a continuum. The able scholar ideally approaches one of these 'obstacles' in the same spirit that a proficient golfer approaches a course hazard.

The first major hurdle ordinarily encountered by the neophyte is the M.A. degree, though in many places he may forego this as a step toward the Ph.D. if he so chooses. The extraordinary 'success' of the doctorate has considerably lessened the prestige of the M.A., so that at present it has lost standing as a badge of scholarship and has become little more than a somewhat apologetic and ill-defined symbol. (This is due in part to the depreciation in value of all symbols in inverse ratio to their scarcity.) In fact, the M.A. has now become mainly a training degree for secondary school teaching, and is useful mainly as an alphabetical indicator of exposure to some graduate conditioning. A number of universities substitute an extra course as an alternative to the thesis requirement, but the master's degree usually entails a final examination, written or oral in major and minor subjects, and 'a thesis due at a certain date, typed in a certain way, fully decorated with foot-notes, charts, graphs, and bibliographies. In the unrealistic language of graduate school catalogues, the thesis must present a contribution to the sum of human knowledge, as evidence of the candidate's capacity for independent and original investigation. . .' [3]

After the candidate has met a certain number of course requirements he presents himself for the preliminary doctoral examination as the first overt step toward acquiring what someone has called 'the indispensable prehensile tail for academic climbing.' The manifest function of this examination is

[3] *The American State University*, p. 110. For a discussion of the present status of the master's degree, see the *A.A.U.P. Bulletin*, xviii, No. 3, 1932; for formal requirements, consult the *Biennial Survey of Education in the United States*, Vol. i, Ch. iii, p. 48.

to determine his worthiness for continuing up the rungs of the ladder of academic apprenticeship. Although the examiners are usually well aware in advance of the particular recruit's merits and demerits, the examination may serve to increase their insight, and regardless of whether it meets this end, it unquestionably has the ritual value of an ordeal. It is an *event* in the graduate career of the student, an event that affords a sportive occasion for inflating the ego of the bantering type of professor and at the same time deflating the ego of the candidate sufficiently to enhance in his mind's eye the status he hopes eventually to assume.

Moreover, examinations constitute a means of title protection, and if they are of the oral type with no rigidly fixed standards of performance or objectified means of measurement, the in-group can well use this method of debarring candidates who meet course requirements, but who are objectionable as professional prospects on other grounds. The examinee is typically aware of the arbitrariness of the whole procedure, and if he can choose his examining committee, he is inclined to select only those professors who regard him favorably or who at least have a vested interest in his successful performance as a vindication of their own pedagogical efficiency.

This hurdle once surmounted, the next advance toward the Ph.D. is some demonstration of the neophyte's ability 'to read acceptably the literature of his field or fields in both French and German.' Such a requirement is in force in nearly all graduate schools, although in many cases another language may be substituted for either French or German. The nominal purpose of the requirement, which usually must be met at least a year before the candidate presents himself for his final doctoral examination, is to make certain that he has sufficient facility in these languages to utilize them in his research. Actually, the requirement is just another dreaded hurdle as far as the average individual is concerned. In practice, two or three efforts are frequently necessary before he succeeds in passing, after a period of intensive 'boning,' private tutoring, and sweating to acquire linguistic facilities that should have been learned in earlier years. The wide prevalence of this *modus operandi* is witnessed in the fact that little or no stigma attaches to repeated trials.

Whatever its apparent purpose, then, the language requirement increases the difficulties in the way of attaining the degree to the extent that many who otherwise might go on are effectively dissuaded, or else take one of the several substitutes for the Ph.D. For those who are determined to compensate for previous background inadequacies it serves as another event viewed in retrospect with more of a sense of relief than of positive accomplishment.

Purely quantitative requirements such as the number of years of residence, the number of credit hours, and the proportion of major and minor subjects may look forbidding at first, but they are removed by a process of cumulative effort, so that they do not create crisis situations for the average candidate. Three years of resident attendance beyond the bachelor's degree, at least one of which must be at the degree-granting institution, are required.

Yet the actual period of lapsed time between the B.A. and the Ph.D. is nearly always greater than the nominal time requirement. For 54 Ph.D.'s granted at the University of California in 1937, the average was 8.74 years, and the modal time 5 years, with more than one-fourth of the total of 54 persons having spent more than 10 years after the bachelor's degree before obtaining the doctorate. For 105 Ph.D.'s at Harvard in 1938, the average lapsed time after the bachelor's degree was 6.85 years, and the modal time was 4 years; but for 33 individuals the period was 10 years or more. Graduate schools are unanimous in refusing to make any explicit statement regarding the precise number of credit hours needed, even when indicating the minimum, the assumption being that the premium is largely upon qualitative rather than quantitative evidences of scholarship.

In some universities all the student's work may be in his chosen field, in other places at least one minor in a related field is required. Ten members of the Association of American Universities require no minor, thirteen require one minor, and three require two minor subjects outside the special field of concentration.

Despite the lack of precise statements on quantitative requirements, broad specifications do exist as a protection of the title. Protection which in other occupations is often secured through governmental legislation has been achieved within the academic profession largely through in-group control and agreements secured through institutional consensus and sanction by the power of accrediting agencies to which these institutions belong. Since the honorary Ph.D. was abolished by agreement among universities in 1896, it is now exclusively a professional degree which represents that its possessor has gone through a systematic form of higher training to achieve his status.[4]

Denotations and Connotations of the Ph.D.

Since the degree of doctor of philosophy has come to imply research competence as well as general understanding (in contrast to mere technical proficiency, which is the main criterion of many other professional degrees), the candidate is expected to acquire: (1) a thorough mastery of a section of a selected field, (2) an extensive familiarity with his special field as a

[4] In addition to the Ph.D., there are other types of doctorates, such as: doctor of science, doctor of engineering, doctor of juridical science, doctor of jurisprudence, doctor of the science of law, doctor of canon law, doctor of law, doctor of both laws, doctor of medical sciences, doctor of public health, doctor of science in hygiene, doctor of theology, doctor of sacred theology, doctor of letters, doctor of modern languages, doctor of religious education, doctor of commercial science, and doctor of education.

The doctor's degree was originally conferred in the schools of theology, medicine, law, and philosophy, and since the school of philosophy represented the broadest training, the Ph.D. has come to be the usual type of doctorate taken by the generic academic man.

whole, (3) acquaintance with related fields, and (4) the capacity to make original contributions to the advancement of learning. In keeping with the general tendency toward greater specialization in higher education, the main emphasis is now upon aspects (1) and (4).

The most important hurdle is the dissertation. When the future professor is somewhere around the halfway point in his preparatory conditioning, he finds that the dissertation has rather suddenly loomed as a major event in his academic life. His increasingly imperative concern is to find a suitable subject. If his mental caliber is mediocre, or his conditioning has not been stimulating, or if he is too acutely aware of the seriousness of his choice and treatment upon his later career, then his situation may well be a dilemma.

The occupational culture, however, has set up ready means for meeting his dilemma. In many departments the graduate professors have well-marked off domains whose minor corners they relegate to such individuals for explorations which may later contribute anonymously to the professor's larger 'discovery.' In the humanities there are always 'influences' to be traced and 'sources' that are sure to be revealed by patient digging; in the social sciences there are innumerable uncorrelated data to be correlated in proving or disproving this, that, or the other proposition; and the physical sciences too are not lacking in stereotyped projects of their own.

Back in 1902 the Association of American Universities attempted to define the formal pattern of 'dissertation activity':

First, the method must either be invented or adapted to the problem. There are conditions to be controlled; principles of selection must be determined; negative instances rejected; very often machinery must be devised and made . . .

Second, there must be data collected, experiments made and noted, facts gathered, protocol books filled, instances and experiments multiplied, and the basis of induction made broad and deep . . .

The third and main stage is to think it all out; to apply a rigorous philosophic method; to reason logically on the objective facts; to find their unity; to determine what is central and what is unimportant; to relate and determine the place and bearings of all; and find whether the accumulations are mere agglomerations, or have meaning and value for science.[5]

The topic itself is selected by the student, subject to the advice of the professor chosen to be in charge, and in some instances it must also be approved by the graduate council. The subject is expected to be one in which originality can be shown in proving or discovering something not known before, or by establishing one of several conflicting views already held, or by disproving an existing view widely accepted. The method of discovery, adjudication, or disproof nominally must be with reference to a topic of importance, but academic standards of importance vary from one department to another, and from one institution to another. In mathematics, for example, the candidate normally picks a problem that can be solved, and has not previously been solved. Obviously, just any problem will not do, yet even in this most precise of all disciplines the criteria of adequacy in respect to difficulty and significance vary widely from one judge to another.

The 'unbelievably picayunish' features of doctoral dissertations that satirists have ridiculed are not so much a deliberate choice on the part of candidates as of numerous pressures brought to bear upon them. Professors often set capable students to trivial and minutely specialized tasks to fill in the gaps in their own larger studies, or the candidate himself may pick a narrow topic of relatively little import in order to get positive results in a limited time. Already beset by a mild anxiety neurosis as foreshortened time becomes a more precious commodity, the thesis writer is realistically reluctant to attempt 'great heroic work with large risks and possibilities of infinite delay.'

[5] See the *Proceedings*, Third Annual Conference, pp. 46-51.

These pressures are generated by an academic ideology (widely shared) that tends to measure the worth of a study by its precision rather than its importance. Aping the physical scientists, social scientists do homage to the third decimal point of exactitude. Particularly flagrant in the humanities is the field of English, where the philologists rather than the broad scholars have been in the saddle. According to one authority, the situation is in no small part due to the failure of the humanists to provide young scholars with acceptable problems, whereas those scholars with a highly specialized view of research are full of problems and stereotyped procedures.

Even a very specialized subject may be rejected, however, if it does not fit in with departmental interests, as the following case rather facetiously shows:

Thirty years ago I went to Harvard University to study the antennae of 'palaeozoic cockroaches' . . . I knew there were more palaeozoic cockroaches in Harvard than in any other institution. I divided my time between regular courses and the antennae of palaeozoic cockroaches. At the end of the year I went with my manuscript, quite a bundle of it, dealing with the antennae to the Professor of Cockroaches. I wanted it considered toward the requirements for the doctorate. I was told that Harvard University was not interested in the antennae, that it was interested only in the thorax . . . The Professor would not even look at my manuscript. The manuscript covered really only the first two joints of the antennae of palaeozoic cockroaches. It was afterward published, as the first of a series of occasional volumes by the California Academy of Sciences, and I believe is still the Authority . . .[6]

A number of eminent academicians have proposed that the French type of doctoral dissertation, which stresses intellectual culture, be adopted alternatively as 'a means of softening the hard lines of the academic type,' but the suggestion has had little effect in changing the present vogue. The prevailing

[6] Professor Eigenmann, 'How Can Universities be so Organized as to Stimulate More Work for the Advancement of Science?' *Proceedings of the Association of American Universities*, 1916, pp. 49-50.

sentiment is that the thesis makes the candidate a scholar, and that he knows more about his special subject than anybody else in the world. That his erudite tome may only gather dust on the shelves of the university library does not greatly disturb the candidate himself, so satisfied is his feeling over having the job finished and accepted. Whatever benefits the writer may derive from the intellectual ordeal, the average thesis should be realistically regarded as an intellectual exercise rather than a contribution to knowledge.[7]

Consistent with the idealized view of the thesis as a contribution to knowledge is the practice of requiring a minimum number of copies to be printed. Functional justifications given are the following: (1) it makes accessible a knowledge of the type of work done in a given department and university, and generally furthers dissemination of the higher learning; (2) it makes more accessible the work of the scholar himself; (3) a good piece of scholarship gives favorable publicity to the young Ph.D.; (4) it is a stimulus to more careful endeavor on the part of the investigator and to more scrupulous checking on the part of the department. Arguments against the practice are in the main: (1) the excessive burden of publication costs, which ordinarily must be borne by the writer; (2) the scholar often wants more time to round it out before publication—especially is this true if he has dealt with a complex and significant topic; (3) if the thesis is worth printing, its significant parts may be broken up into separate articles that will be published without cost to the candidate anyway, and thus be made available to a wide audience in the field.

Regardless of the arguments pro and con, some form of publication is usually required. Almost half of the graduate

[7] Doctoral theses in the Widener Library at Harvard for the year 1909 had been read an average of 1.08 times each during the more than thirty years they had been there, many never having been read at all. The median number of readers for the thesis of 1929 was 3.0. A number of these, to be sure, have had their substance appear in scholarly journals, or else have been published complete in revised form.

institutions require the manuscript to be printed in full, about a fourth publish abstracts, and about a fourth require no publication at all. The vast majority of the printed dissertations of 1940, for example, were published privately at the authors' expense or published under university auspices. Of the 3,088 doctoral dissertations written in 1940, only 18 were published during that year by well-known commercial firms. Where publication is not required, however, only a small proportion of dissertations ever get into print. At the University of Michigan, to cite one leading university, only 90 of the 800 dissertations written up to the year 1932 had ever been published.

Most institutions, as we have noted, do stipulate some 'baptism of printer's ink,' even though it be a mere sprinkling in the form of abstracts. The dissertation is presumed to be only the first step in its author's anticipated career of productive writing, but, as caustic critics of the academician have pointed out, as a creative contributor to knowledge he is often so exhausted by the birth pains of the thesis that never again does he bring forth issue.

Timorously or confidently, after having his thesis accepted, the candidate approaches his last hurdle, the doctoral examination. In some instances this is administered solely by department members, in others a representative of an outside department must be present. The examination itself may be written or oral or both, though it is usually oral. It may deal exclusively with the subject matter of the thesis and principles of the major subject, or it may be restricted to the thesis proper, while aiming to reveal the capacities of the candidate in the widest possible way.

Originally this examination took the form of a defense by the candidate of his thesis, whereas the usual practice in America today is for it to assume the more expansive form. (The original type was patterned after the European model; abroad the examination is often public, with complete outsiders among the examiners.) Professor George Lyman Kittredge summarized from his own broad experience the procedure of the examination as follows:

> To sum up: Questions test knowledge of linguistic and literary history (facts and principles); the candidate's reading and thinking; his taste and appreciations; his judgment and critical faculty; his ability to give a good oral account of himself and of what he knows and thinks. Questions are very varied; some are minute, some general, some specific, some vague. Some call for learning, some for nimbleness, some for thought.[8]

Although there is still a possibility that the candidate may be impeded at this late stage, the actual prospect of his failing is remote. During his years in the department there has been a mutually progressive commitment. As Norman Foerster has mentioned, in the absence of absolute standards, mediocrities often get by on the theory of precedent (Mr. Y. is as good as Mr. X. was last year), or through log-rolling, because a vote against the candidate might be interpreted as a vote against his supervisor, or a pass may be given merely on the basis of sympathy.

FINDING OCCUPATIONAL PLACEMENT

Now that the candidate has achieved full eligibility for teaching or research he is ready (and anxious) for a job. In all probability his graduate school department proceeded in personnel training with no clear knowledge of whether its products were going into teaching or into full-time research, and with no accurate estimate of the number of available positions, or of the competition offered by other institutions. For the candidate in turn there is no well-organized open market, and little advance knowledge of the competitive situation.

It is of interest, then, to see what happens to Ph.D.'s. For the period from 1927-35 the following percentages went into teaching: 58 per cent of 201 graduates of Ohio State, 73 per

---

[8] Reported in the *Bulletin of the A.A.U.P.*, XIII, 1927, pp. 182-3.

cent of 574 at Harvard, 50 per cent of 290 at Cornell, 65 per cent of 28 at Nebraska, 75 per cent of 64 at North Carolina, and 68 per cent of those from Chicago.[9] My own tabulation of present occupations of Chicago Ph.D.'s (1893-1938) shows the following percentages in academic work: mathematics, 95.1; English, 86.8; sociology, 80.7; physics, 75.4; economics, 70.2; psychology, 65.9; political science, 64.7; chemistry, 44.8. The doctorate is thus predominantly a preparation for an academic berth. In fact, for some of the fields in which the candidate may have specialized, the possibility of remuneration outside the college or university is almost non-existent. If he majored in English and finds employment, the chances are about nine to one that he will get an academic job, and chemistry is one of the few fields in which the chances are more than even that he will go into non-academic work.

How and where does he get a position? Nominally he is thrown on the market along with more than 3,000 other Ph.D.'s produced annually.[10] Some of his potential competitors will be persons without the highest degree, others will be individuals who have lost their jobs or who desire to make a change, but he is competing mainly with similar specialists who have just secured the degree in his own and in other universities. The competition for placement, moreover, is by no means completely open. The vast majority of qualified men are not in actual competition for the same openings, and some are not even potential competitors. Aside from the personal factors which delimit free competition (in-group selection or

[9] Data from Edgar Dale, 'The Training of Ph.D.'s,' *The Journal of Higher Education*, Vol. i, pp. 198-202.

[10] The rank order and the number of degrees granted in the twenty leading fields in 1940 were as follows: (1) chemistry, 527; (2) education, 309; (3) English literature, 183; (4) physics, 148; (5) history, 143; (6) economics, 141; (7) bio-chemistry, 130; (8) psychology, 120; (9) botany, 112, and zoology, 112; (10) mathematics, 103; (11) political science, 78; (12) engineering, 77; (13) romance literature, 75; (14) physiology, 70; (15) sociology, 68; (16) philosophy, 61; (17) bacteriology, 59; (18) agriculture, 58; (19) geology, 55; (20) religion, 54.—Figures from *Doctoral Disserations Accepted by American Universities*, 1939-1940, p. XIII.

inbreeding, to mention but one), regional, institutional and other elements enter into the situation. It would be unusual for graduates of a California university to be in active competition with graduates of a New England institution for a vacancy in a Vermont college.

Yet it is only in exceptional cases that the fledgling Ph.D. is left to fend for himself in obtaining a position, for institutional and departmental prestige must be upheld in the successful placement of their men. Since the supply of men exceeds the number of vacancies in some fields, this task is by no means easy. Assuming that the membership of the American Philosophical Society represents 50 per cent of the total number of academic philosophers in the country, and computing the annual number of vacancies to be 3 per cent of the total number of positions in this relatively stabilized field, one would normally anticipate 42 vacancies in all academic ranks. This means simply that one-third of the 61 men taking their Ph.D. in philosophy in 1940 could not find jobs. Similar situations prevail in English, the classics, and certain other fields. In physics, chemistry, and some of the social sciences, however, the opposite is true.

Academic politics and personal factors make generalizations about supply and demand hazardous, but in the main the placement of the aspirant is directly governed by the following: (1) his placement will not be in a university of higher repute than the one from which he was graduated; (2) his best opportunity is in an institution within the sphere of influence of his university or department; (3) related to the preceding generalization is the fact that if the reputation of his institution is regional, he will find a position in some lesser college or university in that region.

Seldom is a job obtained through a forthright or 'cold' application. Contacts are often made at annual meetings of the various scholarly and scientific societies, which have come to be clearing houses for the older men and 'slave markets' for hopeful graduate students nosing about for instructorships for the next fall. Although there is no open announcement of vacancies, it is remarkable how quickly news of any is disseminated at such meetings. Since convention seems to require the advancement of a candidate's interest by a third party, knowing the 'right people' is exceedingly important. Employment is not especially 'seasonal,' but the prospective June Ph.D. may expect to be kept on tenterhooks until April, and sometimes until mid-summer before securing a contract.

Unlike many English universities, American institutions do not publicly advertise vacancies, nor does the aspirant secure placement in the same way that he does a civil service job. He may register with a teachers' agency and have it act as intermediary in informing him of vacancies, yet about all the agency can do to further his cause is to supply information (for which he pays a percentage of his first year's salary), and vacancies brought to his attention by commercial agencies are more likely than not to be rather undesirable posts in teachers colleges or obscure private institutions.

In the absence of any well-organized market, institutional or departmental prestige is vital. Even the mediocre person from a major university or renowned department may be in a better bargaining position than the truly brilliant man from a less central place, since it is to the central institutions that presidents, deans, and department heads of the smaller colleges and universities make inquiries. Particularly is this true of the lower bracket openings for which the young man is eligible. Here it may be observed that the inexperienced Ph.D. enjoys a better situation than young men already out in the field, for unless these latter individuals have attracted attention to themselves by research activity (since teaching skill rarely receives more than local notice), they are likely to drop out of 'circulation.' Once it has placed them, the parent university must discharge its obligation to the current group of unplaced graduates. Hence, though employers might prefer more experienced young men, they often have no knowledge of where to find them.

An inquiry conducted by the American Association of University Professors yields the following specific sources of supply for staff replacements and additions in 117 institutions: own college or graduate school, 26 per cent; other graduate schools, 23 per cent; friends in other institutions, 22 per cent; college and university appointment bureaus, 11 per cent; personal, written applications, 10 per cent; commercial agencies, 5.3 per cent; chance recommendations from other schools, 2.6 per cent.[11]

During the period of rapid expansion in the larger and better-established universities, the exceptional graduate could often expect permanent placement in his own institution; today many of these have reached the feasible limit of inbreeding, or else are undergoing stabilization, or even staff curtailment. The slow rate of turnover that may be anticipated in all places except the expanding state institutions has been stated by President Conant: 'It is expected that there will be [at Harvard] approximately one vacancy in the permanent staff available every four years for a department containing normally eight permanent professors; smaller departments will have vacancies less frequently, larger ones more often.'[12]

Some universities have a policy of retaining at temporary employment those Ph.D.'s who cannot be immediately placed, but the bulk of them can and do find employment in other colleges and universities, and in almost all cases the placement is not on an openly competitive basis. Although the candidate with a high record and unqualified recommendations from competent judges stands a better chance than the less meritorious, between eligible individuals of apparently equal ability and training, preferment is always shown for 'connections.'

It has been noted that sentiments and practices regarding

[11] 'Methods of Appointment and Promotion in American Colleges and Universities,' *Bulletin of the A.A.U.P.*, xv, 1929, pp. 178-9.
[12] *Report of the President of Harvard University to the Board of Overseers*, Cambridge, Harvard University Press, 1940, p. 17.

incentives, rewards, and penalties in selecting and conditioning recruits show a standardized tendency but not complete
uniformity or consistency. While many of these elements may
be arbitrarily established by any given university, all universities are subject to certain inter- and intra-institutional pressures that minimize the factor of arbitrariness in the selection
and training of men. The apprenticeship has its uses and abuses,
both of which derive from institutional determinants. A competitive system enforces quantitative as well as qualitative requirements, and erects hurdles for the prospective academic
man to surmount; while securing training he is brought closer
to the professional type. Throughout the process there are de-
flecting pressures, but the individual finally emerges from his
apprentice role to his initial status as a full-fledged academician.

At this stage he is likely to be about thirty years of age,[13]
as compared with starting ages of 27 in medicine, 25 in the
ministry, and 22 in engineering. Not infrequently he has acquired a wife and incurred sizeable personal indebtedness. Occupational conditioning in the academic profession is more
often interrupted by full- or part-time employment and re-
tarded by marriage than in other professions, marriage usually
deterring the highest degree by five yeas. It thus appears that
far from being a mere callow youth, our 'fledgling' academician has already spent the most vigorous years of his life before he ever begins permanent employment.

[13] The median ages for acquisition of the Ph.D. by present staff members of Chicago and Columbia were 28 and 29, respectively. The gross
average age of men taking doctorates at Harvard between 1931 and 1935
(inclusive) was 30.86, ranging from 28.50 in physics to 31.11 in English.
All three of these groups represent persons somewhat more fortunately
situated than the bulk of persons taking the doctorate; hence, the age
is probably higher for universities as a whole.

IV. STAFF MEMBER

His previous student and apprentice roles have set a permanent stamp upon our typological individual, and without being fully aware of it he already bears unmistakable earmarks of the academic profession even before assuming his initial status as a regular staff member of the university. Although his long and arduous conditioning may have had traumatic effects upon his psyche, the young employee typically mounts the first rung of the occupational ladder with zest and pleasant anticipations.

However unique and important his new status may seem to him, it appears institutionally as a mere part of the process of general metabolism, or gradual change in membership of the university. To provide for continuity of organization, new members are selected to fill vacancies resulting from the loss of old members or from the creation of new positions. Vacancies are filled both from within and without the local organization. For higher ranks, with the exception in many places of departmental headships and other major posts, vacancies are more often than not filled by promotion of men already on the staff. This kind of in-group selection has no reference, though, to where the individual got his training. There is another type of in-group selection known as 'inbreeding,' which refers to the initial placement and later treatment of individuals in the university that graduated them. Since administrative policy in this regard vitally affects the employee status of the academic man, it is important to give the matter a cursory review.

Employment Policy and Favoritism

A college or university presumably employs staff members according to the following more or less loosely formulated considerations: ability and training in teaching and research, intellectual caliber, capacity for leadership, general reputation, originality, personality and character, and probable future performance.[1] In the case of the beginning instructor, evidences of these are sought in his scholastic record, the judgments of those who know him, his written or published work, and the general impression made upon his employers through correspondence or interview. The utilization of objective, impersonal criteria of competency, nonetheless, is hindered by three factors: (1) the absence of an openly competitive market; (2) the difficulty of judging the intangible qualities of candidates on the basis of written statements, brief interviews, and limited evidence; (3) the intrusion of personal elements favoring candidates within geographic and social proximity.

The first of these factors has already been discussed as a peculiarity of the American system, and as a correlate of the sentiment of professional 'dignity.' Interviews to some extent mitigate institutional risks in employing novices, but the requisite information is often difficult to obtain. Most important among the factors operating against a wide selection on the basis of competency is the intrusion of personal elements. While acknowledging the desirability of considering an optimum number of candidates, administrators are prone to fill vacancies before their existence becomes widely known, because of the desire to avoid being flooded with applications from unqualified persons. And too, academic in-groups fre-

[1] For a discussion of these items, see the *Harvard Report on Some Problems of Personnel in the Faculty of Arts and Sciences*, Cambridge, Harvard University Press, 1939, p. 51 ff.
The criteria nominally employed in a large number of colleges and universities are given in the *Bulletin of the A.A.U.P.*, xv, 1929, pp. 177-80.

quently influence selection by weighting the choice in favor of eligible friends, kinsmen, and individuals they have trained themselves. Such practices are minimized in the leading universities; however, an investigation in a more or less typical university of the middle rank revealed that personal elements account for at least four-fifths of all appointments, leaving only a small proportion of vacancies to be filled through open competition.[2]

According to institutional ideologies, this type of selection may be rationalized as 'desirable' in the maintenance of traditional standards. Certainly the policy is consistent with the continuity of localized cultural values, for the inbred candidate has been conditioned in precisely these terms. The local man already understands what is expected of him, is known as a 'co-operative' person, and is readily accessible without the financial expenditure and added effort necessary in securing an outsider. All of these considerations, to be sure, are not necessarily a reflection upon the competency of the recruit, except where a friend, dependent, or relative is assigned a status without due regard for his other qualifications.

It is estimated that more than one-third of all faculty members (proportions are highest for instructors and assistant professors) throughout the country are products of inbreeding.[3] According to the competitive standards of a semi-bureaucratic type of organization it is unlikely that such a high percentage of the 'best qualified' should have received their training where they are now employed. Inbreeding is more prevalent in the East than in the South or West, in private than in public institutions, in Catholic than in protestant universities, in colleges for men than in those for women, and in large institutions than in small ones. Administrators are supposed to wield

[2] A. B. Hollingshead, 'Ingroup Membership and Academic Selection,' *American Sociological Review*, Vol. 3, 1938, pp. 826-33.

[3] For more detailed information, see the *Bulletin of the A.A.U.P.*, XXI, 1935, p. 496, and also John H. McNeely, *Faculty Inbreeding in Land-Grant Colleges and Universities*, U. S. Dept. of the Interior, No. 31, 1932.

the authority of their offices with technical impartiality, yet these offices are always held by people with innumerable relations to other people. Hence it is that complete insulation from favoritism, of the university as a social structure, however desirable ideally is practicably impossible.

Extenuating circumstances undoubtedly exist, and there is obviously no positive advantage in appointing an outsider when a qualified person is already at hand. With reference to institutional efficiency, appointment in this way is likely to function beneficially in direct ratio to the size of the department and university, and their general eminence. Whatever may be the utility in exceptional cases, in the long run non-universal standards narrow the range of choice, groove intellectual backgrounds, break down the reciprocity between universities, give primacy to personal traits over scholarship, and foster a general provincialism.

The whole problem of inbreeding has its individual as well as institutional aspects. Subordinate status is likely to attach itself to the young scholar much longer than it would if he came in as an outsider, and the 'immaturity' of his student period lingers as a survival in the minds of his former teachers, so that he attains his professorship three or four years later than if he had started at another university. (Young physicians and lawyers often find themselves similarly handicapped when starting out in their home towns.) Likewise, since he is chosen because of his 'adaptability' as well as his promise, greater accommodation is demanded of him than would be expected from an outsider.

Climbing the Occupational Ladder

The novice, regardless of whether he came in through inside or outside selection, usually starts on the bottom rung of the academic ladder. There is a definite presumption that the average entrant will rise. As a beginner he uses the 'prehensile tail' he has acquired for academic climbing. He begins quickly to distinguish between nominal and actual practices. He slowly learns the set of attitudes and roles to play consistently if he is to make a successful ascent. Though there is a tendency later to eschew the role of the tyro, such would be hazardous in the earlier stages of the academic career.

In his dual role as teacher and researcher, the beginner encounters an occupational hierarchy. It is a different sort of hierarchy, however, from that presented by the army or by a large business corporation, where there is functional justification for an elaborate gradation of authority. Among academicians there is ideally no question of superiors directing the work of others, but only a question of rank with reference to relative degrees of maturity and distinction. Yet there is a hierarchical principle in university organization. Like the army officer, the civil servant, and the priest, the academic man feels that he has a normal expectation of advancement according to seniority and service. Although there is much ill will provoked by status competition, from the point of view of the administration, the various gradations function as modes of stimulating and recognizing individual activity. Advancement is rarely in terms of a rigidly codified seniority; even so, a normal expectancy within the profession minimizes the element of financial uncertainty inimical to intellectual work, and to some extent offsets moderate remuneration.

The occupational hierarchy consists typically of four ranks: instructor, assistant professor, associate professor, and full professor. (The fourfold division seems to have the weight of tradition behind it, for the same ranking scheme is found in most European countries.) In the average major university, about 31 per cent of the staff is on the first level, 23 per cent on the second, 14 per cent on the third, and 32 per cent on the fourth. In lesser institutions, the percentage distribution among these same ranks is as follows: 9.3, 15.6, 15.6, and 56.7 (2.8 per cent being inactive).[4]

---

[4] *Bulletin of the A.A.U.P.*, xxiv, 1938, p. 249; averages for member groups.

Between the ages of thirty and thirty-two, the individual enters this hierarchy as an instructor on a one- to five-year appointment. All persons, to be sure, do not begin at the lowest level; for example, in sociology nearly 13 per cent enter as professors, 10.5 per cent do so in engineering, 9.6 in the classics, 7.5 in economics, 6.0 in biology, 4.3 in English, and 3.2 in modern languages (see ibid. p. 259). These percentages, however, are lower in the instance of major universities, where the young Ph.D. almost invariably starts at the foot of the ladder. The academician ordinarily remains an instructor from three to five years, the average expectancy of promotion being such that he is likely to achieve the assistant professorship at thirty-four to thirty-five, the associate professorship at thirty-eight, and the full professorship shortly after forty.[5] Average ages at the different levels vary from one university to another and from field to field (being lowest in the physical sciences). At the University of Chicago in 1928-9, the average age of professors was 51.4; of associate professors, 44.0; of assistant professors, 36.8; of instructors, 32.2. At every rank it was lower than in 1918-19. Excepting the professorship, the median number of years for remaining in each rank was 4.3, 4.6, 3.5 (data from *The University Faculty*, pp. 55 ff.).

Because of the absence of completely codified seniority in most institutions, some persons may jump intervening ranks —others may be delayed or permanently halted along the line. (Aside from the question of competence, women teachers and staff members making the complete ascent in the same insti-

[5] An investigation covering the period from 1885 to 1935 in Indiana University, a fairly representative institution of the middle rank, has ascertained the following information: (1) nine out of ten persons promoted are raised to the next higher rank; (2) the chances are eleven to one against movement from the instructorship to the professorship in that university, but the associate professor's chances of promotion are almost even; (4) about twelve to fifteen years are required to make the complete ascent; (5) salary raises are not always connected with promotion, but are in 72 per cent of the cases.—From A. B. Hollingshead, 'Climbing the Academic Ladder,' *American Sociological Review*, Vol. 5, No. 3, 1940, p. 394.

tution are slower in rising.) Although many universities have the 'up or out' policy as far as instructors are concerned, dismissal for mediocre performance is not common above the lowest rank, so that not-too-marginal mediocrities are usually shelved at the middle ranks or else side-tracked into minor administrative work. The full professorship is ordinarily the highest staff status to be achieved, except where distinguished professorships exist as a form of special recognition for exceptional persons.

This whole movement, to repeat, appears institutionally as general and differential metabolism. There is little or no downward movement (demotion) except that department heads are occasionally 'relieved' of their administrative duties; outward movement takes place through the death, resignation, or dismissal of members. One study of this process has shown that each higher stratum is recruited largely from below by promotion, that with the passage of time there is a progressive enlargement of the top stratum (the center of gravity, where metabolism is lowest), and that in recent years the differential metabolism is becoming greater in the lower ranks.[6]

Both general and differential metabolism manifest wide institutional differences. On the whole, the more mediocre the university, the higher the annual turnover of staff. The 'here today and gone tomorrow' attitude which some institutions force upon their faculties gives no opportunity for group coherence and morale to develop, and where there is no reasonable continuity, membership is consequently devalued.

Major universities have a lower metabolism or staff turnover than minor ones, but this difference is not explicable in terms of the greater benevolence of the former. Rather, it is because their staff members can seldom better their positions by shifting to another university, and because initial selection is more rigorous. At the University of Chicago, for example,

[6] P. A. Sorokin and C. A. Anderson, 'Metabolism of Different Strata of Social Institutions and Institutional Continuity,' Roma, *Instituto Poligrafico Dello Stato*, Anno IX, 1931.

60 per cent of the staff members in 1918-19 were still there a decade later, 29 per cent had died, 11 per cent had resigned for various reasons, and less than 1 per cent had resigned to go to other universities. (*The University Faculty*, pp. 55 ff.) Also, it is logical to assume the existence of colleges and universities with such weak staffs that their members receive few offers elsewhere. For any given university faculty the metabolism will be less marked in the higher ranks. This is explicable largely in terms of age,[7] duration of service, and administrative devices for maintaining an optimum or relatively low turnover.

PROBLEMS OF TENURE AND STATUS

To turn now from these general matters, it is pertinent to note the problems attached to each of the temporal statuses. It is quite true that the rights and duties of an instructor and a full professor do no differ as much as those of a private and a general, a bench worker and a chairman of the board of directors, yet there are significant differences. In its prototype the university may have been a society of fellows, and it is still felt that formal organizations should not lay stress on the comparative status of different men. A society of equals lays stress upon individual spheres of technical competence. Academic men are almost unanimously opposed to any permanent differentiation of ranks creating a stratification of classes within the faculty, or a caste system that would be a relation of superiors and subordinates counter to professional tradition.

As complexity of organization has increased, equalitarianism has been undermined, and the modern university has tended more and more toward a semi-bureaucratic pattern. Within this semi-bureaucratic organization, some problems of person-

[7] In 35 smaller institutions, the median percentages for age distributions without reference to rank are: aged 20-29, 21 per cent; 30-39, 31; 40-49, 37; 50-59, 12; 60-64, 4; 65-69, 0.—From Floyd W. Reeves and others, *The Liberal Arts College*, Chicago, University of Chicago Press, 1932, p. 123.

nel are diffuse in their relevance, whereas others are of primary importance at particular levels of the hierarchy. Questions of appointment, tenure, promotion, and remuneration are a concern of the whole institution, to be sure, but for organization personalities they have a different import in the lower statuses. Problems of research and teaching likewise permeate the whole structure, though differing in their nature for instructors and for full professors.

The Instructor

It is a matter of common observation that the largest number of critical issues of personnel problems arises in the instructorial rank. Here the tenure is brief or uncertain, the turnover highest, the remuneration lowest, the criteria for advancement vague or confused, the duties manifold, and the future full of doubt. In most institutions this status is regarded as a trial period and the appointment is for only one year. There are always more aspirants for higher positions than there are vacancies, so that within the intensely competitive system of a large university the individual fear of exclusion is as pronounced as the hope of inclusion where the 'up or out' policy is in force. The mental anxiety may be prolonged by repeated short-term appointments, with the threat of eventual failure of renewal hanging over the instructor after seven or eight years of service. Meantime, he and his family must subsist on a low rate of remuneration, and he in turn must prove himself in an environment not conducive to the best intellectual work.

A great deal of unadmitted exploitation goes on. In this lowest rank the teaching load is usually heaviest and most onerous; to the instructor are relegated the introductory sections (except where it is the policy to give these to the best teachers in the department), where large enrollments necessitate much paper grading, entail many student conferences, allow less freedom in course planning, and so on. Within most

departments, the preferred subjects are already the prerogatives of the older men, so that when the instructor is given
advanced courses in his own right they are often those nobody else wants to teach. Because of heavy demands upon his
time, his research activities tend to become piecemeal, and
because of his unestablished reputation he finds difficulty in
securing backing for projects requiring subsidy. In view of the
vague and conflicting criteria by which his work is judged,
he is uncertain in the allocation of his energies. He knows that
he is a competitor, but often is not clear regarding the terms
of competition.

One of the few faculty inquiries candidly and incisively at-
tacking personnel problems is the Harvard *Report* mentioned
earlier. In answer to one item on the questionnaire to younger
teachers at that institution, 'Have you been given a clear
definition of what you should do, in scholarly work and teaching, in order to merit appointment or promotion?' the 164
replies were as follows: yes, 21; qualified, 20; answer not clear,
7; no, 116 (ibid. p. 46). Illustrative of the difficulties of
younger men are these quotations (p. 46 ff.):

'I should say that the most crying need, so far as the instructors on annual appointment are concerned, is for some
definition of this kind . . . At least there ought to be some
specific understanding on what importance is attached to success in teaching.'

.   .   .

'Suggestions: Clear statement of basis for promotion. A
merit system cannot work unless merit is clearly defined.
And it must be watched carefully in order to keep out favoritism, nepotism and socalled politics . . . All should know
exactly where they stand, and what is expected of them for a
permanent job.'

.   .   .

'If I were asked to offer a one-word diagnosis of the present situation, I should simply say, "uncertainty." Uncertainty
of every sort surrounds the junior instructor,—uncertainty as
to the policy of tenure, necessity of publication, remuneration,
advisability of engaging in outside activities, etc., etc.'

The reactions of the instructors also mention other sources of tension—the 'lip service to teaching,' departmental policies resting on 'caprice rather than considered judgment . . . and a balanced view,' the issue of judgment on intrinsic merits or cultivation of special fields, emphasis on 'quantity rather than quality' in publication, the 'publish or perish' legend. Because of his precarious situation, the instructor is under a variety of pressures to 'make good' in the institutional scheme of things. Few of the junior members would question the fact that temporary insecurity for the individual has a functional value for the institution, hence the main strain in the instructorship seems to be the uncertain criteria for advancement.

Incompatibilities abound between the immediate demands of the instructor's situation and the anticipated satisfactions of an academic career. Neither the wish for security nor the wish for recognition is adequately met. Being past thirty, he is at an age when the young doctor and lawyer are beginning to send out permanent roots in the community and are establishing themselves in life careers. The high geographic mobility of the young academician, on the other hand, precludes feelings of permanence and security. It is not inexplicable that he should come to regard the university hierarchy as a sort of gerontocracy setting the rules of a competitive game in which he is allowed to play only for the smaller stakes, and without knowing precisely the value of the cards.

The Intermediate Statuses

For most individuals who remain permanently in the academic profession, the assistant and associate professorships represent intermediate statuses. Since the model term of appointment for assistant professors is three years and the limit of tenure six years, the same stresses and strains continue upon this level. In the academic hierarchy the assistant professor ranks little above the instructor and is in the disadvantageous position of being neither fish nor fowl. The first word of his title is often a misnomer, for his 'assistance' is often not called for. Like the instructor, he is, in many larger universities, debarred from participation in the more important decisions of the 'inner circle' composed of associate and full professors. The opportunities for securing placement elsewhere may actually be fewer than those for instructors, and his security is little greater. He belongs to an in-between status group, which feels unjustly treated by being placed on a level with the younger and less experienced men who are instructors, and which is also 'insulted' by deliberate exclusions perpetrated from above. The main solace of the assistant professor is that he has at least one foot in the hierarchy.

Although there is precedent for limiting the tenure of associate professors (as of professors) to a first appointment of five years, subject to review for discharge or permanent status at the end of the period, the first permanent tenure is usually achieved with this rank. The employee's chief remaining source of anxiety is that he may be permanently shelved at this stage, since most institutions hesitate to reward mere time-servers with full professorships. After spending several years at this stage he has been in the system long enough to build up definite career expectations, and any pause that threatens to be permanent inevitably causes him to feel let down, frustrated, and even injured. Ordinarily, however, he has reached a mutual compatibility with his institution and begins to take permanent root in the community.

This is the house-and-garden stage for the academician in the large urban university, a stage attained with the assistant professorship in the more complacent atmosphere of lesser institutions, where the feeling of permanency is greater in lower ranks. Arrival at this status also has marked expansive effects upon the egoistic side of the organization personality. The use of the personal pronoun becomes more prominent in his writing, and reference to the work of contemporaries is less deferential. Eccentricities and mannerisms may be cultivated with impunity: the goatee, the cane or umbrella, the *pince-nez*, and numerous other studied affectations of the academician are now permissible symbols of his éclat.

THE FULL PROFESSOR

When the academician has achieved the professorship, his adjustment to the organization is so complete and his status so secure that there are few individual problems derived from mere occupancy of this status. It is an achieved rather than an ascribed status, and once he is there, the competitive pressure shifts from rising and is transmuted into the urgency of living up to the expectations of one's position. Hence it is by no means a fixed position entirely removed from the competitive game. The control forces behind such a status can be strong, and create internalized drives through such negative sanctions as a sense of shame, fear of moral condemnation, or through such a positive sanction as pride. Gossip and other control mechanisms remind him that strains are created in an organization when symbols of achievement are felt to be unjustly held.

It is true that his responsibilities have been increased along with his rights and privileges, yet his position as an employee is sufficiently certain to remove the constant pressure of stresses and strains that fraught his situation on lower levels. Barring serious misconduct, he will not be removed from office, so that almost the only pressure he may experience is the desire to sustain or enhance his established reputation. His position is assuredly no sinecure, for special demands upon his time are likely to be greater than on those below him. Administrative tasks, committee work, public service, and numerous other duties in addition to teaching and research draw upon his energies. These exactions are somewhat offset by research and teaching assistance, hence much of his routine work may be delegated to subordinates; but if he does not resist deflections he can easily devote the major portion of his time to committee work, conferences, correspondence, speeches, and other incidental activities.

Yet he has security, and is beyond the local stigma of non-promotion. The continuity of his position is no longer directly dependent upon the verdict of his compatriots, and aside from the dean and the president he may have no official superiors. In his employee status the principal appraisal he knows about directly is his own self-appraisal. His best scholastic work may still be ahead of him, though ordinarily he has set his own stereotype. As a teacher, he planc his work and checks its results. He is usually convinced of tı.: effectiveness of his own methods, and about the only check upon his complacency is an alarming drop in enrollment or veiled hints from other members of the department. Likewise, the appraisal given by others of his research ceases to be of value as a means of raising his employee status, for, unless there is a distinguished professorship or possibility of transfer to a better university in the offing, he has already 'arrived.'

In short, his situation has largely ceased to involve unknown and uncertain quantities. His institutional lot can still be made very uncomfortable in devious ways, yet inoffensive behavior with a not-too-low minimal performance is sufficient to secure it. This is not to say that the full professor invariably or even typically 'eases up,' for the prestige mechanism may operate more potently in his case than it does below him. The professor represents the final product of a careful and ingenious selective and conditioning system that takes into account both past and probable future performance, so that it is an anomaly to find an individual who has completely lost his sensitivity to the opinions of others.

INSTITUTIONAL ASPECTS OF TENURE AND STATUS

Problems of tenure and status have been considered from the point of view of the typological academician—what are their implications under a rubric that is primarily institutional? It is not intended here to posit a spurious opposition between the individual and the group; however, it is patent that personal and organizational objectives are not always identical. What is desirable in the way of tenure, rank, and so on from one aspect may not be from the other. The university is interested in getting the maximum of performance from its staff, and in finding out where this optimum is among a complex set of variables. Permanent tenure in all ranks might be a boon to the more insecure employees, but it would be a liability to the institution employing them and to the profession as a whole. Up to a certain point the organization must rely upon the fear of loss of position and systematically yet subtly invoke this fear for purposes of stimulus and control. It utilizes both positive and negative sanctions, pride in participation and fear of loss. Informal controls may be in certain instances inadequate, so that a central authority is necessary.

A frequently noted defect in the academic system of tenure is that a sinecure is provided for coasting incompetents in the upper ranks.[8] A defect noted just as frequently but more vociferously is that tenure is not really secure. Institutional needs require provision of the best working conditions for competent functionaries and noiseless riddance schemes for the incompetents; still, it is just at this point that the whole issue of academic freedom arises. From the university angle, non-co-operation is a form of incompetence, and by ingenious definition the 'safe' yet mediocre drone may be deemed competent, and the intellectually alert, conscientious, but socially unorthodox person may be branded as incompetent. The most widely publicized instances of violations of academic freedom have often been those in which tenure was abrogated as a

[8] In lesser colleges and universities where advancement is often largely a matter of seniority, the 'dead wood' and otherwise objectionable members of the faculty provide a favorite indoor game for private faculty parties. This pastime is known as 'Firing the Faculty.' Each participant draws up a list of colleagues he would discharge if he were president, the winner being the person providing the list with the largest number of names found on other lists.

result of outside pressures, yet other pressures just as pernicious may well arise within the institution.

Even if the academic profession were able to enforce a uniform system of tenure such as that advocated by the American Association of University Professors, let us say, this enforcement might eventually defeat some of its purposes by causing the initial selection of 'safe' recruits, and thus stifling individualism. Hence, forcing tenure demands too far is necessarily detrimental to the profession itself. The complexity of the whole issue appears when professional associations find themselves inadvertently defending exhibitionists and incompetents who are ever ready to fall back upon real or alleged violations of the ethics of tenure. In short, tenure is a necessary but not a sufficient condition for academic freedom in its broadest sense.

Another institutional problem involving both tenure and promotion (largely the latter) is that the present system ultimately produces a disproportionate number of employees in the highest status. If the rule of seniority were complete, all individuals who remained in the system long enough would be full professors. Although such a situation is more hypothetical than real, universities often find themselves with too many full professors, and the consequent closure of opportunities for younger men, budgetary difficulties, and other perplexities. The presence of a large number of persons in the highest ranks usually implies advancement on length of service rather than merit, and ultimately cheapens the professorship. Since it becomes impossible for the institution to recognize exceptional individuals, its bargaining power is weakened and it is able neither to hold its own best men nor to attract outstanding persons from other places.

In its efforts to control both general and differential staff metabolism or turnover, the administrative organization guards against routine and stagnation by a graduated 'system' of qualifications. Present methods are certainly far from systematic, but there are periods of review and crisis situations to determine status changes. Leading universities are careful in the advancement of their faculty members, and therefore in many cases the ceremony of status elevation is postponed as long as is feasible in order to heighten competition for placement in the upper brackets. Multiple aspects of this problem are ably put in the following statement:

Conceding that it is neither expedient nor desirable that permanence of tenure should be awarded until after a period of trial, the committee has sought to reconcile the inevitable rigors of a competitive system with that freedom from anxiety which is a condition of wholehearted devotion to present duties and to a full utilization of present opportunities. The system of rank and tenure which is now in force . . . is . . . both too complicated and too protracted. It sometimes leads the teacher to feel that he is entitled to permanent tenure on the ground of his length of service and the multiple hazards which he has survived. His department and the University naturally share his feeling, and sometimes acknowledge a moral obligation to retain for life a man whom they have never at any point explicitly and affirmatively chosen for permanent rank. The time for the crucial decision has been postponed until it is no longer a free decision, the teacher having acquired a cumulative expectation, and the University a cumulative commitment. (Reprinted by permission of the President and Fellows of Harvard College from the *Report*, p. 1.)

Delinquent persons commonly stress their extenuating circumstances, and even average persons like to think of themselves as special cases, so that the concrete individual is always more interested in seeing absolute standards applied to others than to himself, when such an application is not to his own interests.

Each lower member of the staff normally considers himself in line for the rank just above his own, and there is a constant pressure by departments upon the central administration for the promotion of their own younger men. This pressure is brought to bear in type situations where the candidate in question receives an outside offer. In such situations, whether the candidate seriously considers taking the outside offer or not, his bargaining power is enhanced. Indeed, these offers may be solicited with no other purpose than using them as levers to elevate the receiver's local status. It is a game which both sides play, however, for there are universities where faculty members are rarely advanced within a reasonable length of time unless they get bids from elsewhere. When this policy becomes generally known to the local group it plays havoc with morale and the building of institutional *rapport* and loyalty.

To maintain a peak of efficiency, the university has to steer a fine line in order to spur on and not lose its best men, yet concurrently to avoid attaching symbols of recognition to the undeserving. Symbols of recognition and professional status should be in harmony with technical standards of achievement as nearly as possible. Any considerable discrepancy promoting a widespread feeling that men are securing recognition who deserve it less than others, or that the deserving are not being rewarded, is bound to introduce serious strains into any social structure, and to surround each status of the hierarchy with anxiety sentiments that are inimical to effective social organization.

V. PROFESSOR ADMINISTRANT

ACADEMICIANS like to think of themselves as free agents, and are inclined to underestimate the place of administrative functions in directing and holding together the complex social organization of higher learning. In fact, as one college president has pointed out,[1] there is a ubiquitous tendency among professors to belittle the administrative task, so that 'when a man becomes dean or president the reaction of many of his colleagues is from the start, and continues to be, adverse and suspicious. They seem to think that the man, by virtue of his acceptance of administrative responsibility, has suffered some sinister metamorphosis, has been transmogrified.' The functional importance of general administration is attested, however, by the existence of one administrative officer for every six persons employed in instructional work.

The principal administrative statuses we need to consider are those of presidents, deans, and department heads. Since such officers are commonly recruited from the staff, and, in the case of deans and department heads, usually serve concurrently as professors, they are properly deemed academic men. What are the various statuses and functions of the professor administrant? The answer to this question is determined largely by the social structure and organization of the university. Before dealing individually with the administrative statuses, it is necessary to outline the framework into which they are fitted.

[1] Ernest H. Wilkins, 'The Professor Administrant,' *Bulletin of the A.A.U.P.*, XXVII, February 1941, pp. 18-28.

Social Structure of the University

The academician's employee status and his occupational culture are inextricably bound up with the nature of the university, and the real boundaries of his enterprise are set by its social organization. It will be useful here to give a summary typological contrast between the university and other kinds of social structures. Its organization provides an occupational milieu somewhere between the private practitioner type and the highly elaborated administrative hierarchy. The private practitioner type of occupational organization is seen in law and medicine. Both are highly individualistic in their organization, the professional being ordinarily self-employed, responsible to no immediate superiors, and having considerable latitude in the exercise of his own judgment. Superordination and subordination are minimized, as there is no formal scalar principle or hierarchical arrangement in such occupations.

At the opposite pole is the authoritarian type of organization represented by the more or less rigid administrative hierarchy. This appears graphically as a pyramid symbolizing a unitary end, centralized control, and increasing numbers of members toward the bottom. Authority is elaborately graded and functions minutely delegated. As in the Catholic Church and in the army, authority is typically delegated downward. The subordinate exercises little individual authority, but at most a certain discretion. Average individuals begin employment at or near the bottom of the occupational hierarchy; there is no presumption that they will pass on to much higher positions, and seldom is there a definite career goal. Variations of this basic pattern are found in most business corporations and in the non-professional divisions of civil service.

Between the individualistic and the hierarchical poles, the social organization of the university occupies a rather anomalous position. Although the presence of large numbers of functionaries within a single framework nullifies the possibility of an individualistic pattern, their being professional men introduces a new note that mitigates against the rigidity of authoritarianism or hierarchical fixity. Where employees are specialists of a high order of complexity, those persons in purely administrative capacities are ordinarily incompetent to perform, delegate, supervise, or even evaluate detailed activities. The differences between the teacher-researcher and the administrator are more analogous to those between the infantry officer and the artillery officer than to those between the captain and the general. Or, technically put, the difference is primarily functional rather than scalar.

A rigid administrative hierarchy that elaborately delegates functions and issues orders makes competence impossible. By its very nature, professional work requires a large sphere of individual authority, and necessitates the employment of specialists who are 'turned loose on their jobs.' Morale, discipline, and a division of labor are highly desirable, but these must be according to general guiding principles rather than set rules. The specialist cannot be under detailed supervision, and at most can be subjected only to a general checking up. The university faculty, according to the ideal type, appears as a body of equals. With this initial generalization in mind it will later become clear why certain stresses and strains develop within the occupational structure.

It is commonly known that university faculties embody wide differences in attainments as reflected in prestige and reputation, and that these may be made the basis for corresponding differences in rank (not to mention gradations superimposed by gerontocracy, seniority, and other principles). Nevertheless, two things may be pointed out here: first, a close approach to the structure of an administrative hierarchy is without functional basis; and second, authoritarianism is counter to the main traditions of university organization in the Western world. A corporate body of equals making collective decisions, much in the manner of the medieval guild, is the tradition.

To mention an antecedent form, the medieval university was for the most part an unhierarchical and democratic organization consisting solely of professors and students. J. M. Cattell has shown a number of conspicuous features of the earlier type:

> The professors, of course, had complete control of the conditions under which degrees were given and in the selection of their colleagues and successors. The doctor earned the *jus ubique docendi;* he was not employed or dismissed. There was an elected council and rectors were elected for a year or for some other short period. Only later there came to be a single rector for the entire studium. The whole paraphernalia of the modern university—endowments, buildings and grounds, trustees and president, heads of departments and deans, curricula, grades and examinations—were absent or subordinated. There were indeed all sorts of routine, customs and limitations, but the university, in an age of feudalism and of absolutism of state and church, attained a remarkable freedom.[2]

Despite the common medieval pattern, there are today variations in the structure of universities. Oxford and Cambridge are groups of independent colleges, with master and fellows forming the corporation, which owns the plant and divides the endowment income among the members. Organization shows little authoritative gradation, as executive powers are delegated by the members themselves, and control is largely in the hands of elected committees. In pre-Nazi Germany there was also a diffusion of formal control; each faculty elected its own dean, and the votes of all full professors elected the rector. New staff appointments, nominally made through the Minister of Education, were actually made upon the recommendations of colleagues in related departments.[3] In the pro-

---

[2] *Science and Education,* Vol. III, N. Y., The Science Press, 1913, p. 5.
[3] For changes under the Nazi regime, see E. Y. Hartshorne, *The German Universities and National Socialism,* Cambridge, Harvard University Press, 1937.

vincial universities or more recent English institutions of higher learning, control is in the hands of a court, a council, and a senate or faculty; the opinion of the faculty guides the selection of all executives.

The American Association of University Professors and other professional organizations such as the Teachers Union generally advocate a greater diffusion of authority in universities here. A loosely organized fellowship of scholars is the expressed preference over against the corporation modeled on the pattern of an industrial concern. Committee T of the Association has made the following recommendations, which are representative of widespread academic sentiment:

I. There ought to be a close understanding between the faculty and the board of trustees and to this end agencies other than the president are required for joint conference between the two bodies.

II. The general faculty should participate with the trustees in the nomination of a president, and the faculty of a school or division should have a voice in selecting the dean who presides over that school.[4]

This same report further advocates faculty participation in such matters of policy as appointments, promotions, dismissals, and budgets. Collective rather than centralized authority is deemed the better practice. In many leading institutions the faculty has a large measure of control; particularly is this true where tenure is permanent for those of professorial rank, and there are enough individuals with sufficiently established reputations to insure bargaining power.

Departures from the Prototype

Many lesser and more autocratic universities (a frequent combination) maintain the general faculty meeting merely as

[4] 'The Place and Function of Faculties in University and College Government,' *Bulletin of the A.A.U.P.*, XXIV, 1938, p. 141.

a democratic gesture on the part of the administration. No realist would hold that any important matters of policy are ever decided on such occasions. A prevalent low regard for the effectiveness of the faculty meeting is seen in the following professorial analysis:

The faculty of an American college was holding, in May, its second meeting of the academic year. 'The administrative officers of the college,' announced the president, 'have gone carefully into the semester system as contrasted with the quarter system. After consultation with some members of the faculty it has been decided that the quarter system will be abandoned and the semester system adopted, beginning when college opens in the fall. I believe that this change will improve our teaching.'
'The necessary reorganization and renumbering of courses has not yet been completed. If any of you have any suggestions to make at this point please communicate with the dean.'
The moral disintegration of the faculty of the college had proceeded so far that no persons arose to protest so autocratic a statement. There was a time when the faculty of the college met every Monday, sometimes for the entire afternoon. These meetings were devoted to the consideration of the most pressing problems which confronted the institution . . . But, unfortunately, picayune matters also came in for consideration at these weekly sessions . . . A limit was too seldom put on debate, details were too infrequently referred to committees, there was too indefinite an idea of the functions of the faculty meeting. As a result they fell into disrepute . . . More and more busy teachers failed to attend. That made great administrative control inevitable. Today the faculty of the college meets about twice a year and sits passively and listens to announcements and to remarks-for-the-good-of-the-order made by an able but aggressive president.[5]

The place and function of faculties in college and university government has been extensively investigated by Committee T of the A.A.U.P. over a period of years. Its most recent re-

[5] John P. Williams, 'The Faculty Meeting and Democracy,' ibid. pp. 418-19.

sults [6] (as of 1939) give the following pattern for the typical college and university:

1. It has no operating plan for facilitating exchange of opinion between the faculty and the trustees or regents.

2. It lacks definite procedure for consultation between the faculty and the board of control in the choice of a president.

3. It provides for the consultation of departmental chairmen or heads with appointment officers regarding appointments, promotions, and dismissals of teaching staff.

4. It has no provision for faculty consultation in reference to the appointment of deans.

5. It provides for the consultation of department heads in reference to all departmental budgetary needs involving equipment, supplies, and personnel.

6. It makes the appointment of departmental heads or chairmen through the dean or president upon delegated authority (of the board of control) without faculty consultation.

The major findings of this entire inquiry have been summarized by Paul W. Ward, the Chairman:

(1) As a group, state universities in their procedures provide for significantly more faculty participation in budgetary procedures than does the total group; but specific universities may have either democratic or autocratic administrative structures. (2) Among women's colleges there is a significantly larger amount of trustee-faculty cooperation, and of faculty participation in appointments, promotions, and dismissals than is characteristic of the total 177 institutions; but a slightly smaller degree of consultation with faculty concerning budgetary matters is to be observed. These colleges vary widely in their procedures. (3) Engineering colleges vary less than the total group, approximating modal usage in their procedures, but tending to be slightly more democratic than the total group in dealing with appointments, promotions, dismissals and with budgetary procedures. (4) The teachers colleges, in general,

[6] 'Place and Function of Faculties in College and University Government,' ibid. xxvi, April 1940, pp. 171-85.

are autocratic in their administrative procedures. Since these colleges equip many teachers, a careful study . . . will give cause for reflection to anyone interested in conserving the traditional democratic procedures of community life in this country. The replies of this group also indicate that 16 of 23 faculties do not elect any faculty committee. (5) The sampling of large endowed universities with graduate schools indicates that they are significantly more democratic in their usages than the total group, although conspicuously less so than the most democratic state universities. (Ibid. pp. 185-6.)

These data and their implications bear out the common impression that leading universities are on the whole more democratic in their government than are lesser institutions. Any random sample of institutions of higher learning would reveal some in which there is a trend away from faculty participation, others which show procedural stability, and still others moving in the direction of more self-government by their faculties. At present, there seems to be no clear indication of a general trend in all universities, even though faculties expressing a desire for change usually show a preference for more democratic forms.

It seems almost self-evident that the effectiveness of a competent faculty should depend to a large extent upon its administrative organization. Yet, in many places scant utilization is made of professorial capacities in the matter of policy making. With reference to fiscal relations, personnel problems, and even the determination of educational and research objectives and procedures, the administration may place the staff in the passive role of a discussion body, while denying it the prerogatives of invention and proposal, acceptance or rejection. A shrewdly paternalistic administration may, of course, enlist understanding and support from the ranks without providing for their effective representation in controlling emphases in the institution's educational activities. Again, there is some question whether or not prompt and effective action is possible in the face of delays and frustrations arising from vested interests, staff members of low morale and inert tendencies, and others who retard the efficacy of democratic processes.

Without a more exhaustive inquiry than has yet been made it would be hazardous to state that there is a persistent correlation between the democratic organizations of the major institutions in this country and their educational eminence. On the other hand, it is equally fallacious to conclude that democracy is a 'luxury' that the lesser colleges and universities cannot afford.

Sources of Authoritarianism

What many critics fail to see or to acknowledge is that existing hierarchical forms of university organization develop from both internal and external pressures. Faculty indifference, lassitude, or impotence in matters of control are more often the result of gradually changed conditions than they are of administrative Machiavellism. The necessity for fund raising, for keeping a growing but loosely integrated structure from falling apart, and the deficiencies of scholars in collectively administering a complex organization have led to a semi-bureaucratic framework where most types of authority filter down from above. Funds, investments, and their general allotment are usually handled by trustees. Educational policy, standards of scholarship, and direction of research are still determined by the faculty in most leading institutions. The modern university with its multifarious activities is far removed from its medieval counterpart.

Upon weighing the dire possibilities of a lack of unity, and the general inefficiency of collective action against the dangers of arbitrary or incompetent action on the part of a single individual or small group, most professors are willing to concede a large measure of authority (mitigated by responsibility) to individuals who make business methods and academic statesmanship their major employment. A great many academicians would agree with A. Lawrence Lowell that

. . . the non-professional board is the only body, or the most satisfactory body, to act as arbiter between the different groups of experts. Everyone knows that in an American university or college there is a ceaseless struggle for the means of development between different departments, and someone must decide upon the relative merits of their claims. In a university with good traditions the professors would be more ready to rely on the fairness and wisdom of a well constituted board of trustees than on one composed of some of their own number, each affected almost unavoidably by a bias in favor of his particular subject.[7]

Regardless of its importance in making or breaking the prestige of a university in one regime, traditionally and ideally the administrative hierarchy has only secondary functions. The legal position of university trustees is the same as that of a business corporation board, but with more circumscribed functions. The 'club' pattern of ultimate control adequate for a medieval university or a modern institute for advanced study would hardly function in co-ordinating the complex activities of the average university. In effect, however, university organization is seldom a pure type of autocracy, democracy, or bureaucracy—the actual pattern differing from one institution to another, depending upon size, historical development, financial resources, and a number of other factors. A division of labor inevitably follows growth, and what in the beginning was everybody's business becomes a distribution of responsibilities as the club pattern gives way to a semi-bureaucratic pattern. What are the points at which such a break occurs?

The effect of a capitalistic economy upon the university structure has been stressed by numerous critics. It is easy to overemphasize materialistic influences, even though they are undoubtedly at work. Immediate results are seen in course standardization, departmental administrative systems, hierarchical gradations of staff, and lay board controls.

[7] *At War with Academic Traditions in America*, Cambridge, Harvard University Press, 1934, p. 287. (Reprinted by permission of the President and Fellows of Harvard College.)

Hierarchical gradation and bureaucratic subordination, as Veblen has mentioned, have little direct relation to the everyday work of higher learning. Widely divergent student capacities and vast numbers necessitate the parceling out of 'standard units of erudition' that lend themselves to a detailed accountancy. Abraham Flexner, who has been greatly influenced by Veblen, likens the organization of a modern American university to that of a department store purveying 'excellence as well as mediocrity and inferiority.' Although the expensive and non-functional piles of collegiate Gothic are seldom the professors' own choosing, there must be a place to work. There must be also a rather costly library, apparatus, means of publication, and so on, in addition to students and assistants. All of this requires a somewhat elaborate administrative machinery. Administration multiplication in turn necessitates a clerical force, which employs hundreds of office workers merely to keep track of the activities of students and teachers (the former reaching a peak of almost 40,000 in one American university).

Heterogeneity and sheer size break down elasticity of structure and informality of relations as the social system becomes more formalized. A corps of secretaries insulates the president from faculty contacts; many of his lesser functions are delegated to deans, who in turn have assistant deans. Even professors themselves take on the pattern and surround their desks with dictaphones, office assistants, and metal file cases. The click of the typewriter and the whir of the Hollerith machine become a substitute for leisurely talk and the 'personal touch.' Promptly at hour intervals, myriad students bustle from one carefully timed lecture to another, and professors hastily fasten their portfolios to return to research projects and to minor administrative tasks.

WEAKNESSES OF THE CONTEMPORARY PATTERN

Weber, Mannheim, and others have shown that the fundamental tendency of bureaucratic thought is to turn all sorts of problems into administrative problems. A keenly iconoclastic mind (such as Veblen's was) is prone to seize upon the inherent weaknesses of such a structure and bring them into prominence. That the test of competency under materialistic principles tends to become statistical, that departmental rivalries should spring up like weeds, that there should be a competition for students, funds, and numerical 'results' is to some extent inevitable.

Yet, to say that 'the university is conceived as a business house dealing in merchantable knowledge, placed under the governing hand of a captain of erudition, whose office it is to turn the means in hand to account in the largest feasible output,' as Veblen states it, is rather a crotchety conclusion. Whatever may be the apparent importance of the officials and of the red tape that swathes the social body of the university, it is still rather generally recognized that the professors form the life blood.

There are many functional weaknesses in the cumbersome semi-bureaucratic pattern. It becomes more difficult for the staff to modify objectives to meet changed circumstances, and procedures take precedence over principles, as principles give way to rules. The loose integration possible with a small, homogeneous group is supplanted in many instances by subordination and superordination; horizontal contacts are diminished as the scalar chain is lengthened. Communality of interests and purposes is broken down, and the human beings for whom the structure was originally formed are lost sight of. Routine administrative tasks multiply in geometric ratio, teaching and research energy are deflected into them, and concurrently most staff members are deprived of any opportunity for shaping important institutional policies.

A number of administrative units divide labor within the larger university organization, but the most important for the ordinary academic man is the department. His daily activities are determined by its organization, and it is at this point of reference that his most constant and vital interests are found. The organization of higher learning by subject-matter departments is apparently the most logical and certainly the most prevalent scheme yet evolved. Notwithstanding, it has been widely condemned for various shortcomings. That it produces anarchic effects such as the duplication of efforts, lack of planning and co-ordination, minimization of outside contacts and mutual interaction, a dispersal of effort and pottering away at isolated problems has often been pointed out. However necessary such an intellectual division of labor, it inadvertently creates staff tensions within the university, and often has some of the following results:

1. Rivalry between the various departments in securing students for their classes, by appealing either to administrative organization which decides upon required portions of the curriculum or to the students themselves who decide upon elective courses at the registration period.

2. Rivalry between departments in securing administrative favor in the apportionment of funds for maintenance and expansion, or in the effort to enhance their academic prestige in the institution as a whole.

3. The narrowing of the interests and activities of the members of a department to problems wholly related to the development of the subject of that department.

4. The sharpening of the lines of specialized knowledge for the student—the building of tightly compartmented units in the education of the student.[8]

What has been termed the 'scramble for a place in the academic sun' is institutional, departmental, and personal. Departments compete for preferment, power, and general importance. Conversely, 'buck passing,' shirking, and short cut-

[8] From James S. Kinder, *The Internal Administration of the Liberal Arts College*, N. Y., Teachers College, Columbia University, 1934, p. 7.

ting occur when formal organization is weak, duties not sufficiently explicit, and 'politics' is permitted to define situations. Events appearing to the outsider as purely intellectual controversies are frequently instigated not so much by a genuine concern with knowledge *per se* as by vested interests engaging in internecine warfare.

These tempests in the academic teapot are quite often promulgated by picayune and petty issues having little or nothing to do with the advancement of learning, as the pressure toward competitive rather than co-operative activity magnifies the rivalries of contiguous departments and steps up the jealous guardianship of respective frontiers by cliques and intrigues. Favored departments use every device to maintain their positions and keep down rivals, less favored departments often resort to unorthodox procedures to elevate their status, and university problems tend to be regarded first of all in terms of departmental prestige.

Major Administrative Statuses

The king-pin in the social organization of the university is the president. No other employee occupies a status involving duties so diverse, complex, and far-flung; in fact, as one occupant of the status has remarked, the demands are almost too unrealistic to be met by 'one single specimen of human clay.' President H. W. Dodds, of Princeton University, has aptly said, 'I once saw a complete job specification drawn by the trustees of a university in search of a president. Talk about dual personalities! The gifts of a financier, business man, scholar, preacher, salesman, diplomat, politician, administrator, Y.M.C.A. secretary, were some of the qualifications enumerated in addition to high moral character and a happy marriage to a charming wife.' [9]

[9] For a compilation of the speech-reactions of presidents to their numerous roles, consult Edgar W. Knight's *What College Presidents Say*, Chapel Hill, University of North Carolina Press, 1940.

Strictly speaking, the university president is not an academic man in our sense of the word, and the treatment of his roles will therefore be cursory. In the vast majority of instances, however, he has been a professor at some time during his career. A number of years ago, the membership of the office was recruited largely from the clergy; today, except in denominational institutions, only a small proportion of individuals is furnished by the ministry. Aside from the professorship as a source of supply, the office draws recruits from general executive work, such as deanships, foundation directorates, editorships, secretaryships, and so on.

There is a widespread but mistaken notion that stands in need of correction with reference to the backgrounds of college and university presidents. One well-known commentator has stated that not more than a third of the group is derived from the ranks of professors. An investigation of the occupational experience of presidents of the thirty leading graduate institutions in this country reveals that only two of the major executives have had no professorial experience. Of these two, one had been the comptroller of his university, and the other had been a corporation lawyer. Most of the twenty-eight former professors, it is true, had not achieved pre-eminence as scientists or scholars before going into administrative work, but several have stood at or near the top as specialists in their respective subject-matter fields. In major universities there is a premium for administrators who combine executive ability and high scholarship. Elsewhere, the major executive is more often selected primarily for his business abilities and personal contacts, and only secondarily for anything that he may signify in the universe of pure intellect.

Although the president may have begun as a scholar or scientist, the chances of his continuing as such are almost nil, so manifold are pressures upon his time. In 1902, J. McKeen Cattell foresaw an inevitable division of labor in what were formerly the president's sole prerogatives.

He cannot be *in loco parentis* for 5,000 students; select and control 400 officers; coordinate the conflicting demands of incommensurable schools and departments; arrange diverse curricula in accordance with changing needs; superintend buildings and grounds; manage an estate of $10,000,000, and secure additional funds always needed; be a public orator and monthly contributor to magazines; attend bicentennials, sesquicentennials and semi-sesquicentennials; occupy positions of honor and trust whenever called upon by the community or nation, and all the rest. It has become necessary to delegate part of these duties to deans and other officers, and it seems probable that the office of president should be divided and filled by two men of different type: one an educational expert, in charge of internal administration; the other a man of prominence and weight in the community, in charge of external affairs.[10]

Professors are hyper-critical of the mistakes and shortcomings of all administrators, and the president is always a particular cynosure. Publicly lauded, he is often privately categorized by truculent subordinates as 'one who preaches democracy but practices autocracy,' a 'crude bully,' 'a wily political manipulator,' 'a bulldozer of his faculty, but a sycophant of millionaires and politicians,' or 'a bedeviled weakling who means well at first but gradually falls into bad ways under pressure.'

The consensus is that ideally he should be the 'benevolent head' of a society of scholars and scientists who are treated as equals. Yet in America there is a high premium on executive work; this being true there is a strong tendency for other parts of the social structure to be assimilated to such a dominant part. Academic men, like other men, relish authority, so that functional cleavages easily turn into relationships of superiors and subordinates. Just as the average doctor has a stereotyped fear of not being his own boss under socialized medicine, so does the academician dislike the sort of administrative pattern that he fears will put lower employees under orders.

[10] 'Concerning the American University,' *Popular Science Monthly*, June 1902, p. 180.

No doubt faculty shortcomings have contributed to the shift of many controls from scholars to full-time administrators. Furthermore, it should be borne in mind that the professional executive is seldom one who has no first-hand understanding of the scholar's point of view. Whether an administrative post is the salvation of a poor scholar-scientist or the ruination of a good one is beside the point here; what should be stressed is that administrators are under situational imperatives to place emphasis upon practical efficiency and even short-cut methods. These imperatives may result in actions ranging from mild paternalism to complete tyranny, with regents or trustees lending support to or forcing 'business-like methods.' Moreover, certain functionaries must be vested with over-all responsibilties, since power for helpful administration cannot be conferred without the corollary risk of harmful administration.

The president is in an aloof position as the highest executive, and is plainly regarded by the faculty as one apart. The dean, on the other hand, is something of a hybrid: he is apart from the rank and file of the staff, and still is not on a par with the president as an administrator. Ordinarily he is a professor administrant in that he typically occupies a professorship in some department, and in many instances teaches one or two classes. (The American Association of University Professors will not admit presidents to membership, but does include deans who are actively engaged in other than administrative functions.)

Excluding miscellaneous deans of student personnel and the numerous assistant varieties whose titles merely dignify clerical tasks, deans are the most important liaison officers between the staff and the president. Unlike the presidency, which is always the most important status in any college or university, irrespective of its occupant, the deanship varies widely in power and importance according to the capacities of the office holder. With some persons, the office becomes a mere clearing house; with others, it becomes a positive source of university policy. Correspondingly, there is a standing joke among deans that the dean is a man 'who doesn't know quite enough to be a university professor, but who knows too much to be a university president.'

Within the colleges, schools, and divisions of the university over which the deans preside are found the related subject-matter departments. The key position in departmental organization is that of the head or chairman. The holder of this office may be appointed by the president, chosen by the division, selected by department members, or the chairmanship may follow a regular rotation among staff members above a certain rank. How the head or chairman is chosen and what authority he exercises is essentially a problem in power distribution. ('Power' may be here defined as the chance to influence the conduct of others in accordance with the intentions of the power holder, whether those in a subordinate position like it or not.) An autocratic policy concentrates individual power, whereas a democratic policy diffuses it. Regardless of the selection method or scope of authority, the head is the liaison officer between the department and the next administrative unit.

It is interesting to note at this juncture the various means by which this or that alternative may be achieved, such as long tenure versus rotation of office, appointment from above versus selection by equals, and so on. The longer and more nearly permanent the tenure of office, the more authority the head customarily assumes or is delegated. In autocratic institutions he is likely to have many of his nominal powers usurped by the president or dean, and in democratic institutions he often finds them curtailed by other department or division members of professorial rank, so that in actual situations he may fall between two stools. His power and privileges, however, are usually greater than those of the rank and file, and being human he endeavors to extend them.

Much of his authority, even when important decisions are arrived at collectively, lies in the ultimately decisive factor of his recommendations for appointments, promotions, assignment of courses and teaching loads. For example, an A.A.U.P. study of member groups found that in 35 per cent of the institutions the department head alone is responsible for appointments, in 15 per cent in association with the dean or president, and in 10 per cent of the instances with other department members. His decision is therefore the vital one in about 60 per cent of all appointments.[11] Whether departmental distribution of power is more democratic in practice than in form, or *vice versa*, often depends upon the aims and tactics of the head.

His position is such that disgruntled subordinates are inclined to make him a scapegoat—hence the prevailing sentiment among many is that his function should be 'ministrative rather than administrative,' and that the emphasis should be switched from the unit to be managed to the unit to be served. A recent investigation has shown that in most actual situations subordinates do not consider that department heads abuse their powers. Of 188 reports to an A.A.U.P. committee, 75 gave a categorical answer of no abuse, past abuses were indicated by 4, and 20 reports were made of occasional and really serious abuses.[12]

Regardless of the formal definition of the department head's

[11] 'Committee Report,' *Bulletin*, xv, 1929, p. 182.

[12] 'The Place and Functions of Faculties in University Organization,' *Bulletin*, xxiii, 1937, pp. 220-28. As indicated by this report, common charges against the department head are: favoritism; undue influence on younger teachers and students; interference with other men's work; selfishness in taking best courses or lightest loads; habitual autocracy, with no consultation of approximate equals. These abuses are almost invariably regarded as a 'consequence of the personal characteristics of the offenders.' The problem is seen to be one of personalities, which cannot be met by legislation.

With reference to authority, only 20 of 118 institutions indicated existence of written regulations of power. Authority usually follows customs, or is determined by delegation from deans and presidents. Three-fifths of the groups report consultation on course scheduling; three-fifths indicate no direction of course teaching.

At some institutions the office is regularly rotated; at others it is elective; in some places committees govern; no single model for all departments is the scheme at many universities.

functions, in order to be satisfactory to his colleagues he must justify the institutional fixation of authority upon him through genuine leadership, and effect *rapport* not only by word but also by the stimulus of example, since he is in face-to-face contact with members of the department.

SOME EFFECTS OF POWER DISTRIBUTION

Those who dispense largesse are certain to make dependants, if not create disciples, for much of the academician's immediate welfare, irrespective of his technical competence, depends on administrative policy and how he fits into the scheme of things. The actual courses taught by him complement the offerings of colleagues, and thus a group of men all working in the same subdivision of a field is indeed rare. New men are brought into a department with a view of their specialized abilities, but there is also a selection on the basis of an academic traditionalism which causes like to breed like. A department of literature in which linguists are in the saddle is not likely initially to select or later to promote the humanist type of scholar. A political science department noted for its conservatism does not foster radicalism among its members.

As the recent faculty report at Harvard has mentioned, there is even the inheritance by successive generations of techniques and approaches that may ultimately have a narrowing and stifling effect upon individual initiative. In other words, the department takes on the *status quo* stereotype of conditioning which develops conformity of an intellectually inbred type:

The common tendency is to over-value the qualities that make a young man a merely 'sound,' industrious, technically proficient, and 'productive' man of research in an established specialty, and one who does efficient and reliable, routine work as a scholar and teacher, fits obligingly into the niche or groove his department provides for him, is always 'cooperative' in the work of the department, accepts all the aims and standards for his work approved by his elders, and is in no way a nuisance, problem, or disturbing influence; to over-value all these respectable and convenient qualities, and under-value the different qualities . . . of the young man who above all is vigorously, intellectually alive and independent, whose aspiration and bent is to be primarily a thinker rather than a 'scholar,' who boldly challenges accepted ideas in his general field and related fields and is provocative or stimulating in discussions with his colleagues and with students, and who, in a word, chiefly 'shines' not by efficient, routine industry, and conformity, but rather as an invigorating, intellectual force within the university community.[13]

The non-conformist within the system, whether he be a new member of the staff or an old member with new ideas, by virtue of his actions implies that there are other ways just as good as the traditional modes, or even better, and hence tends to devaluate precedent. If he is a 'good fellow' his associates tend to be tolerant, but if he proves personally obnoxious, a wall of social ostracism may be gradually built around him, until he finds himself not being recommended for promotion, or even being dismissed because of his 'non-cooperative' attitudes. In less extreme cases, however, the individual merely encounters annoying obstacles or indifference to his efforts.[14]

By way of summary, it may be said that we now have reviewed the principal employee statuses that the academician

[13] *Report on Some Problems of Personnel in the Faculty of Arts and Sciences*, p. 72. (Reprinted by permission of the President and Fellows of Harvard College.) The quotation is from an assistant professor in the social sciences.

[14] Such a case is illustrated by the following experience of a well-known psychologist.

'Princeton tradition favored a strong staff in philosophy. Any progressive suggestion on my part was overwhelmingly voted down in the Department meetings. When I asked for a second assistant they would express sympathy, but at the same time they would point out that a fourth or fifth assistant in philosophy was needed more. It was with difficulty that I succeeded in getting permission to introduce a new course in genetic psychology. Some years later, after repeated efforts, we were able to get the name of the Department changed to include psychology.' From Howard C. Warren's autobiographical sketch in *A History of Psychology in Autobiography*, Carl Murchison, ed., Worcester, Mass., Clark University Press, 1930, p. 460.

encounters in the social organization of the university. Seldom does the 'club' type of informal organization prevail; equally rare is the complete autocracy; and even the purely bureaucratic type of structure, with its rigid departmentalization of activities, minute delegation of responsibilities, and fully formulated rules of procedure, is an uncommon type. Yet these typological constructs afford unambiguous extreme schemes against which the deviations of concrete universities may be measured. The weight of sheer numbers usually, but not invariably, veers university organization in the direction of the bureaucratic pattern.

There are so many variables involved, notwithstanding, that it is hazardous to set forth generalizations concerning the relations of structure in absolute terms to other factors. Knowing that a university is privately endowed or publicly supported and controlled, for instance, does not enable one to predict its social organization. Even with respect to size categories, universities exhibit no uniformity of structure. Vastly more important than such quantifiable variables for the social organization of the university are factors of a more intangible nature.

Lesser colleges and universities often tend toward authoritarianism in structure when their financial support is insecure and inadequate. Personnel turn-over is high and staff competence and bargaining power low, so that democratic organization represents a 'luxury' that the rank and file cannot forcefully demand. In these weaker institutions, administrators are not as frequently men of broad scholastic background and genuine eminence as in the case of major universities, but are more often political appointees, fund raisers, manipulators, and others who have ascended from the rungs of quasi-academic posts whence they have acquired characteristics that mark the 'go getter.' The methods of such men more closely approximate those of business executives handling subordinates than of the ideal type of academic administrator dealing with equals. In the major or more reputable universities, on the other hand, there is a stronger bargaining power on the part of a superior staff usually protected by security of tenure, a firmly established tradition of power distribution, a more adequate outside support together with looser control, and a correspondingly smaller need for martinet-salesman mentality in executive positions.

PART II

ACADEMIC STATUS

VI. STATUS APPRAISAL

In the chapters of Part I we described the various rungs of the occupational ladder, and observed our academician as he ascended them. The normal expectancy within the profession is that an individual entering as a recruit shall eventually become a professor or professor administrant. Each of the temporal statuses of the career has its special problems, but there are other problems of status that are spatial as well as temporal. They are spatial because they affect all functionaries of the university, irrespective of rank. These are the problems centering about status appraisal or evaluation, status protection or professional organization, and socio-economic status or the class position of members of the academic profession in the larger community. These will be our main concerns in Part II. Let us first consider, then, the matter of status appraisal.

Every social status carries with it rights and duties; occupancy of a status means that a person is expected to perform certain functions. Thus translated into action, a status becomes a role. In his numerous roles, the academician may merely fulfil the demands placed upon him, he may fall short of meeting them, or he may go beyond them. Since he functions in a competitive system, it is necessary to know what these expectancies are and how his performance of them is judged. What is the typical activity pattern, and how is he rewarded or penalized for success or failure? In Part III we shall see how the answer to this question is affected by the process of competition and by the prestige values of the university world. Our immediate purpose is to inquire into the administrative evaluation of faculty services.

Before going into the complexities of appraisal, we should remind ourselves that the social organization of a university is a quite different thing from that of a factory. To return to the earlier contention that a university is ideally a 'society of equals,' two functional reasons for this view may be mentioned. First, from the perspective of academic freedom there is the danger that lower people will be put under orders, and second, the functioning of an elaborate status hierarchy presupposes relatively infallible methods of attaching symbols of achievement to achievement. Any attempt to tie these latter up too closely necessarily creates results inimical to the smooth functioning of an intricate social system, since there is at present no precise mechanism for determining distinctions for a large and diverse group of men.

Personnel managers of industrial enterprises have found that even piece workers cannot be treated as robots, and university administrators know that the proper evaluation of faculty achievement is one of their most crucial concerns. Indeed, this is a prime source of dilemma for the professor administrant. If a single criterion be demanded, then technical competence is the most satisfactory, but age, maturity, length of service, and peculiarities of each individual situation can hardly be ignored. No basis for promotion has yet evolved which provides ready-made answers to all employer and employee perplexities. Fundamental disharmonies result from the 'up or out' system, carefully codified rules of seniority, or rigid adherence to any inflexible system (not to mention arbitrariness, the most disliked of all policies) which ignores the fact that university people, like all other human beings, do not like to be treated as mere instrumentalities.

Type Situations

We are here concerned less with general cautions and admonitions, however, than with actual and proposed procedures to be observed in existing universities. What are the more im-

portant problems of type situations found with reference to
evaluation of what the academician does and is expected to
do? Whom does an institution dismiss, retard, or promote,
and how does it determine who its best men are? The real
state of affairs is less well integrated than it superficially appears to be, and attaching recognition symbols to achievement,
though institutionally valued, is not well articulated. Any administrator will grant the verisimilitude of the following hypothetical instance:

. . . The university president in his swivel chair is still confronted by the enigma of qualitative evaluation. A promotion
is to be made, and there are four available candidates. One
has written two books, but the pundits in his field call them
'unsound' and 'theoretical.' Is he a genius or a fool? The other
has written only three somewhat incomprehensible articles on
esoteric subjects, but the wise men and great consider them
promising of better things to come. The third has written
nothing, but the great professor whom he is assisting swears
that he possesses the most searching mind he has ever come
in contact with. Number four has written one book which is
declared fair, one article which suggests the same promise as
number two. One and three are acclaimed by students as brilliant teachers; two, one hears, is a dull lecturer; four has had
little teaching experience. What is the administrator going to
do? Evidently, all four are men of some ability; appointing
any one of them will not wreck the university. Yet, he is
supposed to pick the one who will be most brilliant and distinguished at fifty. I am glad I do not have to make that selection.[1]

In his further analysis of the problem of selection, Professor
Friedrich points out that Kant, who published nothing of consequence until he was fifty-seven, would have been eliminated
in the modern American university long before beginning
The Critique of Pure Reason. An opposite type of career is
represented by Hume, who did his most important work at
the age of twenty-seven. Administrative selection faces a diffi-

[1] Carl J. Friedrich, 'The Selection of Professors,' The Atlantic, January 1938, p. 112.

cult problem in predicting when the best work will be done. In the physical sciences the academician matures earlier than in the humanities and social sciences, where wide reading and experience are as essential to important work as empirical research. Along with many other writers on the subject, Friedrich advocates more objective selection, with democratic, open competition, instead of the method of secretive consultation between small faculty groups and the president. Neither teaching, scholarship, nor public acclaim would be the sole test of ability, but there would be test lectures before the faculty, open advertising of vacancies, and submission of writings to leading authorities.

THE EVALUATION OF SERVICES

Despite the inherent difficulties in evaluating faculty services and the admitted impossibility of attaining perfect discrimination in attaching symbols of achievement to actual performance, individual academicians are nonetheless rewarded or 'punished'[2] for what is regarded as success or failure in living up to the requirements of their various statuses. That prevailing systems are imperfect or their operation faulty is beside the point here; our interest is in what happens. One way of determining what actually occurs is to note factors conditioning promotion as seen from administrative points of view. A report from the University of Minnesota indicates, for example, that the factors entering into promotions made there

[2] An A.A.U.P. study of dismissals in 31 different institutions gives reasons cited for the negative evaluation of faculty services in the following order of importance: (1) poor teaching coupled with some other shortcoming; (2) personal incompatibility or failure to get along with colleagues; (3) failure to show positive excellence in any direction; (4) lack of scholarly output, together with some other weakness; (5) lack of scholarly output as the sole factor; (6) poor teaching as the sole factor; (7) 'race'; (8) religion. Other reasons occasionally mentioned were 'erratic judgment and tactlessness,' 'sex,' and 'feud in the department.' (*Bulletin*, 1929, p. 177 ff.)

between 1913 and 1931 were in the following order of importance: 'teaching, 43.4 per cent; productive scholarship, 27.6 per cent; student counseling, 11.6 per cent; administrative work, 11 per cent; and public service, 6.4 per cent.'[3] Similar findings for Indiana University give almost the same order: 'teaching, 35.4 per cent; productive scholarship, 22.9 per cent; administrative work, 9.9 per cent; student counseling, 7.1 per cent; and public service, 5.1 per cent.'[4] The complete reliability of formally ascribed reasons for promotions assumes accuracy of self-imputation and candor of revelation on the part of the department heads, deans, and presidents, to be sure, but the close comparability of results from these two institutions indicates a marked similarity of practice. Teaching and productive scholarship assume a priority over all other factors in each place, and both of these items are considered proportionately more significant at Minnesota, the larger university. Though no statistical compilations are available for universities that outrank either Minnesota or Indiana in general prestige, a sampling of subjective opinions indicates that productive scholarship or research would loom much larger as a factor at such institutions as Chicago, Harvard, and Columbia.

At the University of Michigan the A.A.U.P. chapter has circulated the following criteria to be used in evaluating faculty services: (1) teaching, (2) research, (3) standing in the profession, (4) personal qualities, (5) departmental and university administrative work, (6) public and community

[3] F. S. Chapin, *Contemporary American Institutions*, N. Y., Harper & Bros., 1935, p. 157.

[4] 'Climbing the Academic Ladder,' p. 393.
'There is an inverse relation between the proportionate share teaching has played in promotion and the rank to which a person was advanced. The higher the rank, the less influence it had; nevertheless, it remains the main conditioner, even from associate professor to professor. Productive scholarship, that is, publication, ranked second. Publication, in comparison with teaching, is only approximately one half as important for promotions from instructor to assistant professor; two thirds for promotions from assistant professor to associate professor; but almost as important in promotions from associate professor to professor.' Ibid.

services.[5] It is acknowledged that some of these are of primary and some of secondary importance, yet no attempt is made to assign an absolute value to each item. To establish more definite evaluations of teaching ability and to improve it, the committee recommends that all departments at Michigan put into practice a procedure already in use there. This involves: having more experienced men visit the classes of young teachers, reciprocal ratings by colleagues within a department ('best teacher in department—one of the better teachers in department—reasonably good teacher—poor teacher'), and student evaluations in terms of a definite questionnaire on teaching effectiveness.

The faculty consensus at Michigan is that in the matter of promotions more emphasis is placed upon research than upon teaching, a practice in part explained by the fact that publication is more tangible than direct proof of teaching ability. To improve the 'rather haphazard methods now used in appraising research capacity and contributions,' while admitting the difficulty of 'satisfactory and practicable standards and policies of general applicability,' the committee recommends: (1) giving notice of publication and of work in progress by individual members; (2) maintenance of a current faculty bibliography of publications in a central office and in departments; (3) a departmental appraisal of research ability as often as the need arises or when requested by an administrative officer.

Professional standing of faculty members is to be appraised by colleagues in terms of reputation ('stands highest in department—is well and favorably known—is only slightly known outside this University—is practically unknown outside this University'), participation in learned societies, and through the opinion of qualified men outside the institution.

It is the opinion of the Michigan group that too little attention is paid to personal qualities, and that faculty members' colleagues should express their considered opinions in such

[5] 'The Evaluation of Faculty Services,' *University of Michigan Administrative Studies*, Vol. I, No. 3, p. 9 ff.

matters as co-operation, manner, industry, and health. Since a university should be a co-operative organization, it is recommended that faculty members be given proper credit for performance of necessary administrative duties. The value of the individual in administration is to be stated by the department head, and the value of public and community services is to be stated by the department head or a committee. Although extra-mural service is to receive credit, it is of secondary importance and 'should not be weighted in such a way as to make up for deficiencies in teaching, research, and services directly to the University.'

As far as employee status is concerned, the main burden of staff evaluation for purposes of status assignment falls upon administrative officers almost exclusively, and seldom do the rank and file of faculty members have much voice in determining the relative importance of different types of performance, or which colleagues are entitled to promotion. One large Eastern university tried the democratic experiment of having no individual promotions except by unanimous recommendation from departmental colleagues of equal and superior rank. The scheme was abandoned, however, when it inadvertently led to a perennial round of faculty dinner parties and other forms of obsequiousness, which proved mutually expensive and burdensome!

Since one-third of all academicians are employed in colleges or universities having 500 or more faculty members, and one-half of the total number in institutions having 200 or more, it is obviously impossible for deans and presidents to know personally a great many of the employees upon whom they pass ultimate judgment. Thus, when the Dean of one of the largest state universities states with reference to promotion, 'I put first, competency in research, next teaching competence, and next strength of character and personality,' [6] the implica-

---

[6] The statement is from Dean George F. Arps, of Ohio State University, and is quoted in Jesse L. Ward's 'Promotional Factors in Col-

tion is that in many instances he must rely entirely upon indirect sources as bases of evaluation. Judgment can be no more valid, of course, than the materials upon which it is formed and the criteria that are used.

SERVICE LOAD AND PRODUCTIVITY

In any evaluation of faculty services the time budgets of staff members must be taken into account. The problem of how academicians spend their time in performing various functions has been studied carefully in a survey of 407 staff members at the University of Chicago (see *The University Faculty*, p. 158 ff.). It was found that for the average man, 41.6 per cent of the service load is for teaching, 24.6 for research without special compensation, 12.7 for departmental services, 5.4 for administration, 4.5 for extra-mural activities without compensation, and the remaining lesser percentages for miscellaneous activities. (For staff members specializing in a given type of service, any one of these figures may outweigh all the others; those persons reporting special administrative work, for example, indicated that it occupied an average of 20 per cent of their total time.)

How time budgets differ from one subject-matter division to another may be ascertained from Table 1. Although this tabular presentation rather over-simplifies matters by equating time with energy, and affords no infallible index to the relative importance of different types of service, it is useful in showing how clock time (an inelastic quantity!) is distributed.

Studies in other universities, most of which are less exhaustive than the Chicago survey, indicate that teaching accounts for the largest time consumption of any activity. One

lege Teaching,' *Journal of Higher Education*, Vol. 8, 1937, pp. 475-9. This investigation reports that 31 prominent administrators and personnel men in higher institutions of learning ranked publication first as a criterion for promotion. None of them mentioned teaching competence, 'not because it is not at least first or second in importance, but because, as many admitted, it is useless to put in as a criterion, something about which so little can be determined.'

Table I

Relative Demands of Different Types of Service upon Time and Energy of the Academic Staff [7]

Percentage of Time and Energy of Entire Staff Required by Different Services

Field of Study	I Research Without Special Compensation	II Research Under Subsidy	III Teaching service on the Quadrangles	IV Departmental Services	V General University Services	VI Administration	VII Extramural Activities Without Compensation	VIII University College and Home Study	IX Extramural Activities with Compensation
Humanities	23.1	2.3	48.2	6.3	4.2	2.7	3.7	4.6	4.9
Social Sciences	19.1	1.2	40.3	7.2	4.7	9.1	5.4	5.0	8.0
Physical Sciences	35.3		42.9	7.1	2.6	6.3	1.5	1.5	2.8
Biological Sciences	28.7	1.1	32.3	25.6	2.2	4.3	3.2	0.8	1.8
Professional Schools	13.3	0.2	49.4	12.4	4.7	6.6	5.2	1.8	6.4
Average	24.6	1.1	41.6	12.7	3.6	5.4	3.7	2.8	4.5

[7] Ibid. p. 163.

investigation gives the average number of hours per day spent in teaching duties as 5.8, with a range for individual teachers from 2 to 14. The total working day, as indicated by a number of inquiries, appears to average around 8.5 hours, with a range of from 4 to 15. Next to teaching come research and writing in the time budgets of academicians in major universities. A constant complaint of professors is that the tasks to be done are too numerous, and that their energy must be spread over too many activities. It is true that versatile and obliging individuals may be called upon to engage in a wide variety of functions. The harried professor is a familiar spectacle on every campus; familiar also is the type who, like Chaucer's Sergeant of the Lawe, 'semed bisier than he was,' is so immersed in educational 'busywork' that his teaching and research are neglected.

Generalizations about the academic working day are indeed difficult. The university community supports both workers and drones, and in this respect is like every other community. For the professor who uses routine classroom procedures and is under no pressure to do research or to perform other major functions, employment in the higher learning is one of the easiest of all sinecures. For the diligent, however, the academic profession can become the most strenuous of all the intellectualized occupations. A principal difference between the university professor and other employees is that he enjoys a greater freedom in the planning of his work, and is subjected to a less constant appraisal from above.

Teaching, research, miscellaneous administrative and public service functions are recognized everywhere as essential parts of the academic man's work, but the university ordinarily defines only the teaching load in quantitative terms. Regardless of how efficiently or inefficiently the faculty member discharges this duty, the effect of a quantitative requirement is to insure his doing a specified minimum *amount* of classroom teaching. For the person who is completely absorbed in teaching or who is not interested in research, an inadvertent result of this requirement is to make scholarly productivity a residual activity. Although institutions exert many indirect pressures to overcome this tendency, few go so far as to specify any given amount of research expected from individual staff members. (A report to the A.A.U.P., however, mentions one institution in which the president would not raise the salary of any professor who did not publish at least three papers a year!) Consequently at institutions where no formal or informal pressures are exerted upon staff members to do research, and where it is not valued highly, very little gets done.

A survey of 35 lesser institutions found, for example, that only 32 per cent of all staff members made any contribution to printed literature over a five-year period, and that the median number of contributions was only 1.3 items.[8] An inquiry conducted by the American Historical Association in various types of colleges and universities revealed that only 25 per cent of doctors of philosophy in history are consistent producers.[9] Similarly, 'among 1,888 persons in the United States who took the Ph.D. in mathematics between 1862 and 1933, after graduation 46 per cent prepared no published papers; 19 per cent only 1 paper; 8 per cent only 2 papers; 11 per cent 3 to 5 papers; 6 per cent 6 to 10 papers; 2 per cent 21 to 30 papers; and 2 per cent more than 30 papers.' [10] These figures indicate that if the average academician in the typical college or university depended on his quantitative scholarly output for employee advancement, in rank and status, the hierarchical pyramid would show very few members at or near the top. The actual situation in such institutions proves, therefore, that the research function is not participated in extensively by most faculty members—a partial corol-

[8] See *The Liberal Arts College.*
[9] Jernegan, op. cit. pp. 1-22.
[10] Figures cited in the *Biennial Survey of Education in the United States,* Vol. I, 1938, p. 51.

lary of its being considered less essential than teaching and other kinds of performance appraised by the administration.[11]

Nowhere does the contrast between the lesser college or university and the major university come out more markedly than in the performance and evaluation of the research function. The University of Chicago affords a case in point of a leading institution in the field of scholarly productivity; during the period from 1924 to 1929, 70.6 per cent of the total faculty contributed to technical journals, association proceedings, or had materials published in the form of books, bulletins, and monographs.[12]

The types and average number of published studies may be ascertained from the following table:

TABLE II

Average Number of Published Studies of Each Type during the Five-Year Period by Members of the Faculties Who Were Connected with the University during the Entire Period [13]

	Average Number per Faculty Member in Five-Year Period
Books, bulletins, monographs	0.7
Articles in technical journals	3.9
Articles in association proceedings	0.4
Articles in local journals	0.3
Articles in collaboration	1.4
Reviews	3.8
Other publications	0.3
Total	10.8

[11] At Indiana University, for example, Hollingshead's investigation found no close relation between publication and promotion, and, astonishingly enough, 'on the average, the person who has reported on a piece of research or formulated some creative or interpretative writing and has either published or had it accepted for publication has not been promoted as rapidly as the person who confined his activities to classroom teaching and social affairs.'—Op. cit. p. 390.

[12] *The University Faculty,* p. 45.

[13] Loc. cit.

As may be deduced from the percentage of those making contributions, only 29.4 per cent of the Chicago group made no contributions. How productivity was distributed by the percentages of all faculty members contributing a given number of items during the five-year period is reported as follows: 26.9, 1-3 items; 17.4, 4-6; 10.4, 7-9; 5.8, 10-12; 5.8, 13-20; 4.3, 21 or more (page 46).

Not only does this official Survey of the University of Chicago give compilations for the entire staff, but also it makes comparisons of quantitative productivity by ranks, departments, and divisions. In addition, the percentages of faculty members in *Who's Who in America* or in *American Men of Science* are also noted by ranks, departments, and divisions. This Chicago survey does not state the administrative utilization of such invidious comparisons, but it goes without saying that they must be used extensively in determining individual promotions, allocating departmental funds, and in making administrative changes of personnel. The authors of the study do state, however, that

Any attempt to evaluate the services rendered to their departments and to the University by the individual members of the Faculties or to compare the relative success of different departments in attaining scholarly leadership must of necessity be incomplete and imperfect. Nevertheless, in addition to the basis of estimate afforded by the higher degrees held by staff members, the recognition accorded to members of the university staff by extramural agencies is of considerable significance.[14]

THE QUALITATIVE JUDGMENT OF ACHIEVEMENT

Lacking precise qualitative means of judging productivity, administrators are prone to fall back upon rather crude quantitative measures as a partial substitute. Departmental budgets are increased, staffs enlarged, and promotions expedited for

[14] Page 39.

those departments showing power to attract the largest number of students. A *post hoc* judgment of successful teaching
is frequently rendered for those staff members who build up
the largest following of students. Likewise, in research the
most 'productive' academician is often considered to be the
one with the most extensive yardage in his bibliography of
published material. Sometimes published materials are divided
into categories and weights are assigned. As indicated by the
Indiana study, the following weighting procedure is apparently
used there: '(1) research articles published in professional or
scholarly journals, or in a university series, 5; (2) popular
articles and pamphlets, 3; (3) monographs. This class includes
research contributions, creative writings, and scholarly compilations not specifically designed as textbooks for classroom
use, 15; (4) textbooks, 10; (5) essays, poems, and short
stories, 5.' [15]

As is well known, there is no completely objective basis for
judging the qualitative achievement of the academician.
Though the quantity of his output is of some importance, it
is a relatively meaningless thing when divorced from qualitative significance. Administrators are to some extent war-
ranted in assuming that any piece of work has to be of some
merit in order to get published, but there certainly is no
objective basis for the notion that the staff member who produces a dozen titles during a year has been four times as
productive as the one who turned out only three. Actually,
there is no way of equating monographs, articles, and textbooks. Even a book review may involve only a couple of hours
of work and result in a superficial summary, or it may be a
penetrative critical analysis resulting from many hours of concentrated effort. In actual practice, therefore, discriminating
administrators are forced to turn to personal estimates of a
man's worth. These may come from extra-mural sources as
well as from colleagues within the university, and ordinarily

[15] 'Climbing the Academic Ladder,' p. 390.

involve so many intangibles as to render them incapable of
any purely quantitative or statistical summation.

Thus, the testing of intellectual and scientific endeavor cannot be entirely clear-cut and impersonal, and reputation is
not reducible to precise categories. The unfortunate aspect of
the whole situation is that objective orientation for the individual is rendered difficult by tangential and often conflicting demands; his teaching, research, and other work is judged
by a number of standards, one set often being at variance
with another. And the hierarchy of prestige in academic fields,
as in all others, is never identical with merit. Judgments of
merit, in turn, as well as the capacity to assess it, differ according to the level and segment of the hierarchy rendering the
verdict. The competitive system and whatever scale of values
he may choose or have forced upon him determine the academician's ideology of success. Situational pressures vary from
department to department and institution to institution, so that
the functionary works toward the kind of attainable results
that bring approval from those whose verdict is worth most.

Everywhere there are to be found a few rare individuals
so absorbed in performance for its own sake as to be relatively indifferent to the symbols that may be attached for
achievement. Even the most perfunctory performers experience occasional moments of real zest, for much institutionalized activity proceeds in the form of voluntary projects to be
carried forward rather than as assigned tasks to be finished.
Yet a competitive system necessitates expediency in the allocation of time and energy and causes the functionary to concentrate upon teaching if this brings the greatest rewards, or
upon research if the local stress lies in this direction. In lesser
colleges and universities most staff members are relatively non-
productive of published work (the primary basis of national
reputation); hence it cannot be made a generalized criterion
for the evaluation of staff services in respect to employee
status. On the other hand, the staff member of a major university is placed in a situation where the innovative function

is on a par with the disseminative function, and, because of the universality of science and productive scholarship, he is judged according to competitive standards that come from outside as well as inside the institution.

In these central institutions the wish for recognition is tacitly backed by administrative imperatives, so that the intensity of competition and the large number of competitors multiply enormously the real and alleged contributions to the advancement of learning. That a strong emphasis upon scholarly productivity results in tremendous positive values from leading universities is generally known. That it interferes with the performance of other functions, and in marginal cases produces flamboyancy, exhibitionism, quantitativeness without regard for quality, and results indirectly inimical to knowledge itself is not so generally acknowledged. When the evaluative system prevailing in leading universities is indiscriminately forced upon the staffs of lesser colleges and universities it cannot but multiply such consequences. Indeed, it is no exaggeration to say that the most critical problem confronted in the social organization of any university is the proper evaluation of faculty services, and giving due recognition through the impartial assignment of status. Not to mention its utility in removing unnecessary sources of *anomie* and frustration in many organization personalities, a more adequate and rational basis for the differential appraisal of faculty services would unquestionably afford a less wasteful division of labor.

VII. PROFESSIONAL STATUS

ACADEMICIANS are a heterogeneous lot of individuals engaged in diverse duties, but they all have a common locus as employees of the university and as members of that broad occupational grouping known in our society as the professions. Our purpose here is to inquire into the meaning of professional status. What is the social significance of being a professional man? Important in the structure of any profession is its written or unwritten code of ethics. What is the code of the academic group? Every profession is also organized. How is the academic group organized for protecting and advancing the status of its members? Is the bargaining power of the typical individual within the system strong or weak? Further, we want to know how much agreement there is within the profession on objectives and procedures, and how effective organization is in attaining them. And finally, there is the relation of all these concerns to academic freedom and to professional solidarity.

The rather peculiar position of the academician as both a professional man and an employee imposes limitations not found in the absence of this combination. It will be of interest, therefore, to see how problems common to functionaries of the higher learning are met by professional organization.

THE MEANING OF PROFESSIONAL STATUS

The academician participates with the members of all major professions in a behavior system distinguished by the following criteria:

1. Prolonged and specialized training based upon a systematized intellectual tradition that rarely can be acquired through mere apprenticeship.

2. Rigorous standards of licensure, fulfilment of which often confers upon the functionary a degree or title [1] signifying specialized competence.

3. Application of techniques of such intricacy that competency tests cannot be deduced upon any simple continuum scale, nor can supervision be more than loosely applied.

4. Absence of precise contractual terms of work, which might otherwise imply a calculated limitation of output and an exploitative attitude toward productivity.

5. A limitation upon the self-interest of the practitioner, and a careful insulation of professional considerations from extraneous matters, such as private opinions, economic interests, and class position.

6. Certain positive obligations to the profession and its clientele.

Not every profession embodies all of these common elements, yet taken together they form a *Gestalt* or whole that enables one to differentiate the profession from other generic types of occupations. Professional work, unlike most business and industrial enterprise, has no simple unitary end such as the production of goods for profit. Common practices often fall short of ideals, and individuals have difficulty in drawing the line, but in economic enterprise, the professional aspect stresses service and the business aspect profits.

[1] It is interesting to note that although the Ph.D. certainly requires as rigorous training to achieve as any professional degree carrying a title, academic men are rarely as insistent upon being called 'Doctor' in any and every context as are dentists and medical doctors. In major universities, 'Professor' carries more encomium than 'Doctor,' but this situation is usually reversed in lesser colleges and universities where more staff members are in the former category than in the latter.

PROFESSIONAL ETHICS

Professional ideology supports the tradition of a body of equals, making corporate decisions (whenever enterprise is collaborative), and being judged in terms of individual competence. The relative non-interference on the part of society presupposes, in turn, self-imposed as well as professionally enforced duties and obligations. Though not isolated, the academic man is insulated—the assumption being that he will do his work disinterestedly or objectively. As men have known since the time of Francis Bacon, however, objectivity in scholarly enterprise is not simply a matter of writing in the third person singular. Higher education is ideally organized to minimize bias, careerism, and other factors injurious to the disinterestedness necessary for best professional performance, but the academic ethic is a result of the combination of certain positive factors and of the negation of others. Thus the scholar-scientist is not a person with no values, but one with disciplined values, and objectivity is a term that is always relative to wider values.[2]

To insure the unfettered pursuit of learning, an optimum of free association must be maintained. The liberal tradition and the intellectual tradition are closely coupled, and disinter-

[2] This judgment leaves open the question what disinterestedness and competence (knowledge and skill) are to be used for, so that from a pragmatic point of view, disinterestedness is merely an attitude serving as a tangential rather than an ultimate end.

'Generalizations, laws, hypotheses, do not, that is to say, proceed either by some self-revelation of phenomena, or by some equal and impartial treatment of them by the human mind, but by a method of approach and handling which is definitely "interested," in the sense of putting preconceived questions to which answers are sought. In this sense all Science is qualified by human interest. So when we speak of "disinterested science" we mean, either that the questions are valued merely as knowledge, or that, if behind that knowledge lies the sense of the need to utilize it, that utility is conceived in terms of general human welfare, not in terms of some particular gain. Specific utilities must come as implications, or by-products . . .' From J. A. Hobson, *Free Thought in the Social Sciences*, N. Y., The Macmillan Co., 1926, pp. 61-2. (Reprinted by permission of the publishers.)

estedness as a normative pattern means that values must be universalized and divorced from contexts where they are distorted by prejudices and sentiments. The universalism of the academic world, as in that of ideal-experimental economic theory, assumes that actions shall be rational (most efficient in the choice of means). Any primacy of ulterior motives of personal gain and success is definitely dysfunctional. As one analyst of the professions has observed, 'In the professions and their great tradition is to be found one of the principal reserves against that false conception of utility, in its close connection with the love of money . . . encouragement of the professions is one of the most effective ways of promoting disinterestedness in contemporary society . . .' [3]

Ethical codes are to some extent unenforceable in a legal sense, and their sanctions are usually non-legal. Laws in the main apply to territorial groups, whereas professional codes apply to functional groupings. Sanctions exist positively in the desire for approval and negatively in the sense of shame; tabus, publicity, education, and the effects of clarifying and interpreting individual cases all serve as sanctions of a sort.

Although moral aspects of professional behavior are regulated more by ethics than by law, professors, doctors, and lawyers are in no sense beyond economics and the ultimate value system of the community except when they become déclassés. Standards of licensure and ethical codes are not merely arbitrary in-group formulations, and must have a general social acceptance. Group opportunism, esoteric cultism, or monkish idealism in small, independent associations may be tolerated by society, but it is hardly conceivable that these tendencies would be allowed to develop unrestrained in the academic or any other major profession.

The professor's independence is limited by his institutional connection, and especially so if he cannot distinguish between freedom and license, yet there are in most universities few

[3] Talcott Parsons, 'Remarks on Education and the Professions,' *The International Journal of Ethics*, xlvii, 3, April 1937, p. 356.

positive hindrances upon his intellectual initiative. (That this is true may be due in large part to the prevailing factual situation that his political and social views seldom go beyond the preconceptions of the middle class to which he belongs.) There is no universal acceptance in the academic profession of any explicit statement analogous to the Hippocratic oath, and for many members there is merely a vague understanding of those ideals or norms of conduct that overreach the satisfaction of individual desires. Be they explicit or implicit, however, institutional codes help to define situations for individual members; they set up rules that insist upon something more than 'a merely economic logic of production,' and the fact that many verbalized codes are nothing more than empty ideologies in no way negates the importance of having them. For a group to maintain itself, special conditions of success must be formulated, error penalized, and deliberate deviation punished.

The A.A.U.P. has a code containing rather explicit norms for each of the following categories: (1) relations of the teacher to his profession; (2) relations of the teacher to his students; (3) relations of the teacher to his colleagues; (4) relations of the teacher to his institution and its administrators; (5) relations of the teacher to the non-academic world.[4]

How ethical standards should govern the various ranks in their conduct toward one another within the profession is suggested by an item in the Association's *Bulletin*.[5] Though lacking the sanction of formal adoption, it is an interesting document for its suggestion of points of tension in intra-departmental affairs. The following statements represent a condensation of its most important recommendations:

Publication: ownership and authorship. Research assistants who do work involving little or no originality have no claims to ownership in the product. Where initiative of the assistant is utilized, a claim to part ownership arises, and should be

[4] For the complete code, see Appendix III.
[5] Henry S. Conard, 'Ethics Among Professors,' XIX, 1933, pp. 144-8.

established. An assistant may publish independently only with consent of the research director. Professors should refrain from lending too much assistance to students writing theses that pretend to be original.

Freedom of teaching and research: Assistants and instructors should follow the method and procedure assigned by the professor in charge of teaching or research. It is wiser to allow freedom to competent assistants, but where a certain method is essential, no compromise should be made. Teachers of professorial rank, or any teacher in charge of a course, should have the same authority as the head professor. In case of serious disagreement, the person of lower rank may take the matter directly to the dean or president, get a transfer to another department, resign. Should such situations be repeated the department head should be demoted. Subordinate members of a department are entitled to the same freedom of opinion that the head claims for himself. A person out of sympathy with the field of research set by a department should follow the same procedure mentioned above in cases of disagreement. Both before and after publication, controversy should proceed as freely and impersonally both in print and in speech between members of the staff as with outsiders.

PROFESSIONAL ORGANIZATION

Regardless of, or in addition to, what any professional organization may say about its out-group service functions, it exists primarily for the protection and advancement of in-group status. Though academicians are accused of being a timorous lot when it comes to protecting and enhancing their professional status, they are not without organization designed for this purpose. While cognizant of altruistic objectives, realistic members of the profession recognize that only through the solidarity of organization can status be protected in a society where equilibrium is maintained through the counterbalance of pressure groups.

The American Association of University Professors has other purposes than increasing the bargaining power of members, but this is its most important objective, as it is the only widely recognized association of this type. Since its formation in 1915, the Association has concerned itself actively with the general welfare of the profession, and by 1937 had 13,390 members and 322 chapters throughout the United States. That its membership is made up neither of parvenus nor of malcontents is witnessed in the fact that of 26 past presidents of the American Association for the Advancement of Science, 10 were charter members of the A.A.U.P., 4 others active members, and 7 ineligible for membership.[6]

The general functions of this organization are to establish and articulate criteria and sanctions governing the mutual relations of members, to control the relations of members and non-members, and, if possible, to affect the behavior of non-members toward members. With certain restrictions, the membership is open to all engaged actively in the academic profession, as is testified in this official statement:

The Association is an organization for the formulation and expression of the opinion of those members of the staffs of universities and colleges who are primarily teachers and investigators, rather than administrators. Deans who are also teachers are eligible, as well as heads of departments. The purely administrative officers already have organization through which they can express their opinions. In expressing this view the Committee wishes to emphasize that the present form is not based upon any hostility to administrators but merely a belief that it is desirable to have an organization through which the opinion of those who are primarily teachers and investigators can be formulated and expressed. The Committee believes that bringing in persons who are primarily administra-

[6] Membership of past presidents of leading associations of scholars has been as follows: past presidents of the American Economic Association, 25 of 34; American Historical Association, 15 of 26; American Sociological Society, 15 of 16; Modern Language Association, 31 of 45; American Philological Association, 15 of 15; Mathematical Association of America, all.

tors might well defeat its own end and tend to promote rather than decrease hostility to those in administrative positions. (*Bulletin of the A.A.U.P.*, XXIII, 1937, p. 202)

Upon its formation the A.A.U.P. established fifteen special committees, whose reports, when sanctioned at the annual national meeting, represent the approved professional opinion of the entire organization. The number of these committees has now increased to eighteen, the most important being: A. Academic Freedom and Tenure; B. Freedom of Speech; D. Educational Standards; I. Professional Ethics; O. Organization and Policy; Q. Preparation and Qualification of Teachers; R. Encouragement of University Research; T. Place and Function of Faculties in College and University Government; Z. Economic Welfare of the Profession.

The intellectual worker, inside or outside the university world, however, has been more individualistic in his methods than the followers of most vocations. Consequently he often works under informal agreements, and legal obligations are usually vague or entirely absent.[7] Unlike many other professional intellectual workers, the professor is always an employee and has to conform to basic administrative controls common

---

[7] J. E. Kirkpatrick gives the following resumé of the legal status of the professor:

'This study of the legal rights of the teacher may perhaps be best summed up by reviewing further the findings of the court majority in the West Virginia case of Hartigan vs. Board of Regents, 1901. The professor in a state university is not, it was then decided, a public officer, neither is he a semi-public officer. He is like a teacher in the public schools, a subordinate of the board of education, responsible to such board and not to the public or to the patrons. The professor takes no oath, gives no bond, does not account for misfeasance or nonfeasance in a legal sense, has no term and no duties of a determinate character fixed by law. He does not share in the "sovereign" power of the state. For these reasons he was regarded by this court as a "mere employee," "however distinguished and learned" he might be. Here, it may be said, is clearly, if brutally, stated the present position of the American academic person. So far has he fallen from the high estate that belonged to his colonial predecessors.

Early in our national period, as we have seen, the professor was not entirely without the rights and dignities of office. The common law accorded him the right of a hearing upon specific charges and the

to all organized undertakings. Because of the nature of the calling, there has long been a sentiment, both within and without the academic profession, that its members should present themselves as individuals and not as members of a labor union. In the past this has largely been the case, and partially as a consequence the professor has developed little bargaining power. During periods of economic retrenchment he has had his status rendered precarious by the fact that his labor is not an absolute necessity in the usual sense, and during periods of prosperity his wages are slow to rise. On the whole, academic men as a professional body have been slow to realize that their being employed in a dependent capacity supersedes many other economic considerations.

Although it is argued by many that the policies and practices of trade unionism are highly undesirable in intellectual work, there is also an increased awareness of the difficulty of maintaining an intermediate class position. Confronted by other organized groups protecting their own special interests, irrespective of the common welfare, the rank and file of academic men are highly dependent on the discretion of superiors, while at the same time being generically different from the

courts were ready, in part at least, to defend these rights. In Webster's estimate the Dartmouth professor was not without a "free hold" right in his office and the Massachusetts court, in the Andover case, was not ready to limit the professor under charges merely to the rights of a hired man. But toward the close of the last century, all right of office and all rights at common law, had disappeared from the view of the courts. Whatever statutes, ordinances, and contracts prescribed the courts would consider. But right of office, freeholds, dignities, judicial power, legislative power, once the possession of the teacher in the school world, had passed to a new class—the lay governor of the school.'
Academic Organization and Control. Yellow Springs, Ohio, The Antioch Press, 1931, p. 199.
For further information on legal status see M. M. Chambers, 'The Legal Status of Professors,' *The Journal of Higher Education*, Vol. 11, 1931, p. 481; Hardin Craig, 'Methods of Appointment and Promotion,' *Bulletin of the A.A.U.P.*, xv, 1929, pp. 175-217; Alexander Brody, *The American State and Higher Education; The Legal, Political and Constitutional Relationships*, Washington, American Council on Education, 1935. The last-mentioned work gives a good historical treatment, a full bibliography, and is replete with citations from court decisions.

craftsman and the clerk. In the matter of bargaining, academicians must submit their requests to a tribunal which must also be their foremost opponent.

BARGAINING POWER

The absence of such an organization is looked upon with favor by some professors and deplored by others. (Some few even regard the A.A.U.P. as 'undignified'!) A number of years ago Cattell said:

I am not, however, here raising the question of general ethics; I refer to the philosophical belief, to the special theory of *professorial* ethics which forbids a professor to protect his colleague. I invite controversy on this subject; for I should like to know what the professors of the country have to say on it. It seems to me that there exists a special prohibitory code, which prevents the college professor from using his reason and his pen as actively as he ought in protecting himself, in pushing his interests and in enlightening the community about our educational abuses. The professor in America seems to think that self-respect requires silence and discretion on his part. He thinks that by nursing this gigantic reverence for the idea of professordom, such reverence will, somehow, be extended all over society, till the professor becomes a creature of power, of public notoriety, of independent reputation as he is in Germany. In the meantime, the professor is trampled upon, his interests are of no social consequence, he is kept at menial employments and the leisure to do good work is denied him. A change is certainly needed in all of these aspects of the American professor's life. My own opinion is that this change can only come about through the enlightenment of the great public. The public must be appealed to by the professor himself in all ways and upon all occasions.[8]

The implication of Cattell's statement is that professors should organize into a militant group. His views were set forth several decades ago, but in certain quarters the agitation for a professional organization with more sweeping powers

[8] *Science and Education*, Vol. III, p. 457.

occasionally flares up, as is witnessed in the activity of men like George S. Counts, of Columbia University.[9] It is easily possible that such an organization could become incompatible with the present status of the profession, for it is generally considered that public officials, ministers, and professors are compensated in general esteem for whatever deficiencies they may suffer on the pecuniary level.[10]

Critics of the present bargaining position of the professor believe it is a mistake to think that he is exempt from the operation of the ordinary economic laws that govern the activities of others, and that the 'profession is somehow above and beyond and superior to the labor problem which bedevils the existence of the rest of humankind, or that, because teachers may not be "all out" for money-making, they are therefore automatically immune to exploitation by those who hire them.'[11] The authors of this same view point out a second misconception in the idea that collective bargaining is out of place in colleges and universities, for salaries in teaching go up and down like all others in response to supply and demand. Since the university is no longer a free company of scholars as was the medieval university,[12] such euphemisms as 'honorarium' and 'call to a wider field of usefulness' are considered as indicative of the hypocrisy prevalent in economic matters.

Thorstein Veblen likewise comments on the lack of a strong bargaining organization in the academic profession, and shows

[9] At a meeting of the National Education Association in 1934, Professors William H. Kilpatrick and John K. Norton, of Columbia, demanded a 'pressure group of a million teachers.'

[10] See F. W. Taussig's *Inventors and Money-Makers*, N. Y., The Macmillan Co., 1930.

[11] Earl E. Cummins and Harold A. Larrabee, 'Individual versus Collective Bargaining for Professors,' *Bulletin of the A.A.U.P.*, xxiv, 1938, p. 487.

[12] 'If, as some reformers maintain, the social position and self-respect of professors involve their management of university affairs, the Middle Ages were the great age of professorial control. The university itself was a society of masters when it was not a society of students.' Charles H. Haskins, *The Rise of Universities*, N. Y., Henry Holt & Co., 1923, pp. 68-9.

that certain definite substitutes are offered in lieu of pecuniary rewards. There is a feeling prevalent among university teachers that salaries are not in the nature of wages and that there would be a 'species of moral obliquity implied in overtly dealing with the matter.' The rate of pay is usually established by individual bargaining and the university employee is often constrained to accept, 'as part payment, an expensive increment of dignity attaching to a higher rank than this salary account would indicate.' Veblen calls attention to the common institutional plea of being in want of necessary funds, and to the lack of any settled code of professional ethics governing many aspects of academic management.[13]

The 'hush-hush' attitude toward money matters among professors of the old school and the attendant exaggerated notion of the dignity of the profession may be accounted for psychologically as a compensation for the generally emasculated status which the public assigned to them.[14] There is quite a contrast, however, between the old generation and the new.

PROFESSIONAL ASSOCIATION OR UNION

To return to the question of a militant organization of the trade union type, it is evident that there is still no consensus in the whole profession on what sort of association is best

[13] See *The Higher Learning*, N. Y., B. W. Huebsch, 1918, p. 162 ff.

[14] This notion of the 'dignity' of the profession developed a whole complex of attitudes, which here will be mentioned only in passing. Many accepted forms of behavior were formerly taboo in public for the academician in his conduct. The popular stereotype demanded that he refrain from public smoking, drinking, and any sort of bohemianism. Even the theoretical radical was usually a timid individual in his personal behavior.

That there may still be personalities who rebel against the norms of university life is seen in the following quotation from Watson's *Scientists are Human:* ' "Industry," I am told by a scientist who has tried all three, "does not inquire into my intellectual life or into my private personal life." Thus General Electric or Eastman Kodak may provide professional avenues for many whose gonads and hatred for hypocrisy have made them ineligible for the marble colonnades of the university.' (P. 52, London, Watts & Co., 1938.)

suited to academic ends. In an article entitled 'Professional Association or Trade Union?' [15] Professor Arthur O. Lovejoy shows that in some respects the A.A.U.P. is analogous to a trade union because the economic status of teachers is legally the same as that of most industrial workers. Teachers are not individual entrepreneurs, like most doctors and lawyers, because their livelihoods are nominally dependent upon the decisions of those who control the funds. Most trade unions are not interested in more, or better, or cheaper production, or in general that 'the distinctive function of that industry as a whole—employers and employed together—in relation to the rest of society shall be better and more adequately performed.' In a university the situation is different; the trustees do not enhance their own pecuniary status by keeping salaries down, and the funds they dispense are not their property, but tax-free public funds. The professor, therefore, does not stand in a competitive economic relation in the complete sense to the corporation that employs him. Lovejoy concludes his remarks with the opinion that unionism would seriously split the ranks of the profession. Unquestionably there is absent the same collective ulterior ambition; this does not imply that there is something intrinsically different between the businessman and the professional man, but merely that the difference is in the institutional aspects.

Dissatisfaction by a minority with alleged inadequacies of the A.A.U.P. and other organizations in existence, moreover, has led to the formation of the American Federation of Teachers, an organization not hostile to other teachers associations, but rather one that professes a wish merely to enlarge the sphere of professional activity. There are now local chapters of this organization in some of the central universities, but it is only within the last few years that the movement has gained any headway. An item in the *Bulletin of the A.A.U.P.* cites a statement from *The American Teacher* (official pub-

[15] *Bulletin of the A.A.U.P.*, 1938, pp. 409-17.

lication of the American Federation of Teachers) concerning the purpose of the union:

The American Association of University Professors does not perform the functions which the teachers' federation aspires to perform. Although it offers a junior membership to assistants and instructors, it has never made an appeal to this group. The professors' organization for the most part does not focus upon local campus issues. It offers no protection to its members so far as their economic status is concerned. The organization is a strictly professional one and has no outside affiliations. Most important of all, perhaps, the Association has no point of view and holds no opinions regarding economic institutions. As previously stated the teachers' federation has a point of view and does take a side on at least some very fundamental economic issues.[16]

A fuller statement of general union objectives is represented by the following recent itemization from the Cambridge Union of University Teachers:

1. In affiliating with the organized labor movement we express our desire to contribute to and receive support from this progressive force; to reduce the segregation of teachers from the rest of the workers who constitute the great mass of the community, and increase thereby the sense of common purpose among them; and in particular to cooperate in this field in the advancement of education and resistance to all reaction.

2. We intend to work with other organizations for the preservation and extension of academic freedom, by which we mean freedom to investigate all problems in a scientific spirit and to present the conclusions of such researches.

3. We are sensible of the fact that the interests of University education are best promoted by preserving to administrative officials wide latitude in the appointment and advancement of teachers—a latitude which we wish to see preserved. But where issues arise which are clearly those of academic freedom or discrimination against individuals on grounds of race, or of social, religious, economic, political opinions or activi-

[16] From Vol. xx, 1934, pp. 253-4. (The Federation is affiliated with the A. F. of L.)

ties, the Teachers' Union will be prepared to have a fair investigation made and appropriate proposals brought forward.

4. Convinced that retrenchment in education is deplorable, especially at a time when the world is beset by problems requiring the highest measure of public intelligence for their solution, we intend to resist all efforts to reduce the amount and quality of education now provided in this country. We believe that an expansion of educational opportunities and an improvement of the quality of instruction are needed, and we shall do all we can to promote them.[17]

ACADEMIC FREEDOM

This present study is purposely ignoring the usual issue of academic freedom: still, it must be briefly considered in relation to appointment, tenure, and other variables that are inseparable from the problem of the academic man as a professional. Many basic faculty questions are centered about tenure, unemployment, appointment, and promotion. Even a superficial study of the publications of the Federation and of the A.A.U.P. reveals that their chief concerns are with these problems.[18]

With reference to academic freedom it is important to modalize that not only are there in the objective situation pressures brought to bear on whoever has to make decisions concerning individual employees, but also that persons about whom such issues arise rather generally tend to be deviant individuals in their personal characteristics as well as their institutional behavior. In other words, they are more commonly than not 'difficult' people. It usually takes a combination of such personality traits with academic unorthodoxy to make a

[17] From folder distributed to members.
[18] It may be mentioned here that in 47 of 96 institutions studied by the U. S. Office of Education, all appointments are made for one year regardless of rank. At 48 of the institutions some differential prevails. The model pattern for differential appointments is: professors and associate professors, indefinite terms; assistant professors, 2 to 3 years; instructors, 1 year. *Biennial Survey of Education in the United States*, 1934-6, Vol. I, Ch. III, p. 36.

problem case. If an academician has the combination, he usually undergoes considerable inter-institutional mobility during his professional career; perhaps the most important factor in publicized cases is inept handling by the university president or executive responsible for his dismissal.

Though the American Association of University Professors is organized for many purposes other than making adjustments in conflict situations, it is the sole available professional agency of this type for most men within the group, and hence inevitably finds itself confronted with a large number of such cases. Its codes provide enactments for guidance in such situations, its officers are prepared to act in a judiciary capacity, and in addition there are sanctions which may be brought to bear upon the offending institution, but no formalized measures for dealing with miscreant individual members who may prove to be at fault. Since negative pressures are normally the prerogative of employers, however, it is logical that the professional association should assume employee protective functions which otherwise would devolve upon no organized group.

Like the general public, professional associations have their attention called primarily to actual dismissals, and the higher the 'visibility' of the person dismissed, of course, the greater the amount of comment. Individuals in the larger institutions usually have their cases better publicized, yet most of the cases coming before the A.A.U.P. Committee on Academic Freedom and Tenure are from the 400 smaller colleges. (In 1932 one of every six smaller institutions of learning had a case appealed to the General Secretary or to the Chairman of Committee A.) The extensity of this phenomenon over a representative period may be judged from the table on page 129.

How the Association reacts is apparent from data in the second part of the table. More specifically, it may bring a positive sanction to bear by placing the institution at fault on a non-recommended list, or occasionally, and without making

TABLE III

Cases Relating to Academic Freedom and Tenure between 1928 and 1935 [19]

	1928	1929	1930	1931	1932	1933	1934	1935
1	2	3	4	5	6	7	8	9
Cases pending Jan. 1 ..	10	5	10	8	20	7	8	11
New cases opened during the year	19	17	27	63	66	69	40	56
Old cases removed		3	1	4		9	12	7
Total cases dealt with during the year	29	25	38	75	86	85	60	74
Cases apparently closed during the year	24	15	30	55	79	77	49	61
Cases pending Dec. 31 .	5	10	8	20	7	8	11	13

METHODS OF HANDLING CASES

	1928	1929	1930	1931	1932	1933	1934	1935
1	2	3	4	5	6	7	8	9
Cases withdrawn	2	6	11	7	20	16	5	18
Cases reported requiring no action	14	3	9	42	41	32	28	—
Cases in which statements have been made or planned without visit	6	6	3	7	3	6	0	2
Cases in which visits of inquiry or investigation have been made or planned	2	7	6	9	12	9	10	14
Cases otherwise handled	5	3	9	10	10	22	17	13
Total cases	29	25	38	75	86	85	60	74

known individuals, it has declined to defend men 'in incompetent and exhibitionist groups.' So active has the association been in its efforts to preserve the status of its members that hostile critics have accused it of being a 'mere protective association.'

[19] Data from *Bulletin of the A.A.U.P.*, XIX; 91-2, February 1933; and XXIII, 103-4, February 1937.

(The general definition of the situation concerning academic freedom and tenure by the A.A.U.P. may be ascertained from a conference statement. See Appendix IV.)

Despite its definitive regulations concerning appointment and tenure, and its publicized 'blacklists' of institutions not conforming, the sanctions of the A.A.U.P. are not entirely effective. In a recent magazine article,[20] Professor Donald Slesinger remarks that he cannot recall a single celebrated case defended by the A.A.U.P. who ever got another university job, and cites the instances of Dana, Cattell, Nearing, and Watson. Further, Slesinger thinks that the professors themselves are the greatest enemies of academic freedom, and that 'Nervous Daughters of the American Revolution to the contrary there are no more stodgy defenders of the *status quo* than our university faculties.'[21]

Security of tenure is, indeed, a corollary of academic freedom, for if one were supplied the other could be taken for granted. President Robert M. Hutchins has called the attention of the A.A.U.P. members to another side of tenure which the organization has not stressed.

Indeed it is not too much to say for everything that goes on in the university the professor pays.

He certainly pays for the permanence of his tenure. Perhaps it is worth the price. He pays if the university permits or encourages him to do extension and summer teaching to get enough to live on, when it ought to pay him a regular salary adequate for that purpose. As the Yale Chapter has shown, he pays for the multiplication of the staff.

Particularly does he pay if new appointments are poorly

[20] 'Professor's Freedom,' *Harpers,* October 1937, pp. 546-51.
[21] It should be noted that pressures other than outright dismissal may be brought to bear officially upon the non-conforming academician by the following means: increase in teaching load or class size; failure to renew appointment if not permanent; reduction in money for library, equipment, research; reducing clerical assistance; scheduling classes at awkward hours; reducing salary under other pretenses, etc. These methods may be just as effective as immediate dismissal, but they do not make newspaper headlines.

made and made without regard to the interests of the university as a whole.

The professor pays, not only for additional personnel and incompetent personnel, but also for wasteful organization of instruction and research.[22]

INTERNAL FRICTIONS

That solidarity is not complete within the ranks of the profession may be ascertained from the following unsigned letters to the editor, which are more or less typical of those which occasionally appear in the back pages of the *Bulletin*.

Not all the ill feeling, however, is between the public and the faculty. We on the faculty envy each other. The professor does not want any other teacher to have higher standards than he has, to know more than he does, or to be promoted before he is. If the head of the department, or his jackal, is unproductive, it is dangerous to publish an article; if your senior gives no grade lower than a B, and you give two D's, your job is in jeopardy—you are an inefficient teacher; and if your standards are so low and your ignorance so great that your promotion seems inevitable, you may be sure that some less fortunate colleague is waiting for an opportunity to impugn your morals. Sloth and envy are the sins which dominate the academic scene, not bigotry. A little bigotry would be welcome evidence that someone cared for matters extraneous to his own right to unearned academic distinctions. It would be evidence that someone, besides a few classroom drudges, was concerned about the students.

I do not believe that we are more unscrupulous, lazy, and envious than other men. If there were no laws against short weights and poisoned food, grocers would doubtless be as corrupt as we are. But there is no restraint placed upon us or upon our employers, and consequently we do not have a freedom, far more important than freedom to teach unproven theories—we are not free to work for higher standards. This may sound extreme, but if an administrator were to ask me tomorrow to change the F that I gave Joe Cocktail to an A, I should obey him because I would not know of any repre-

[22] 'The Professor Pays,' *Bulletin of the A.A.U.P.*, 1932, pp. 22-3.

sentative of academic ethics to whom I could appeal for support.

Why cannot the A.A.U.P. support academic standards instead of devoting its best energies to the protection of our right to blow off at the mouth? (Vol. xxiv, 1938, pp. 381-2.)

The second letter differs somewhat in tone:

I have long felt that the Association indulges in too much uncertain beating of the air, and I should be glad to know how many of the members would offer their support to some such simple programme as this:

1. Let us retain the present machinery that concerns itself with the problems of academic tenure and freedom.

2. As a counterweight to this labor-union activity, let us offer every encouragement to the various degree-granting institutions throughout the country to state clearly what they expect of the members of their respective faculties in the way of (a) teaching skill, (b) zeal in study (i.e., in keeping abreast of the progress of the instructor's special field), and (c) research in the strict sense of the word. They might also be asked to name any local academic taboos such as are likely to create trouble if disregarded.

3. Let us use most of our funds in maintaining a great professional 'clearing house' which will supply, on the one hand, full information with regard to academic vacancies and, on the other, complete lists of scholars, with their qualifications, who are available to fill these posts. (Vol. xxiv, 1938, p. 379.)

Granted that ideally there should be a consciousness of the dignity of the profession, an *esprit de corps* among its members, and an unrelenting devotion to the disinterested pursuit of knowledge, one does not have to assume a muck-raking attitude to show that the actual state of affairs differs considerably from what it would be under ideal conditions. Aside from the fact that the employee status of professors places definite limits upon the powers of their professional organization to clarify issues in its own way, there is the additional complication of widely divergent interests. The average academician's time and energy are divided among a number of scholarly and scientific societies, and these often have a priority of interest for him which lessens the amount of attention he can or does give to a strictly professional association, so that the A.A.U.P. labors under heavier odds than does the American Medical Association or the American Bar Association.

VIII. SOCIO-ECONOMIC STATUS

THE academic man occupies a status within the social system of his university and profession, but as a human being he also has a broader socio-economic status, or position in the larger society. He is a participant in an open-class society in which occupation is the most important single factor in determining class position. Not only does the long arm of the job encircle working conditions, but also it reaches out to embrace almost every phase of social life. The university professor is no exception to the general rule that where and how one lives is largely a matter of occupation and one's relative success in it. So long as the division of labor is human, therefore, we must consider employee social and economic statuses as being no less important than functions performed.

In short, we want to know what professional employment in the higher learning does to one's social status. Except in rare instances of esoteric callings, individuals do not follow occupations solely as ends in themselves. What does it mean in the wider community, then, to be a university professor rather than a plumber, merchant, or lawyer? How adequate is income as a criterion of social status? What are the exigencies of standard of living demands? To what extent do university people form a class *sui generis*, independent of other classes? What stereotyped attitudes does the public have toward the academic profession, and what status does it accord members of the profession? Persons of approximately equivalent status within the university system may have extremely disparate social positions in the community at large, to be sure, yet there are on the whole enough similarities to afford generalizations about the socio-economic status of the academic profession. Our major purpose here is to ascertain what generalizations of this nature it is possible to make.

ECONOMIC STATUS

In common with the clergy and certain other vocations, the academic profession stands somewhat apart in not having its general prestige established primarily in terms of monetary remuneration. There are other important common denominators of achievement and usefulness, so that money becomes important only when these are vague or weakened in significance. Success or distinction in university work is a goal comparable with wealth and power in other occupations. This comparison does not appear on the individual level as a distinction between the professional man as 'unselfish' and the business man as 'selfish,' it should be emphasized, but the difference is clear-cut on the institutional level. Professors are no less interested in their pay checks than are other groups, however, and in no case is there a selfless devotion to that amorphous something called 'service,' irrespective of the personal rewards it brings. The academic man is typically a person with a family to support, and even as an unattached individual he is far from being indifferent to the social standing that the community accords him.

Since a great many of the things that go to make up social status must be purchased at a price, the academic man (particularly in his consumer role) finds himself confronted with a multiplicity of problems centering about remuneration. The university expects him to yield dividends in the form of teaching and research, and, in addition to professional satisfactions, he expects material returns for his knowledge and skill.

In the academic profession, as in a number of others, the employee is not remunerated in terms of the absolute worth of his services. An industrial enterprise operating under *laissez faire* principles pays its employees what they are worth, and is free to discharge them when they cease to be worth their wages. Professors, on the other hand, often receive identical salaries for work of vastly different value to the institution employing them. Most academicians also enjoy a measure of tenure security which protects them against discharge when their utility is diminished. Still another peculiarity of university work is that it would be difficult to equate in monetary terms a discovery in Shakespearean sources with one in atomic structure. The modal system is 'that of paying salaries very close to a fixed scale, and letting every professor do as good work as he can.'

Generally recognized is the fact that the competitive order does not reward pure scientific research and scholarly work in the same way it does technology, or the teacher of skills to the same extent as the applier of skills. Or, as Florian Znaniecki has put it, 'The knowledge that is needed as a condition of success in practical activity is always less highly esteemed socially than the success to which it is subservient.' [1] (E.g., academic biologists with four-figure incomes discover the knowledge capitalized upon by physicians with five- and six-figure incomes.) Those who enter the academic profession are fully aware that they are going into an occupation where possibilities for amassing a fortune are almost non-existent,[2] and their prime motivation is usually not financial gain. Able persons are not necessarily deterred by the lack of large financial reward, and feel that the general respect accorded the occupation, the certainty of a reasonable competence, together with other inducements, are partial compensations.

Yet there is no way of completely overcoming income as a

[1] *The Social Role of the Man of Knowledge*, N. Y., Columbia University Press, 1940, p. 91.

[2] I say 'almost' because a few college professors have amassed fortunes, not from their salaries, but by virtue of certain activities carried on as a result of being in the academic profession. Some academicians have made considerable fortunes from textbook writing and from inventions. Most inventions and discoveries of a remunerative sort, however, become public property, property of the university, or of a special corporation set up for this purpose (as·in the case of Wisconsin).

social denominator in a society where wealth is such an important criterion of status. The most highly valued jobs are usually the best paid, and in the long run a university gets about the caliber of talent that it is willing to pay for. It is not merely in a spirit of munificence that Harvard, Columbia, and other leading universities pay their professors almost treble the average salaries that men draw in provincial colleges, or that in most universities the salaries in professional schools are higher than those in non-professional schools.[3]

Without doubt, low remuneration is a source of many stresses and anxieties in the average organization personality, a cause of much energy dissipation in outside activity, and the origin of conflict between multiple roles (university and non-university). The presence of a great many low-paid instructors is a deteriorating influence upon the economic status of the whole profession, and a widespread reliance upon outside work and private incomes operates against those who must derive their livelihoods solely from their salaries. Average salaries are also depressed by the fact that there is a higher percentage (about 25 per cent) of women workers than in any other major profession. It is a practice in our society to pay women less than men for the same work, so that the entrance of women in large numbers as competitors is always both a cause and a result of low wages in an occupation.[4] Moreover, the dubious sop handed the academician in the form of the honor or standing his office is supposed to entail is not

[3] The North Central Association has found that good salaries are associated with institutional excellence. This finding is stated as follows: 'The chances are about 65 in a 100 that the rank-order position of an institution with respect to faculty salaries will be predictive of its rank position in educational excellence within two times the probable error of the distribution of fifty-six institutions [the number investigated] in educational excellence.' *The Evaluation of Higher Institutions*, Vol. 2, p. 131.

[4] The proportion of women teachers varies greatly according to the type of institution. In teachers colleges and non-degree-granting institutions, women outnumber men; women form less than a third of the faculty in publicly controlled universities, and slightly more than a third in privately controlled universities.

willingly accepted as a substitute for an adequate scale of living.

Studies made of the Yale faculty [5] have demonstrated rather conclusively that university employees feel acutely the strain of invidious comparisons with outsiders of comparable social status. It has been found that for a university to get a given level of faculty ability it is only necessary to ascertain the tax values of the residences of the economic class having that . level of ability; half the valuation of their homes is 'the approximate market price in that town for the corresponding level of ability.' Thus, the investigators conclude, a university cannot obtain abilities corresponding to those of successful lawyers and doctors and at the same time pay salaries comparable to those of bank clerks and policemen.

In addition to other strains developed, low income leads to diffusion, not to mention dissipation, of energy. A study conducted by the General Education Board in 302 institutions,[6] representative geographically and educationally, gives the following information. Of total staff members, 69.7 per cent do extra teaching or other institutional service for their own or other institutions; 24.3 per cent do writing; 19.5 per cent lecture; 10 per cent do consulting work; 25.2 per cent are engaged in miscellaneous activity. Teachers in urban institutions have a better opportunity for writing, extra teaching, and consulting. In lecturing and miscellaneous services the comparison is in favor of the more rural colleges and universities. The total supplementary earning of 7,072 persons equalled 23.8 per cent of their regular annual income, the range being from less than $100 to more than $10,000, with a median of

[5] See Yandell Henderson and Maurice R. Davie, *Incomes and Living Costs of a University Faculty*, New Haven, Yale University Press, 1928; and also, Yandell Henderson, 'Quality versus Quantity in University Faculties,' *Science*, LXX, 1929, p. 4.
[6] Trevor Arnett, *Teachers' Salaries in Certain Endowed and State Supported Colleges and Universities, with Special Reference to Colleges of Arts, Literature and Science*, N. Y., General Education Board, 1928.

$522 in supplementary earnings.[7] This inquiry also found a general correlation between salary level and size of the faculty group.

SPECIAL PROBLEMS OF REMUNERATION

There is not only the question of what academicians are to be paid but also how they are to be paid. Inextricably tied up with problems of rank and tenure is the salary scale—whether there is to be a fixed uniform rate, individual bargaining with no fixed schedule, or a scale of salaries, increasing with rank and length of service for each grade, according to a definite schedule.

Each of these systems is now widely followed, each has its merits and demerits, and there is no marked consensus that any one is decidedly superior in most respects to the other two, although the first and last bases may be considered extremes. A flat salary rate disregards age and length of service; it assumes no increase in value with length of service and often results in an 'inferiority complex' for the older men, if not in an actual easing up. Individual bargaining helps the university get better men, and makes possible a differential administrative treatment of outstanding and mediocre individuals or departments. On the other hand it makes for administrative autocracy, for uncertainty, anxiety, and fawning in the ranks; inevitable and unfair discriminations lower morale, and foment bitterness, jealousy, and unco-operativeness. A scale based on rank and length of tenure or seniority disregards individual differences by remunerating according to position, irrespective of the position's occupant. Proposed systems advocated by professors' organizations are likely to prove expen-

---

[7] Henderson and Davie found the relation of salary to total income to be as follows (median per cent): instructors, 79 to 84; assistant professors, 75 to 83; associate professors, 75 to 84.5; full professors, 70 to 83. Thirty-two persons reported no supplementary earnings, 23 from $1 to $499, 20 from $500 to $999, 14 from $1,000 to $1,999, with a successive falling off to only one person earning more than $8,000. (It should be kept in mind, however, that as university faculties go, the Yale group is relatively plutocratic.)

sive from the point of view of the university, whereas those enforced by university administrations often afford scant security for the average academician. The former almost invariably consider professors as ends, whereas the latter too often treat them merely as means.[8]

Remuneration entails a complex set of social conditions that the 'technologically minded' seldom think of. While it is true that few become teachers and scholars merely to gain a livelihood, it is also true that income is not a secondary consideration. In their professional organizations, with the exception of the A.A.U.P. and the American Federation of Teachers, professors have no unified front in the matter of remuneration. The following explanation has been given for this neglect:

First, college professors are enveloped in a 'tradition of dignity,' perhaps a heritage from ecclesiastical days, one aspect of which is that the profession has nothing in common with labor, or the methods of laboring groups in protecting their own interests. A gentleman does not bargain. Hence, organization, outspokenness or mass demands are regarded with disfavor, particularly by administrative officers and the more successful members of the profession. There is, too, a trace of the older notion that a scholar's life is one of sacrifice and poverty . . . Learning is its own reward . . . Second, there is a timidity or an inertia that flows from a spirit of individualism. Faculty members have not, in general, been imbued with a concept of cooperative or unified welfare . . . There is evidence that at some institutions staff members fear reprisals when they discuss matters that run counter to administration practice. There are, also, lines of cleavage within the profession on the basis of rank; instructors and full professors do not always see eye to eye . . . The prevailing departmental set-up has tended to make staff members departmentally

[8] A high proportion of academic men feel that a fixed scale with limits for each rank is the fairest system; such a system reduces the element of bargaining and perhaps lessens purely economic competition. One investigation has found this type of remuneration to prevail among 98 representative institutions in the following distribution: public, 40.0 per cent; private, 50.0 per cent; denominational, 61.1 per cent. (*Depression, Recovery, and Higher Education*, p. 53.)

minded, with each division seeking to advance its own interests. (Ibid. p. 94.)

Inadequate income and low economic status, regardless of the class origins of persons within the academic profession, may engender a general dissatisfaction, cynicism, and revolt against the *status quo*. A study of the leadership and composition of the Nazi party in Germany has shown why persons feel disadvantaged when there is a great disparity between self-esteem and actual status, and how they are readily attracted to movements promising an overthrow of existing conditions. 'The teachers—most elementary-school teachers—are the best represented of all professional groups composing the Nazi party . . . 97 per cent of all German teachers are members of the party or its affiliates.' [9] Thus, an institutionalized 'intelligentsia' that is economically dissatisfied and insecure can as readily become a revolutionary element as the unemployables in the lowest economic stratum.

In any consideration of income it should be noted that, aside from actual buying power, remuneration is valued very significantly as a symbol of status. Indirect testimony for this statement is seen in the practice of giving 'dry raises,' or promotions without increase of salary, a procedure very prevalent during the depression. Under a fairly stabilized promotion system this policy rendered a modicum of satisfaction to those who were due salary increases.

Whether a fixed salary scale prevails or not, however, income is regarded as one symbol of status, both inside and outside of the group. Many universities with established salaries for full professors have special chairs or professorships having a higher remuneration than the usual maximum, and these serve the double purpose of attracting outstanding men and of giving them special recognition. Annual salaries for these distinguished professorships or endowed chairs may range sev-

[9] Hans Gerth, 'The Nazi Party: Its Leadership and Composition,' *The American Journal of Sociology*, XLV, January 1940, pp. 517-41. See p. 525 ff.

eral thousand dollars above the usual top salary scale, which is $12,000 for an ordinary full professorship in the two highest paying American universities.

But the average academician of full professorial rank makes well under $5,000, and the entire salary range for all ordinary ranks is from less than $2,000 to $12,000, with the vast majority of all employees falling toward the bottom end of the scale. There is some overlapping in many places in salaries between ranks, and almost everywhere there is a spread between the lowest and the highest salary paid at a given rank (typically about 20 per cent). Although this practice causes some friction in the personnel, the North Central Association inquiry cited earlier found it to be a procedure characteristic of superior institutions. A comparison of income by the three professorial ranks (1931-2) has been summarized by Wilson Gee, and is condensed in the table on page 143.

'SOCIAL' STATUS

Since one's social position or status always stands in a reciprocal relation to the statuses of other persons, it is impossible not to consider the socio-economic status of the academic man without reference to his non-academic associates. As one observer has put it:

In interests, in tastes, in ambitions, and in the desire for social status and acceptance, the college professor and his family are closely allied to other professional groups: doctors, lawyers, and successful business men. The college teacher seeks to cut the pattern of his life to the same standards that they cut theirs. One can read with understanding and full sympathy the 'haunting thought' of the assistant professor on an income of approximately $2,000 whose 'submediocre financial status' makes it impossible to satisfy his tastes; yet he clings to his one dress shirt, which he launders himself. This situation symbolizes the point that is being made. Yet the fact remains that the salary scale of the faculty group is below the income level of the successful members of the groups whose

Table IV

Average Annual Salaries Paid for Instruction by Ranks in a Sample of 99 American Colleges and Universities [10]

	Actual Salaries Paid			Range of Salaries		
	Prof.	Assoc. Prof.	Asst. Prof.	Prof.	Assoc. Prof.	Asst. Prof.
	$	$	$	$	$	$
47 Southern Institutions	3,663	2,843	2,323	3,131– 4,370	2,602–3,248	2,060–2,724
47 Northern and W. Inst.	4,944	3,637	2,986	3,841– 6,421	3,244–4,245	2,400–3,625
The Univ. of Chicago	7,004	4,724	3,215	4,500–10,000	3,500–4,500	2,700–3,500
Columbia	8,288	5,165	4,012	7,500–12,000	5,000–6,000	3,600–4,500
Harvard	9,729	6,164	4,698	8,000–12,000	6,000–7,000	4,000–5,500
Yale	8,148	5,272	3,971	6,500–10,000	5,000–5,500	3,500–4,500
7 Southern Agr. Col.	3,671	2,882	2,287	2,911– 4,449	2,417–3,565	1,965–2,990
8 Northern & West. Ag. Col.	3,872	3,085	2,646	2,848– 4,956	2,596–3,763	2,103–3,338
7 Southern Smaller Col. for Men ..	3,377	2,470	2,068	3,150– 3,492	2,507–2,893	1,950–2,208
7 N. & W. Smaller Col. for Men ..	5,461	4,130	3,488	4,264– 6,167	3,825–4,620	2,693–4,175

[10] *Research Barriers in the South*, N. Y., The Century Co., 1932, p. 38 ff. A comparison of salaries by universities does not establish the fact, nonetheless, that problems of socio-economic status are most pronounced in those institutions where remuneration is lowest. Many lesser institutions in small towns of the South and West pay the lowest salaries, but their faculty members often enjoy more economic security and a higher comparative social status in their communities than do much better-paid professors in metropolitan centers, where living costs are greater and 'keeping up with the Joneses' is a more strenuous affair.

standards they emulate. Out of this fact apparently arises the pinchpenny psychology to which reference has already been made . . . The emphasis upon 'appearances,' plus the assumption that each salary advancement is a permanent new level of income, naturally leads faculty families to expand their scale of life, as has already been called to attention. There is the attempt to achieve a maximum status, socially and as measured by 'cultural' terms, upon limited income. The desired mode of life, and the income from teaching, are not perfectly harmonized . . .

The desire for status and the emphasis upon those expenditures through which it is achieved involves more than a comparison between members of the teaching profession and those outside of it. Within the profession itself, there is an intense competition which is accentuated by the hierarchical organization and by the intimacy of association. 'The college community' has a connotation that cannot be escaped. The standards that prevail within this community in general apply at all ranks. It is essential to observe that, while the expected standards do not vary greatly from rank to rank, the income for maintaining them does vary widely. It is this fact that is disturbing, especially to the staff members on small income.[11]

Income according to status within the profession has been indicated in Table IV. It is difficult to compare relative achievements in different fields, yet the broad ranking of income hierarchy on the whole expresses society's differential valuation. The tabulation on page 145 furnishes a basis for comparison of the economic standing of the academic man with that of various other professionals:

So much for the various gradations of economic status within the profession, and relative to other professional groups —it does not follow that the professor's wider social status is contained entirely in this one category. What he lacks in pecuniary prestige is to some extent compensated for by prestige of a less mundane nature.

Despite lower incomes, professors in leading universities

[11] *Depression, Recovery, and Higher Education,* pp. 138-9.

TABLE V

Average Annual Income of College Faculty Members at Land-Grant Institutions and Certain Other Professional Groups, 1929-33 [12]

Group	1928-9 Amt.	Index	1929-30 Amt.	Index	1930-31 Amt.	Index	1931-2 Amt.	Index	1932-3 Amt.	Index
	$		$		$		$		$	
Consulting Engineers	10,412	100.0	8,523	81.9	7,220	69.3	4,377	42.0	3,940	37.8
Lawyers	5,560	100.0	5,219	93.9	5,114	92.0	4,170	75.0	3,879	69.8
Physicians & Surgeons	5,389	100.0	5,105	94.7	4,371	81.1	3,311	61.4	3,079	57.1
Dentists	4,575	100.0	4,381	95.8	3,794	82.9	2,776	60.7	2,413	52.7
College faculty members *	3,277	100.0	3,307	100.9	3,343	102.0	—	—	—	—
Clergymen	2,136	100.0	2,014	94.3	1,881	88.1	1,701	79.6	1,573	73.6

* All staff members in 51 land-grant institutions.

[12] This table is adapted from a similar one in *Depression, Recovery, and Higher Education*, p. 50.

and ministers of the more fashionable churches are usually accepted as being on a par with successful lawyers, doctors, and businessmen. Since the primary objective of the pursuits of the former is not the accumulation of wealth, they are judged by standards other than those of pecuniary success. Professors and ministers are not expected to enter into the conspicuous consumption that characterizes the social life of members of other occupations. Yet the characteristic discrepancy between income and tastes is bound to give rise to family strains. Because of his intellectual achievements and the respect that the higher learning commands, the academic man may be accepted everywhere, though his personal appearance and his general mode of life on the material plane are not characteristically prepossessing, but this same acceptance is not accorded to other members of his immediate family.

Whether the dowdiness of academic wives and the penuriousness of family life are what they are imputed to be by some depends upon the vantage point or class perspective of the observer. A rather extreme opinion of the social status of the professoriate is expressed by Flexner:

The truth is that, with exceptions, of course, the American professoriate is a proletariat, lacking the amenities and dignities they are entitled to enjoy. Amenities are provided in plenty for the well-to-do students, who have club houses, fraternity houses, and at times luxurious dormitories; not, however, for the teaching staff. Thus a very small part of our unheard-of national wealth, even in the most cultivated and complacent section of the country, is devoted to the uses to which a civilized society would attach, and assuredly some day much attach, the highest importance. Meanwhile, the mental and physical vigour which should be attracted into universities is in unduly large proportion forced into activities which, if successfully pursued, will yield an adequate return. And this is happening at the very moment when the fortress of intelligence needs to be most strongly defended.

The professoriate is disadvantaged by one more consideration. Time was when it meant something to be a college or university professor, as it meant something to hold a college or university degree. And this legitimate distinction operated as a compensation for the plain living required. Now the situation is reversed. Professors of economics, physics, philosophy, or Sanskrit find themselves in the same boat with professors of business English, advertising, journalism, physical training, and extra-curricular activities. They bear, all alike, the same titles; the second group generally earn more, for they frequently do remunerative outside work. The universities, by sacrificing intellectual purpose, have thus sacrificed the intellectual distinction which counts for more than money. (*Universities*, N. Y., Oxford University Press, 1930, p. 208.)

That the 'professoriate is a proletariat' is very doubtful, for low income does not necessarily mean identity with the proletariat, as this is not simply a matter of *Messer- und Gabelfrage*, or at least the connection between the belly and the head is not so direct. There is no gainsaying, however, that the professoriate is composed of human beings with at least a modicum of material desires and feelings. The professor may spend long hours in the classroom, office, or laboratory, and even in his 'social' life he often finds it difficult to cast aside his professional role; still, in his private life, his tastes, desires, and behavior patterns are not widely different from those displayed by most of his non-academic associates.[13]

As was shown in an earlier chapter, the class origins of average members of the academic profession are such as to preclude the presence of any considerable number of persons of private means. By way of comparison it is interesting to note that moderately paid professorships in pre-Nazi Germany also entailed obligations and the maintenance of a social position beyond the returns of the office; hence, an independent source of income (frequently a wealthy wife) was necessary. In Germany, however, the academic career was held in so much esteem that a wealthy bourgeois family was willing to pay

---

[13] For recent literary treatments of the professor's social life, see Henry S. Canby, *Alma Mater*, James R. Parker, *Academic Procession*, Hester Pine, *Beer for the Kitten*, Lawrence R. Watkin, *Geese in the Forum*, and Kenneth P. Kempton, *So Dream All Night*.

for the prestige of the office by continued subsidy of one of its sons. In America, on the other hand, the profession is often entered via scholarships by those who cannot afford a legal, medical, or engineering training, and must rely upon their own earnings, not only later but also during training and apprenticeship.

Likewise, though the academic profession is a 'prestige' occupation, it entails more arduous work and less glamour than the diplomatic service and other relatively unremunerative occupations that attract scions of the plutocratic classes. One may wonder why in this country the academician commands respect but no great amount of popular envy. As the Dean of an American university has put it,

Why is it, I have been asking myself, that in Europe an ordinary mortal, when he sees a professor, tips his hat, whereas in these United States he taps his forehead? Why is it that in Europe the professor is the jewel of the salon while in the United States he is the skeleton at the feast? Why is it that in Europe a professor is a lion who is diligently hunted by the arbiters of society, while in the United States he is as a lone ass braying in the desert? Such startling differences, my friends, cannot be due to accident or caprice, and therefore cannot be safely ignored. In the name of scholarship, and for the sake of the future American professor, they must be examined and, if possible, explained.[14]

A similar observation has been made by Znaniecki in his recent book, *The Social Role of the Man of Knowledge*. He notes the high position of the Chinese mandarin, and the greater prestige among orthodox Jews of the poor student of the Talmud than of the uncultivated man of wealth. In France, a member of the Academy of Sciences is given the place of honor at the right of a dinner-party hostess; in other European countries (e.g. Poland), the full professor enjoys an

---

[14] Marten ten Hoor, 'The Species Professor Americanus and Some Natural Enemies,' *Association of American Colleges Bulletin*, xxvi, No. 3, November 1940, p. 405.

official rank equal to that of a province governor or a brigadier general.

Various critics of the American professor have made the observation that democratic demands for mass education in all sorts of practical subjects have resulted in many faculty members of mediocre mentality and general cultural attainments. Flexner, ten Hoor, and others have felt that professorial prestige is debased by the inclusion in the academic fold of specialists on such matters as hog-raising, dishwashing, and cheerleading. This point of view overlooks the fact that the American university is conceived as having broader functions than its European counterpart.

It is undoubtedly true that the profession has its general prestige lowered in the eyes of some by a superfluity of persons who rise above the average man neither in intellectual accomplishments nor in style of life. And too, even if this were not true, America, with its lingering frontier heritage and strong ideology of material success, has never made a place for an aristocracy of intellect in the same way it has for an aristocracy of wealth. Family position and affluence are the only two common interpretations of a social hierarchy that have ever had much acceptance here. Some of our professions have attempted to enhance their social status by showing exclusiveness and class bias, but the academic profession has been one of those affording a floodgate for social advancement.

In the matter of social rank, or preferment and degradation of various social groups, it should be remembered that individuals are differently conditioned; the resulting heterogeneity leads separate groupings to refuse to accept one another's standards. Even within the middle class, to which most professors belong, approximate equality in income and social rank may be accompanied by very disparate ideals or value systems. Because of its heterogeneous social composition, the academic profession is on the whole not a highly class-conscious group. This fact is important from two vantage points: first, it means the academic profession recognizes that no class has a monopoly of human talent; [15] and second, there is no super-imposition of a class or caste allegiance, which would interfere with the impartial interpretation of life in dynamic terms.

THE PROFESSOR: TYPE AND STEREOTYPE

For purposes of describing the professor as a social type, a composite based upon statistics is not very helpful. A modal man from a major university would appear somewhat as follows. He would be a teacher of English with a Ph.D. from Chicago. He would be a family man with one or two children, and would have spent his early years in one of the eastern or north-central states. He would have been in his present institution from six to ten years, and would have taught in one other college or university.[16]

Qualitative characterizations are more meaningful and certainly more abundant, however, in the material available at the present time. Many of these qualitative characterizations are impressionistic rather than objective, and are properly designated as stereotypes. The stereotype always pre-judges the policeman as a flatfoot, and the professor as an absent-minded individual. Yet there is no gainsaying that these stereotypes help to determine the social status of any occupational group, whether they be accurate or inaccurate. The press, stage, and screen help to perpetuate erroneous notions, so that in the case of the academic man it is something of a shock to the uninformed outsider to find behavior at luncheon clubs, sporting events, and other social gatherings not in conformity to stereotyped ideas.

Using the professional stereotype as a point of reference, one investigator has culled comments from twenty magazines

[15] The functional value of this recognition is partially witnessed in the superior scholarship of those attracted to the profession. In addition to materials discussed earlier, see B. L. Gambrill, *College Achievement and Vocational Efficiency*, N. Y., Teachers College, Columbia University, 1922.

[16] Kunkel, op. cit. p. 249 ff.

of various sorts over a period of forty-eight years.[17] Academic writers proved to be more adversely critical of the professorial personality type than were laymen. The non-academic writers expressed a disdain for the professor's dullness, social inadequacy, impracticality, and laziness; on the other hand, they admired his intellectual curiosity, unselfishness, dispassion, and humanity. None impugned his moral integrity. More than half of the opinions were from professors themselves, and it was in these comments that the higher percentage (67 per cent) of unfavorable reactions showed up. Some representative epithets were: lacking breadth, monkish, dull, funny little fellows, absent-minded and bigoted, sheepish, stultified, garrulous, queer, lacking virility, fugitives from reality, absurdly theoretical, lacking conviction, unimaginative, oracular, tradition bound, and lazy. Favorable terms were: genuine curiosity, high ideals, studious habits, generously proud, human, cultivated, dignified, unprejudiced, contented, and choicest spirits of the age.

On the whole, academicians are more openly self-critical than the members of most other occupations, and many lean over backwards to avoid conforming to stereotypes. Whether the professor was ever as unusual as popular thought pictured him is questionable, although there is a basis for the impression that specialization in highly abstract intellectual activity and the consequent loss of outside contacts do engender absent-mindedness, impracticality, and other traits attributed to the pedagogue.[18]

Yet the modern college professor has changed considerably from the former pattern, and seems not to be vastly different from other persons in the professional classes. As Dean Otto Heller has remarked,

[17] Claude C. Bowman, *The College Professor in America*, Philadelphia, privately printed, 1938 (Ph.D. thesis).
[18] See Burges Johnson, *Professor at Bay*, N. Y., G. P. Putnam's Sons, 1937.

Go at the noon hour to the pastures of the Elks, the Moose, the Buffaloes, the Bulls and the Bears, and I defy you to spot the sporadic professor among his Loyal, Benevolent and Protective Brethren. Formerly he was alien to their lairs, now he is hail fellow well met there. They did not use to invite the 'highbrow' in, for they felt uncomfortable in the company of literary aspirations. Nowadays, the bookish interests of the collegian run much the same way as theirs: to the volume of business. He frequently lectures to them—on the psychology of salesmanship, by preference, or gives inspiration talks, perchance on Christ as a Rotarian, or on the human side of retailing.[19]

To some academicians, the changed public role seems a loss in professional dignity; by others it is taken as an emancipation from the narrow limits of behavior formerly prescribed for the educator.

Excepting the clergy, the army, and a few callings that retain institutional clothing and other ready marks of identification, superficial differences setting specialists apart from one another have been broken down by trends in modern civilization toward standardization and uniformity. A few professionals retain the *pince-nez*, frock coat, beard or goatee, and other outward symbols of their group, but in the hotel lobby or lounge car it is difficult at a glance to distinguish the professor, doctor, lawyer, clerk, merchant, manufacturer, or salesman. The successful businessman is more likely to show the results of custom tailoring than is the successful scientist; still, the difference is one of degree rather than kind.

Closer acquaintance reveals the indelible stamp of the occupation upon personality, however, and subtle, important manifestations are apparent. Long continued salesman-customer, doctor-patient, officer-private, and teacher-student relations become interiorized and cast their aurae over many spheres of behavior. Work in a bureaucratic system produces

[19] 'The Passing of the Professor,' *The Scientific Monthly*, Vol. 24, 1927, p. 31. See also Edgar J. Goodspeed, 'The Twilight of the Professors,' *The Atlantic*, Vol. 156, 1935, pp. 210-14.

a divergent type of occupational personality from that found in individualistic enterprise. The predominance of persuasive approaches in one type situation is displaced by ordering and forbidding techniques in another; a relation of equals is found in one context and the superordination and subordination of an hierarchical arrangement in another. Some persons work primarily with people, others with ideas and objects; some are accustomed to giving orders, others to taking them; some associate professionally with equals, others with inferiors. Advancement through casual personal contacts makes the salesman affable and dapper; advancement through the impersonal medium of research causes the scientist to be more aloof in manner and indifferent to appearance. Each occupation produces personality vices in extreme cases: the military man becomes a martinet and the academic man a pedant. Each occupation also develops its criminal type—the quack, the plagiarist, the shyster, the traitor, or the fraud. University professors are more commonly agnostic in religion and liberal in politics than are bankers.[20] Even in non-technical contexts, academic and legal speech is loaded with adjectives, and military speech with imperative verbs; business thinking is characteristically in the indicative mood, clerical thinking often in the subjunctive. What each occupational type sees in the same general situation has its economic coloration: the doctor has man's ill health impressed upon him, the professor, man's ignorance.

In these and thousands of other ways occupation stereotypes personality and determines socio-economic status. Common accessibility of standardized forms of recreation, religion,

[20] James M. Leuba has found that of a representative group of individuals from *American Men of Science* (1933 edition), the percentage of those believing in a supreme being was as follows: physicists, 38; biologists, 27; sociologists, 24; psychologists, 10. (From 'Religious Beliefs of American Scientists,' *Harpers*, Vol. 69, 1934, pp. 290-303). A later study by the same author of various occupational groups in *Who's Who in America* yielded the following 'believers in God': bankers, 64 per cent; businessmen, 53 per cent; lawyers, 53 per cent; writers, 32 per cent.

education, and so on, to some extent negates differences promulgated by the division of labor, and an open-class society prevents the accentuation of peculiarities arising from intensive social inbreeding. The decline of the family, church, and other groupings has been accompanied by a rise in the importance of occupational organization in the structure of contemporary society. Considerable attention has been directed in the past toward the attainment of a maximum efficiency in the production of goods, and in ascertaining what the worker can do to participate more effectively in the organization of economic enterprise. Yet it is only recently that scientific attention is being given to the social organization of production in terms of its effects upon the direct participants.

PART III

ACADEMIC PROCESSES AND FUNCTIONS

IX. PRESTIGE AND COMPETITION

It is clear by now that the academician participates in a highly competitive social system. There is necessarily much co-operation, but competition, or individual striving for ends that cannot be equally shared, creates the problems in which we are interested. Those in training for membership, it has been observed, compete for grades, prizes, honors, and fellowships. Selection and promotion are based upon criteria that assume competition. Universities and departments within them are in active and sometimes acrid competition for students, money, and other symbols of achievement. Wherever accomplishment is measured comparatively, there is inevitable competitiveness.

Co-operation is a much lauded process in higher education, and effective organization would be impossible without it, yet no considerable acumen is required to see divergences between professed emphases and actual workings of the system. Major universities compete for their share of the national income. Institutions supported by the same domain compete with one another. Private and public universities are placed in rival positions, and growth in one place may imply decline elsewhere. As the limits of expansion in higher education are approached, the struggle for a place in the sun is even more intensified. The quick tempo of social change prevents stabilization of the position of any university, so that the weakest institutions struggle to keep alive, the average ones to maintain themselves or to improve their status, and the best to stay at the forefront. Levels of institutional aspiration are always relative, and the status of any university is relative to that of comparable universities.

FACTORS IN UNIVERSITY PRESTIGE

Inter-university competition is transmuted into personal competition, for to secure a desirable place in the prestige hierarchy, an institution must be able to bring forward specific claims. To obtain endowments, appropriations, and the other material means of sustaining or advancing its position, the university needs to show evidences of accomplishment. Such evidences are popularly seen in the size of its student body, the magnificence of its physical plant, and the prowess of its athletic teams. Expert judgments, however, are based upon other criteria of prestige.

Qualified judges are interested above all in the general competence, training, and experience of the faculty. An inquiry into fifty-seven co-operating institutions in the North Central Association [1] has ascertained that institutional excellence is dependent largely upon a competent, well-organized faculty, which is provided with a satisfactory working environment. Individual members must be adequately trained, sufficiently experienced in their specialties, and must evidence their scholarship through publication and by participation in learned societies. Effective faculty organization means a well-balanced ratio between student numbers and instructional staff, an adequate representation in the various fields of instruction, and ample opportunity for staff participation in policy making. Good working conditions means that satisfactory provision must be made for the following: 'salary status; tenure; instructional load; recruiting, selection, and appointment; aids to faculty growth; and provisions for leaves of absence, retirement, insurance, housing, and recreation and community life.' (Ibid.)

With reference to faculty competence, a statistical estimate of the relative importance of major items has yielded the table on page 159.

[1] Melvin E. Haggerty, *The Evaluation of Higher Institutions* (Vol. 2, *The Faculty*), Chicago, University of Chicago Press, 1937.

TABLE VI

*Regression Weighting of Items of Importance in
Staff Competence* [2]

Doctor's degrees	.10
Master's degrees	.30
Graduate study	.30
Experience	.30
Books and monographs	.35
Articles	.50
Membership in learned societies	.06
Attending society meetings	.25
Office in learned societies	.20
Part in society programs	.20

In addition to having a competent faculty, as judged by these and other factors, an institution is measured in terms of its laboratory, library, and other facilities, the quality of its undergraduates and graduates,[3] and its administrative leadership. To insure institutional stability, there must be adequate and continued financial support, and a dependable enrollment. Equally important are those intangible items expressed as morale, and an emphasis on the higher reaches of scholarship.

Some of the terms of inter-university competition are set in a rather mechanical way by such accrediting agencies as the Association of American Universities, the National Association of State Universities, and a number of others of national as well as regional scope,[4] which maintain explicit standards.

[2] Ibid., p. 78. The average rank of faculty competence by these criteria, according to types of institutions, is as follows: (1) universities, (2) liberal arts colleges, (3) Catholic colleges, (4) teachers colleges, (5) junior colleges (see p. 89).

[3] The rank order of the first thirteen institutions in the production of graduates of distinction since 1915 has been computed as follows: (1) Harvard, (2) Yale, (3) California, (4) Columbia, (5) Princeton, (6) Chicago, (7) Wisconsin, (8) Michigan, (9) Pennsylvania, (10) Cornell, (11) Dartmouth, (12) Illinois, (13) Indiana. See B. W. Kunkel and D. B. Prentice, 'The Production of Graduates of Distinction by Undergraduate Liberal Arts Colleges and Technical Schools,' *Ass'n. of American Colleges Bulletin*, XXVI, No. 3, 1940, p. 136.

[4] See George F. Zook, *The Evaluation of Higher Institutions*, Chicago, University of Chicago Press, 1936.

Aside from expelling or refusing to admit institutions falling below their standards, these agencies attempt to give no rank order to affiliated and non-affiliated colleges and universities.

INSTITUTIONAL RANKINGS

The general standings of universities become known to the educated classes of laymen largely through informal channels. Specialized excellence, while known to scholars and scientists within a field, is not widely disseminated as information, even among undergraduates who contemplate entering the field. (Appendix I should be useful to such persons.) Harvard, Yale, Columbia, and other leading centers stand as symbols of scholarly prestige with many persons having only vague notions of how such standings are deduced. Even academicians themselves are prone to be swayed by the magic of traditional renown, regardless of how meaningless it may be when applied to the merit of a particular department within a major university.

To provide interested individuals with a more rational basis for their impressions, numerous attempts have been made to rank colleges and universities in various orders of merit. In 1911, for instance, the Bureau of Education prepared a rating of 344 institutions at the request of the Association of American Universities. This list was first distributed semi-confidentially, and aroused such a storm of protest that it was officially withdrawn. Despite objections from various sources to invidious comparisons, later rankings have been made. The best-known of these is one undertaken by the American Council on Education in 1934.[5] This study relied upon the ratings of a presumably representative group of prominent specialists in thirty-odd fields (averaging about sixty-five judges to a

[5] *Report on the Committee on Graduate Instruction*, Washington, American Council on Education, 1934. Whereas this *Report* is the most comprehensive study yet attempted, the sampling procedure was somewhat faulty, and the representativeness of the returns was not checked. Likewise, certain institutional rankings based upon the cumulative totals

field). The derived rank order of universities according to the number of distinguished departments is as follows (as of the year 1934): (1) Harvard, (2) Chicago, (3) Columbia, (4) California, (5) Yale, (6) Michigan, (7) Cornell, (8) Princeton, (9) Johns Hopkins, (10) Wisconsin, (11) Minnesota.

In a commentary on these findings,[6] Edwin R. Embree has pointed out that there is nothing particularly difficult about rating individual departments, since it is constantly done in all university thinking and planning. Although this is perhaps a *non sequitur*, one might assuredly state that contemporary eminence is nothing more than what competent judges think it is. In the case of the eleven institutions just mentioned, it is evident that from the point of view of their total number of distinguished (as well as adequate) departments, Harvard, Chicago, Columbia, and California are pre-eminent. (Note Appendix I.) Cumulative ratings become more difficult as one passes below this group. Some of the larger state universities, for example, have adequate graduate departments in many fields without being adjudged distinguished in any of them. There are other institutions, notably Massachusetts Institute of Technology and the California Institute of Technology, which are unsurpassed in their specialties, but without attempting to compete in all fields. Then again, a few well-known universities which try to spread themselves over the entire field of scholarship and science are not considered by disinterested specialists to be adequate in a single graduate department.

A further means of arriving at the distinction of universities is through the distribution of American Men of Science. Embree shows the close correspondence between institutional eminence and the location of outstanding scientists as follows: Harvard, 78; Chicago, 57; Columbia, 54; Yale, 50; California,

of distinguished departments have rather indiscriminately given the same weighting to relatively minor fields in which few persons are engaged as to those in which thousands of individuals are trained and employed.

[6] 'In Order of Their Eminence.'

46; Johns Hopkins, 39; Cornell, 35; Princeton, 31; Wisconsin, 30; Michigan, 29; Minnesota, 26; Pennsylvania, 26; Stanford, 25. (Ibid.)

Another investigator has used a composite index based on these criteria: institutions at which there are Fellows of the Social Science Research Council, the National Research Council, and so on; the institutional affiliations of officers and members of committees of the American Association for the Advancement of Science, and other learned societies; starred men in *American Men of Science;* institutions from which these men took their degrees, and so on to get a total of twenty-eight items for statistical comparison.[7] The relative standing of the sixteen leading American graduate centers was found to be (figures indicate sum of ranks): Harvard, 63; Chicago, 121; Columbia, 126; Yale, 157; California, 180; Johns Hopkins, 199; Cornell, 234; Princeton, 242; Michigan, 245; Wisconsin, 250; Pennsylvania, 257; Minnesota, 279; M. I. T., 317; Illinois, 329; Stanford, 339; Ohio State, 393.

It is in these and other leading universities within the main stream of higher education that intellectual competition is most intense. Every major university vies for recognition in nearly all the branches of learning. Intellectual competition, to be sure, is more subtle and muted than is athletic competition on the collegiate level, but it is equally evident in disguised or open forms. Most of the central universities already have tremendous resources; hence they are in a position to press their advantages through demands upon their staffs to a much greater extent than would be possible in provincial colleges.

Existing disparities between leading and lesser universities are further intensified by recruitment of the ablest scholars and scientists to such centers, so that this draining off of talent—especially marked in the South—leaves lesser institu-

[7] Walter C. Eells, 'Another Ranking of American Graduate Schools,' *School and Society*, Vol. 46, 1937, pp. 282-4. For another treatment of the subject, see Laurence Foster, *The Functions of a Graduate School in a Democratic Society*, N. Y., Huxley House, 1936.

tions still further weakened. Graduate centers enjoy the marginal advantage of being able to use their prestige to secure more prestige. They can and do bid for outstanding individuals, and their superior resources make them the logical recipients for added resources from foundations and other benefactors.[8] Affiliated institutes for research and advanced study provide an environment where undivided attention is given to cultural discovery and invention.

Since the Ph.D. has been conceived as a research degree, research centers also tend to become centers for training toward the doctorate. In general, there is a close correspondence between the resources of a university and its power to attract graduate students. Offsetting factors exist, however, which cause individual institutions to strain or under-utilize their resources in the production of doctorates. A rough approximation of the utilization being made by various universities of their physical resources may be ascertained from Table VII. Here we get a comparison of leading graduate centers with reference to certain material factors that are necessary though not sufficient conditions for the attainment of prestige in the academic world.

Any comparison of universities in terms of physical resources is inevitably misleading in certain particulars. For example, state and denominational institutions may rank low in endowment, yet have a more stable and adequate financial support than many private institutions with considerably higher endowments. Expenditures for teaching and research cannot be compared fairly until figures are reduced to a per capita basis according to the size of staff and student body. Among the most important material criteria of adequacy with regard to physical resources is the size of a university library,

[8] Consult Appendix II for information on the contributions of foundations to leading universities.

It should be noted that the initial advantage of leading endowed universities is being undermined as lower interest rates and the heavier state absorption of private incomes places the tax-supported institutions in a relatively more favorable competitive position.

but it should be borne in mind that institutes of technology do not require the extensive libraries needed in universities offering advanced training in practically all subject-matter fields. On the whole, however, it may be inferred that a university is straining its resources and emphasizing quantity at the expense of quality when it ranks high in the production of doctorates, while ranking low in value of property, income, expenditures for teaching and research, and size of library. This inference may be verified by comparing the data of Table VII with those of Appendix I.

THE LOCAL SIGNIFICANCE OF INVIDIOUS COMPARISONS

A significant aspect of invidious comparisons between universities is the interpretation made of them within a university. In larger institutions where there are few if any personal contacts between the deans or presidents and average staff members, the principal check upon departmental activities is the annual report made to the central administration. A case in point is afforded by a University of Chicago survey [9] which ranks the four divisions with respect to higher degrees held, extensity of published works, and recognitions accorded in such published lists as *American Men of Science* and *Who's Who in America*. In addition to this comparison, the survey also gives tables showing the average number of published contributions according to subject-matter departments, and academic rank. The authors comment that bibliographical entries obtained from reports to the president are not necessarily complete, but add—perhaps facetiously—that 'faculty members in general feel an interest in having their publications recorded, and few fail to send in the data called for.'

The rapid rise of the University of Chicago to the forefront as a graduate center is attributable in no small measure to its emphasis upon the prestige which accrues from intel-

[9] *The University Faculty, passim.*

TABLE VII

A Comparison of the Physical Resources of the Thirty Leading Graduate Centers

Rank Order of the Thirty Leading Graduate Centers in Terms of Doctorates Conferred between 1929-30 and 1938-9 *	Rank Order with Reference to: †				
	Value of Property	Endowment	Expenditures for Teaching and Non-Budgeted Research	Expenditures for Research Separately Budgeted	Size of Library (Number of Bound Volumes)
1. Columbia 3	4	4	3	3	
2. Chicago 2	3	13	1	5	
3. Wisconsin 16	23	10	6	6	
4. Harvard .... —	1	1	7	1	
5. Cornell 8	11	5	11	8	
6. Yale 1	2	7	9	2	
7. California 4	12	3	2	4	
8. Michigan 7	17	2	14	9	
9. Illinois 10	26	9	4	7	
10. N. Y. U. 18	18	6	27	17	
11. Ohio State 17	25	12	13	18	
12. Iowa 19	27	15	20	16	
13. Johns Hopkins 14	10	19	27	15	
14. Minnesota 13	15	8	5	11	
15. Pennsylvania 9	13	11	10	10	
16. Princeton. .... —	9	21	15	12	
17. Stanford 12	7	16	23	13	
18. M. I. T. 11	6	18	19	24	
19. Pittsburgh 20	21	23	16	28	
20. Iowa St. College 24	28	20	8	26	
21. Catholic 28	20	29	27	22	
22. Northwestern 15	14	14	17	14	
23. Cal. Tech. 23	19	—	12	30	
24. Texas 5	5	22	18	19	
25. Fordham 27	30	27	25	29	
26. North Carolina....... 25	22	28	21	23	
27. Washington (Seattle). 22	29	24	26	21	
28. Virginia 21	16	25	22	25	
29. Duke 6	8	17	27	20	
30. Southern California .. 26	24	26	24	27	

* Rank order is based upon figures obtained from Clarence S. Marsh, *American Colleges and Universities,* Washington, American Council on Education, 1940, Table XIII. The number of doctorates by institutions and by departments is given in Appendix 1 of the present study.

† Institutional rank orders with reference to indicated physical resources are from Henry G. Badger and others, *Abridged Statistics of Higher Education,* 1935-6, Washington, U. S. Dept. of the Interior, 1938 (Bulletin, 1937, No. 2), *passim.* Blank spaces indicate no data reported. (One should bear in mind that the endowment rankings have no particular significance for tax-supported institutions.)

lectual competition. Specific evidence of this attitude is seen in a brochure distributed to the alumni. A few representative passages follow:

As not-too-modest alumni of the University of Chicago, we wish to share with others our pride in the recent announcement that twelve more University faculty members have been voted 'star' ranking by the country's leading scientists.

. . .

Including the twelve scientists newly honored in the 1938 poll, the University of Chicago now has a total of forty-six men on its faculty who have won stars since 1921.

. . .

We blush a bit that Harvard should outrank Chicago, but console ourselves with the reminder that the Crimson has been in the business longer and has a tremendous edge in capital assets.

We thought it would be a good idea to kill two birds with the same chart. So along with Professor Visher's total on starred men we have included several endowment estimates taken from *Fortune* magazine's recent article on the University of Chicago.

When it printed the endowment totals of the four leading privately supported universities, *Fortune* said: '. . . *When you come to equate the endowment and income figures with scholarship, a reasonable case could be made out that Chicago gets more B. T. U.'s of teaching and research energy per dollar than any other U. S. university, even including Harvard.'*

. . .

So, returning to Professor Visher's statistics, we find that among 1,000 men starred since 1921, a *total of 123* received their Ph.D.'s from Chicago.

Only one other university, Harvard, exceeds the University of Chicago in this respect. Harvard has 126, just three more than Chicago.

. . .

Perhaps we sound like alumni extolling their Alma Mater. But the implications of these reports are broader than any local 'pointing with pride.'

We have amassed a good deal of evidence demonstrating that Chicago is a great research institution—one of the greatest. With that accomplished, our final purpose is to point out the place of a great research institution in the pattern of modern life.

A university must not be confused with a college. A college *teaches*. A university *learns*. A college transmits knowledge. A university discovers new knowledge (or recaptures lost knowledge) which colleges presently will interpret and teach . . . But the real test of a great University lies in its *Additions* to human knowledge.[10]

Explicitly or implicitly invidious comparisons with their competitors place tremendous pressures upon major institutions to uphold their reputations. Both administration and staff security depend upon the ability to get maximum results. In marginal instances these may be mere surface results, as there is engendered a misplaced premium upon practical success, spectacular achievements of value for publicity purposes, and even upon mere quantitative productiveness ('dean's research,' as it is colloquially known). The logic of the situation tends to counterbalance keen qualitative discrimination, so that there is a palm for almost any sort of investigative effort, and administrators become prone to judge academicians by the yardage of their publications. As a consequence, there is much hothouse forcing of second-rate material and an intense spirit of rivalry and *reclamé*.

It is within this institutional setting that the academic man seeks his goals. Institutional prestige is translated into personal prestige, and vice versa. The social system of the university abstractly phrases competition in terms of objective technical competence, irrespective of personal rivalries, yet on the concrete level status is made important and there is no way of measuring success except by comparisons. To satisfy individual wishes for security and recognition, scholarly disinterestedness must rest paradoxically upon some form of interestedness.

[10] 'New Stars in the Scientific Firmament,' Chicago, Alumni Committee on Information and Development, 1938.

THE PRESTIGE MECHANISM

Prestige attained within the academic profession usually elevates its possessor in his whole social milieu. To be a champion horseshoe thrower carries no great general prestige, but to be eminent in any of the major professions is to be eminent in every sense of the word. The extension of prestige beyond the immediate group understanding its components is afforded by the lay reputations of such men as Einstein. It should be noted, nonetheless, that the in-group does not always succeed in having its evaluations of importance accepted by outsiders. The leading authority on the *musca domestica* may command the utmost admiration in entomological circles, yet his less learned confreres may consider him a very ordinary mortal.

Since prestige symbols vary from one complex social situation to another, prestige itself is in no sense a metaphysical entity or social force remaining constant. Prestige, whether academic or otherwise, is bound up with a 'complex sign or symbol situation' embodied in whatever is known as success. It accrues to the individual as a result of his possessing qualities or achieving ends envied by the group. As Frank H. Knight has remarked,

Economic activity is at the same time a means of want satisfaction, an agency for want- and character-formation, a field of creative self-expression, and a competitive sport. While men are 'playing the game' of business, they are also moulding their own and other personalities, and creating a civilization whose worthiness to endure cannot be a matter of indifference.[11]

Yet prestige referents are not essentially the same in the academic world as they are in other social universes; likewise, legitimate means of achieving them are differently defined. The academic ethic is not to be reconciled with bandying about knowledge 'as an object of sport, no matter how fasci-

[11] *The Ethics of Competition*, N. Y., Harper & Bros., 1935, p. 47.

nating it may be to leaders.' Knight considers action motivated
by rivalry as being of dubious worth. He feels that the satisfaction of discovery carries with it—if one insists upon hedo-
nism—an elation, kin to true invention, which is sufficient
reward.

It is generally recognized, however, that actual behavior
always falls short of the standards of recommended behavior.
Although scholars and scientists collectively are less given to
ulterior motives than are most occupational groups, deviations
appear on the individual level. The quest for prestige normally
is indirect, in that self-aggrandizement supposedly is only a
by-product of merit, but this is not always the case. It is
easy to exaggerate academic competition as a selfish struggle
of egoists, and concomitantly to minimize the vast amount of
co-operation in higher learning. Notwithstanding the latter,
the outward placidity of academic life belies the intensity of
inner processes. These processes are not naked, neither are
they always sensed by the outside observer, for as Veblen
has noted:

This advancement of learning is in no degree a business
proposition; and yet it must, for the present at least, remain
the sole ostensible purpose of the business-like university. In
the main, therefore, all the competitive endeavors and ma-
noeuvres of the captains of erudition in charge must be made
under cover of an ostensible endeavor to further this non-
competitive advancement of learning, at all costs.[12]

Group interests are complicated by the development of
active but unavowed purposes in many members. That relatively few devote themselves to learning altogether for its
own sake is borne out by the following statement from Einstein:

Many kinds of men devote themselves to Science, and not
all for the sake of Science herself. There are some who come
into her temple because it offers them the opportunity to dis-
play their particular talents. To this class of men science is

[12] *The Higher Learning*, p. 174.

a kind of sport in the practice of which they exult, just as an athlete exults in the exercise of his muscular prowess. There is another class of men who come into the temple to make an offering of their brain pulp in the hope of securing a profitable return. These men are scientists only by chance of circumstance which offered itself when making a choice of career. If the attending circumstances had been different they might have become politicians or captains of business. Should an angel of God descend and drive from the temple of Science all those who belong to the categories I have mentioned, I fear the temple would be nearly emptied. But a few worshipers would still remain—some from former times and some from ours.[13]

Although he might prefer a situation in which materialistic considerations did not have to be taken into account, the savant cannot ignore them entirely, so that in academic pursuits, as in all others forming the basis of livelihood, there must be a working adjustment.

SYMBOLS OF SUCCESS

There are many substantive symbols of status within the higher learning, but income is regarded as only incidental. As in all occupations, there are also in the academic profession persons who are actually being paid more than they could get in any other type of work; this may be due to general incapacity or merely to a trained incapacity for other kinds of pursuits. In all probability there are more instances of highly capable persons on university faculties—chemists, engineers, teachers in medical schools, and others—who could obtain far more remuneration on the outside. At any rate, the individuals who are attracted to teaching or research primarily because it affords a comfortable, leisurely, and re-

[13] 'Prologue,' to Max Planck's *Where Is Science Going?* N. Y., W. W. Norton & Co., Inc., p. 7. For other treatments of the motives of scholars and scientists see Alexander Herzberg, *The Psychology of Philosophers*, N. Y., Harcourt, Brace & Co., 1929, and Bertrand Russell, 'Philosophy's Ulterior Motives,' *The Atlantic*, 159, pp. 149-55.

spectable life seldom achieve much prestige in the profession.

Prestige within the academic world depends upon statuses that are both ascribed and achieved, but the latter are far more numerous and important. Many mediocre men fill important professorships largely by virtue of seniority, but with increasingly keener competition this is becoming less true. Likewise, the professor's prestige is connected with his institutional affiliation, and a faculty member at one of the leading universities has some prestige attached to him regardless of his personal standing among the elite of his field. A fortunate institutional connection is a double asset to the teacher or research man: first, it gives prestige to him by signifying (if status is permanent) that he has already 'arrived'; and second, it places him in an advantageous position further to enhance his reputation. He is aided in this second respect in devious ways; despite the fact that material submitted for publication from, let us say, Yale or Princeton, may not be better than that submitted by an unknown from a second-rate college, it usually *looks* better to the editor or reader because of the institutional prestige and authority behind it.[14] The leading universities, in short, afford more favorable environments for the development of distinction.

Notwithstanding, there is a large mixture of folklore in the ascription of prestige, especially to men in central universities, where their status carries a halo effect. There is a ritual element in the historic nature of office, which causes the occupier to be judged by popular conceptions of what the office should be.[15] Although the professorial office is by no means completely ritualized, objective judgments concerning holders are partially held in abeyance. It is for this reason that a

[14] For example, the author of an outstanding recent book in history had difficulty initially in getting his manuscript considered merely because he happened to be connected with an obscure southern college. His monograph finally received the attention of a leading publishing firm, had its merit recognized, and the book is now widely used as an authoritative reference in its field.

[15] See Everett C. Hughes, 'Institutional Office and the Person,' *The American Jl. of Sociology*, 43, 1937, pp. 404-13.

mediocre Columbia, Chicago, or Harvard professor is more likely to be included in *Who's Who*, called to Washington for consultation, or otherwise signalized, than is a professor of equal achievement in a provincial institution.

The vast majority of the nation's leading scholars and scientists, it is true, are found in the major universities,[16] and the more promising ones in outlying places are constantly being recruited to them. Moreover, the prestige of research centers is so potent that other institutions, established for quite different purposes, indiscriminately try to simulate the pattern, so that teachers almost everywhere must strain to become intellectual innovators and leaders with demonstrated ability to impress, express, and persuade followers.

Regardless of whether the academic man is in a major or a minor university, his need for security as well as his institutionally induced ego demands provide the push from within and the pull from without toward socially valued norms. Lip service is given to the impersonal and unselfish advancement of learning, but at the same time keen personal competition is fostered. Unmitigated strains develop in a defective social structure relying upon an increasingly meaningless credo to secure co-operativeness and objectivity. Individually, all of this appears in the necessity for zealously upholding one's status within the local situation and in the national professional group. In brief, the scholar-scientist is competing against all others in his immediate field for status in the wider arena, and also for status among his local colleagues to gain their acclaim and to secure administrative recognition.

[16] Verification of this generalization in one important field is afforded by an inquiry I recently made in another context. A questionnaire was sent to a random sample of 200 members of the American Economic Association, asking them to name the ten living economists who had made the most valuable contributions to the field of economics. The 98 replies received mentioned a total of 162 different names, many of which appeared on only one individual list. It is interesting to note, however, that with the exception of two economists with a private foundation, the twenty-one men receiving as many as ten or more mentions were all concentrated in seven universities—Columbia, Yale, Harvard, Wisconsin, Chicago, Princeton, and Pennsylvania.

Still, this does not mean that prestige is a function and activity is its variable. The teacher and researcher who is genuinely interested in what he is doing may have little thought of the prestige that may come to him as a by-product. Also, there are many who may be under pressures without being aware of them, or who may enjoy the stimulus of the competitive process, or may find so much pleasure in their activity that they are wholly unconscious of the existence of pressures. There are still others in the academic fold who turn their backs on scholarly fame or recognition; they may have the capacity for significant research work but prefer to remain in colleges where the emphasis is wholly or primarily upon teaching.

It cannot be denied, however, that perversions of the process of competition and overemphases of prestige values tend to make successful teaching and research commodities that are manufactured for the direct purpose of trading them for personal prestige. The university organization within which the academic man functions defines the goals, purposes, and interests for his 'aspirational frame of reference,' and it also sets up a regulative structure. A disproportionate stress on goals at the expense of the legitimacy and adequacy of means serves to promote opportunism and to weaken the efficacy of the regulative structure.[17] The observations of this study should make it quite clear that a disproportionate accent on goals has intensified competition to the extent that satisfactions often cease to be derived from mere participation. In the academic world the symbols of success and the tokens of acclaim are much the same for all participants, and are theoretically attainable by all—in spite of their scarcity. With a limited possibility in sharing the symbols of prestige, warped results and distorted organization personalities are bound to develop, and especially so in light of the wide discrepancies in performers' abilities.

Stress upon goals and lack of attention to regulation generate

[17] Cf. Robert K. Merton, 'Social Structure and Anomie,' *American Sociological Review*, III, 1938, pp. 672-82.

anti-social behavior in the university organization as well as in the wider social organization. Although the 'rules of the game' are not unknown to the competitors, regardless of the principles of legitimacy or the norm of disinterestedness, a significant number of individuals tend to use those means of obtaining prestige that are most easily adapted to institutionally derived ends. The present system creates needs that are neither cared for nor formally acknowledged, and gives rise to problems that are often officially ignored. If the organization of higher education is to persist in its present form as an open social system, then it is very likely that within the near future there will have to be a redefinition of ends or else greater attention to the legitimacy of means.

The preceding analysis of prestige and competition was set forth to show the dynamic processes at work in the social organization of the university. Men must be supplied with motivations in order to get necessary tasks accomplished. These motivations result in both intended and unintended consequences, and within the complex social system of higher learning there is much confusion over means-ends relations. Some of the more important sources of confusion will be traced in the next two chapters, in which it is demonstrated how the processes of prestige and competition affect teaching, research, and other specific functions of the academic man.

X. PRESTIGE AND THE TEACHING FUNCTION

NOWHERE in America is there a university which devotes itself exclusively to a scholarly pattern. In actuality one finds academicians engaged in a wide variety of activities under the name of cultural conservation, dissemination, and innovation. The typical state university, for example, is conceived as a kind of service station for the general public. Medical and legal-aid clinics are provided for the indigent; short courses are held for parents, policemen, and football coaches; research bureaus show farmers how to increase egg production and businessmen how to improve sales volume; radio stations and sports stadia enlighten and entertain the masses; faculty members are on call for luncheon clubs, study groups, and popular forums. As the late President Lotus D. Coffman, of the University of Minnesota, expressed it: 'The state universities hold that there is no intellectual service too undignified for them to perform.' Many private institutions share this democratic credo.

A variegated assortment of staff roles results from the manifold public demands made upon institutions of higher learning. As someone has suggested, the professor selects and rationalizes the roles expected of him, and which he regards as most favorable and most attainable. The specific activities in which he engages depend upon the institution employing him, the kind of position he has, and the components of his wishes for security and recognition. Our purpose in this and the next chapter is to analyze the major functions the academician performs in terms of their prestige or recognition value.

Promotional Activities

The two major functions performed by most staff members of the major university are teaching and research, so that the average man finds occupational advancement along one or both of these avenues. Between the two, however, there is a penumbra of other activities through which recognition may be secured. Although our primary immediate concern is with teaching, it is pertinent to digress briefly upon those functions that may be designated broadly as promotional. Like teaching, promotional work is less impersonal and specialized than research, less an exercise of the intellect alone than of the total personality, and more likely to be of strictly local import.

While recognizing that promotional work is a legitimate function of full-time executives, such as deans and presidents, a great many academicians feel that it is not in the line of ordinary duty for the regular staff member. There is a common sentiment that the professor who devotes considerable energy to promotional activities must fall into one of three categories: (1) he is trying to compensate for incompetence in or indifference toward his own specialty; (2) he would rise on the basis of personality traits or 'pull' rather than technical competence; or (3) he is mistakenly permitting himself to be sidetracked from the 'true' ends of scholarship. In any case, his motives are attributed to guile, ignorance, or error, and the derogatory imputation is that the real motive of action is a discreditable one. He is compared by scornful as well as envious colleagues to the country-club lawyer or the bedside-manner medical specialist.

As one professor puts it, 'The faculty politicians swarm into the committees, with the result that the least intelligent professors are very often the most powerful. Sometimes the president is fooled by a smooth professor, but more often he is balked by the good ones. He wants to put them on committees, and they don't want to serve; they insist that they give their time to study and teaching.'[1]

Regardless of how much some scholars may belittle the promoter as an intellectual parasite and exploiter of the work of others, he is indispensable in co-ordinating and directing university research, both local and national. As J. D. Bernal has remarked:

> It does not follow that the best scientists are the best research directors; some of them are so wrapped up in their own work that they see their students for an hour or so once a year; others are so interested in their students that they are apt to forget that they have not done all the work themselves. It is always a distressing experience for a young man to find that age and genuine eminence are not guarantees against the temptation to enjoy credit for what one has not done. Perhaps the most convenient chiefs are those amiable scoundrels who establish a kind of symbiosis with their research workers, choose good ones with care, see that they are well supplied with apparatus, attach their own names to all their papers, and when at last they are found out, generally manage through their numerous connections to promote their protege into a good position.[2]

Teachers and researchers are frequently annoyed at the type of promoter who reaps more than he sows in passing as a distinguished scholar-scientist in his own right. This is less likely to occur in university work than in private foundation or government projects. It is the common practice in these latter enterprises for the director to receive sole credit or most prominent mention, while subordinates, who often do most or all of the work, are given little or no public mention.[3]

[1] Percy Marks, *Which Way Parnassus?*, N. Y., Harcourt, Brace & Co., 1926, pp. 92-3.

[2] *The Social Function of Science*, N. Y., The Macmillan Co., 1939, p. 84. (Reprinted by permission of the publishers.)

[3] The influence of professional associations, scientific societies, and other organizations of this sort upon university activities ought to be systematically investigated. The same is true of foundations, for E. V. Hollis's pioneer work in *Philanthropic Foundations and Higher Education* (N. Y., Columbia University Press, 1938) merely points the way.

The promoter is seldom given due credit for the fact, nonetheless, that he fulfils a function that teachers and scholars may be unwilling or unable to perform. Deans and presidents cannot make all of the speeches, serve on all of the civic committees, develop all of the useful contacts, and carry out the myriad other promotional functions that devolve upon the university. Thus it happens that staff members are not always simply teachers and researchers.

Teacher Performance

Faculty time budgets show that, irrespective of the relative importance which academicians may attach to their other functions, teaching makes greater time demands than any other single activity. The instructor or professor spends from six to fifteen hours weekly during the school year giving lectures and conducting classroom discussions for undergraduate or graduate students. A still greater amount of time is spent in preparation. Courses must be organized and conducted with respect to analytical insight, breadth, and richness of content. Ideally, much attention is given to clarity in explanation and illustration, originality and stimulus in point of view, skill in eliciting and guiding discussions, and care in the assignment of student tasks. In addition to conducting stimulating and provocative classroom meetings, the teacher is expected to be available for consultation, to take a personal interest in students, to spur them on to their best achievement, to criticize and evaluate their work, and at the same time to aid in maintaining morale.

Teaching is a highly personal activity, so that the teacher, as contrasted to the researcher, is in every sense of the word a person. He may incorporate his lectures into the impersonal medium of textbooks, but he typically functions in face-to-face situations. Most academicians realize that their duties may

Such concerns are beyond the immediate locus of our inquiry, but in Appendix v the general nature of these organizations is indicated.

be thought of with reference to two axes: those activities that bring only local recognition and reward, and those that result in both local and extra-local prestige. Teaching belongs primarily in the former category. Although the nature of teaching is more plainly delimited than that of research, since research is often confused with the most casual and trivial sort of inquiry, the teaching function itself has never been successfully subjected to any objective analysis.

Universities profess to desire good teachers, but will admit having no infallible means of developing or detecting them. For these and other reasons, superior teaching is neither demanded nor rewarded in the same way as distinction in research. Going through various monographs on college and university teaching, one gets the impression that effective instruction is neither definable nor measurable. The characteristics of success are typically expressed by such generalities as 'vision,' 'personality,' 'inspirational power,' 'popularity,' 'general culture,' and other rather ambiguous qualities. Furthermore, administrative ratings of individuals in terms of these characteristics are often based upon unsolicited reports and casual remarks.

An inquiry [4] based on a questionnaire to which 247 members of the Association of American Colleges and several other leading associations responded, ranks the six following characteristics of teaching efficiency as being rated highest by administrators in arts colleges: (1) stimulating intellectual curiosity; (2) broad knowledge of subject matter; (3) sympathetic attitude toward students; (4) wholesome influence on student morale; (5) wide range of general scholarship; (6) carefully planned class work. Distinction in research was considered to have little relation to efficiency in teaching.

The two teacher types judged by administrators to occasion

[4] Anna Y. Reed, *The Effective and Ineffective College Teacher*, N. Y., American Book Co., 1935. See also, Luella Cole, *The Background for College Teaching*, N. Y., Farrar & Rinehart, Inc., 1940; and Frank C. Hockema, 'Earmarks and Question Marks,' *Journal of Higher Education*, Vol. 8, 1937, pp. 471-4.

most difficulties were the 'rusty' teacher and the inexperienced teacher; 231 administrators indicated troubles with the former, and 35 with the latter. Other inefficient teacher types pointed out were: the self-satisfied, self-sufficient, and cocksure; the lazy, indolent, and indifferent; the emotionally unstable, erratic, and 'cranky'; the conventional, 'petrified,' and 'fossilized'; and the narrow specialist. All acknowledged teaching to be in large part a matter of personality, and many spoke of the 'born teacher.'

This same investigation gives administrative sources of information for evaluating teacher efficiency as follows:

TABLE VIII

Bases of Teacher Rating Used by Administrators [5]

Basis of Rating	Weighted Value
Rating by head of department	1.079
Rating by dean	.868
Personal interviews and casual contacts	.636
Comprehensive examinations for seniors	.413
Rating by co-workers	.524
Judgment of colleagues	.535
Questionnaires to graduates	.069
Unsolicited reports	.109
Student opinions	.418
Rating by students	.297
Surveys and observations by outside agencies	.172

A University of Chicago student-faculty committee has ranked the main aspects of teaching in the following order: (1) knowledge and organization of subject matter; (2) instructional skill; (3) personal qualities of the instructor. Some means of recognizing the successful teacher are set forth in the following criteria from the University of Michigan:

I. With respect to subject matter:
    1. Does he know his subject? Is his scholarship sound?
    2. Is he vitally interested in his subject?
    3. Does he view his subject in proper perspective—that

[5] Reed, op cit., pp. 66-7.

is, does he see it (1) as a whole and (2) as a part of the broader areas of knowledge? Or does he grovel in a mass of particulars in a field which he appears to regard as a little isolated world of its own?

4. Does he have lively interests and valid information outside of his subject?
5. Does he have potentialities for growth? Is he actually growing in his subject and in general mental power?

II. With respect to the classroom:
   1. Does he have the gift of clear exposition?
   2. Does he have ability to illuminate his subject through concrete illustration, pertinent subsidiary information, applications to life situations, etc.?
   3. Does he have the ability to engage his class in lively, well-directed discussion?
   4. Is he able to interest his students in his subject and to stimulate them to independent thought and effort?
   5. Does he show evidence that he has organized his course well and that he plans each day's work with care?
   6. Does he have a sense of humor?
   7. Is he *en rapport* with his class?

III. With respect to general matters:
   1. Does he have the professional spirit?
   2. Does he regard teaching in itself as a worthwhile job or does he look upon classroom duties merely as a way to meet monthly bills, while his real interests are elsewhere?
   3. Is he co-operative in departmental matters, willing to give and take, ready to shoulder his share of responsibilities, etc.?
   4. (a) Is he interested in students?
      (b) Is he generally fair and decent in dealing with them?
      (c) Is he willing to give time to personal conferences?
   5. Is he conscientious in performing duties?
   6. Does he have a healthy outlook on life?
   7. Is he *alive?*
   8. Does he have any negative personal qualities that might interfere with his success?[6]

6 *The Evaluation of Faculty Services,* pp. 19-20.

Although the vast majority of academic men acknowledge the importance of the teaching function and profess to recognize good performance when they encounter it, they have difficulty in stating precisely what it is. The only consensus to be obtained from various polls and expert opinions is that the *sine qua non* of effective instruction is a thorough knowledge of the subject. 'Personality' is always mentioned prominently, but is generally used as a blanket designation to cover those factors deemed desirable, though not readily definable.

One reason for the lack of objective knowledge is that the professor plans his own work, tests the results of his teaching, and passes a verdict upon his accomplishment. His self-appraisal, particularly in colleges of liberal arts, seldom receives any careful outside checking up. If his courses are popular he assumes the *non sequitur* that his teaching is effective; if they are not, he rationalizes in such terms as their uncompromising difficulty for undergraduates, student inability to recognize merit, low standards and catering to popular demand on the part of colleagues, and so on. Few teachers presume their own perfection, yet universities have still to devise completely acceptable and satisfactory ways of demonstrating to laggard staff members how improvement is to be effected.

University men are aware that the instructor who can hold a large freshman lecture section spellbound may be woefully inadequate in conducting a graduate seminar, and that successful graduate teachers may merely bore and confuse undergraduates. Indeed, many of the techniques that are positive on one level become negative on another, and the assets of one personality configuration may be liabilities in another. No pedagogue can succeed in being all things to all students, but with wide differences in student abilities and interests he is nonetheless forced to try, and it is no wonder that there is much falling between stools.

Poor teaching goes on in spite of careful attention to content and method, and good teaching follows from a variety of approaches. The dull but driving taskmaster often effects a massive amount of assimilation, and the scintillating lecturer sometimes gives his classes nothing more than a higher form of vaudeville. Large elective sections of low-grade students render a professor suspect, and courses that consistently draw those of high scholastic standing suggest intrinsic merit, yet in neither case is there final evidence of poor or good teaching. No matter how well taught, an early morning class in Greek or Latin will attract few students, whereas a required course in English or some other subject, no matter who teaches it or when it is scheduled, will have a large enrollment.[7]

The A.A.U.P. chapter at Johns Hopkins has expressed its conviction that there is no such thing as good teaching in the abstract.[8] Teacher, student, course, and institution variables, they contend, must be taken into account. Various teachers may use different methods with equal success (since the whole is more than the sum of its parts). Effectiveness of instruction is conditioned by the composition, social backgrounds, and aims of the student body, as well as the preparation and age of individual students. Teaching problems differ from one department to another, and from one course to another within a department. The same methods would not be equally successful in the North and South, the East and West, in technological schools and in liberal arts colleges. These factors, it is concluded, are not mutually exclusive, but are certainly prerequisite to any final analysis of the disseminative function.

TEACHER IMPROVEMENT

It has been suggested that since students are the only persons who meet the professor in his capacity as a teacher, student

[7] It is often difficult to ascertain whether student attitudes are primarily toward the teacher or the course. One inquiry found that in a total of 470 courses both teacher and subject were liked in 62 per cent of the instances and both disliked in 17 per cent—the agreement of attitudes being 79 per cent. See S. M. Corey and G. S. Beery, 'Effect of Teacher Popularity upon Attitude toward School Subjects,' *Journal of Educational Psychology*, Vol. 29, 1938, pp. 665-70.

[8] *Bulletin of the A.A.U.P.*, XVIII, 1932, pp. 454-5.

opinions and ratings should be utilized as the primary source of guidance in individual improvement. Other persons necessarily judge largely by inference, yet it is very doubtful that professors would be willing to accept undergraduate judgments as conclusive, or, for that matter, any except a multiple rating basis. Many questions have been raised as to the reliability of student ratings according to scales and other measures. The coefficient of reliability for the well-known Purdue Scale is .95, and students who use it feel that they are rating something that is tangible to them. Notwithstanding this, reliability and validity are not the same thing, for students' evaluations, though consistent, may be wrong, so long as they rest upon incorrect premises. Another weakness of ratings, irrespective of who makes them, is that they are of little functional value unless professors use them for improvement purposes. They may be useful to the administration in locating the problem professor, but if no benefit accrues to good teachers and no penalties to poor ones, then these ratings merely have an ineffectual police function.

Nearly everybody can listen to a teacher and give some judgment of his ability, but apparently nobody can tell precisely what the characteristics of the successful teacher are, much less how to attain them. The National Survey of the Education of Teachers was unable to delimit them, and concluded that no very reliable measures of teaching success have yet been worked out. Approximately 500 investigations have been made within the last several decades in an effort to get at the factors in good teaching. A summary of recent investigations concludes that few advances have been made in measuring teaching success, and no new techniques have been devised for the study of related problems.[9]

Time budgets and the great amount of critical literature on the subject attest perennial concern with teaching as a professional problem. Although academicians on the whole show a

[9] Consult the *Review of Educational Research*, Vol. 7, 1937.

certain antipathy toward any guidance from their colleagues (especially those in departments of education, for whom many pundits have a low regard), the profession cannot be accused of group indifference. The A.A.U.P. has a standing Committee on College and University Teaching, and the Committee makes reports and recommendations from time to time.

The essence of good instruction may be so intangible as to defy reduction to any abstract formulation, and thus far experiments to produce good teachers synthetically have not been notably successful—still, there are many minor procedures that can be reduced to definite principles. Public schools, and to some extent smaller colleges and universities, have given more formal attention to such matters than have many of the major universities. (It is a common experience for freshmen from good secondary schools and transfers from small colleges to be quite astonished at the indifferent quality of instruction they receive from many famous scholars in major institutions.) Perhaps the caliber of student personnel in the leading universities is high enough, especially in advanced courses, not to require much solicitude for pedagogy, so that slipshod methods and obviously faulty techniques are forgiven in an otherwise able man, whose instructional shortcomings would make him completely inadequate for less able students.

Many professors appear to regard teaching as a non-communicable technique, or an art acquired only through experience, if at all. Except in teachers colleges or in the preparation of secondary school teachers in other institutions, little or no formal attention is given to teaching practices during the apprentice stage. Research methods and techniques are carefully inculcated and their use is subjected to rigid scrutiny and criticism, while teaching methods develop in a random trial and error way without benefit of direct guidance. Courses in pedagogy have in isolated instances been specifically designed for the prospective college or university teacher, but academicians traditionally object to placing such responsibilities in the hands of the educationists.

The A.A.U.P. Committee on Training of Graduate Students for College Teaching has expressed a very lukewarm attitude toward compulsory education courses, and feels that if courses in practice teaching and methods are offered, the subject matter departments should give them. The Report states: 'In some institutions, notably Wisconsin, one teacher in the department who is a good teacher and who is particularly interested in teaching problems is placed in charge of the graduate students in the department who plan to teach. Whether formal courses are offered or whether a series of discussions or seminars are held, it is believed . . . that much good may come of such training.' [10] At the University of Michigan, where it has been established that the average faculty member devotes 55 to 60 per cent of his time to teaching or teaching preparation, A.A.U.P. members indicate that there is too little care given to teaching, and that more definite procedures need to be established for ascertaining effective and ineffective performance. Class visiting, evaluation and criticism by colleagues, and student questionnaires are proposed as specific measures.

TEACHING AND OTHER FUNCTIONS

Numerous suggestions have been made for the improvement of teaching by relating it more closely to scholarship. An able statement of this point of view was made in a speech by President H. W. Dodds, of Princeton University, in 1936:

To make teaching most effective, scholarship should be encouraged and time and facilities provided for faculty research. Lest you charge me at once with confusing the small college and the university let me remind you that scholarship and inspirational teaching are not incompatible but complementary. The true teacher is a man of inquiring mind, not satisfied with a parasitical intellectual life but eager to discover truth as yet unknown. The college teacher who views knowledge as something in a dish to pass around among his students without spill-

[10] *Bulletin*, XIX, 1933, p. 127.

ing any of it is promptly exposed by undergraduates quick to detect the bluffer.[11]

Others have pointed out that teaching is after all merely a form of communication, or sharing knowledge with students. One of the most important though least-mentioned features of the division of academic labor is the unavoidable conflict arising from the allocation of time and energy. Many critics speak as if there were no necessary conflict between teaching and research activities, and it is true that in individual cases they are mutually beneficial, but such a view overlooks the fact that time and energy are not infinite.

So fundamental is the conflict, in fact, that a number of universities have reorganized with the college division as an autonomous unit. The University of Chicago has done this. Harvard, Princeton, and Yale have attempted to keep teaching from becoming a residual staff activity by setting up the preceptorial system. Stanford has set up an independent study plan, whereby students may receive special attention. Despite such schemes, the major university establishes type situations in which the instructional aspect of higher education comes to be considered much more haphazardly than are research processes. Major institutions assert that their staff members devote as much energy to teaching as to research, but it is very doubtful that instruction gets the best energies of the staff. It goes without saying that any social system that extols values without defining or inculcating them is likely to find them neglected in actual behavior.

Whether teaching assumes a primacy over research as the academic man's main function, or vice versa, depends on many factors. Most of the current statistical studies of promotion policies, as we have seen, indicate a greater nominal stress upon teaching in the average university. Yet there is a widespread belief, based upon what happens in most major universities,

[11] Quoted in Edgar W. Knight's *What College Presidents Say*, p. 263.

that these averages, heavily weighted as they are by individuals benefiting from past policies, blur the true contemporary picture. In many places today, only a modicum of efficiency is demanded in teaching, and even meritorious achievement in performance seldom brings the prestige awarded for outstanding research. In lesser institutions and on lower levels in leading universities, the teaching function still has a primacy over the research function, yet everywhere there is an attitude among the academic elite that dismisses meticulous attention to instruction as a deflection from the 'higher' purposes of scholarship and science.

Many academicians take their classroom duties seriously and even enthusiastically. Both patient systematizers and brilliant showmen are rewarded by prestige and promotion in the primary group, but it is printed dissemination that is of greater importance in spreading the professor's renown beyond the confines of his own campus. Moreover, the individual who chooses or permits his energies to be directed into other channels to the exclusion of research gives hostages to fortune. The highest prestige values, exclusive of major executive posts, are in the field of research, and the ambitious professor concentrates his best energies upon this form of activity because it supplies the highest rewards. Typical of a large segment of academic reaction is the implication of the following statement from a faculty member at the University of California: 'I challenge —— to name a single member of the faculty who has been promoted to an associate or full professorship during the period 1920-1937 solely or primarily because he has been an excellent teacher or because he has had a beneficial, elevating influence on the student body.' [12]

A questionnaire was recently sent to a random sample of 200 academicians in each of the main fields of the arts and sciences. Respondents were asked to list the ten living Ameri-

[12] Quoted in Franz Schneider, *Teaching and Scholarship and the Res Publica,* Berkeley, California, The Pestalozzi Press, 1938, p. 16.

cans whom they considered to have made the most valuable contributions in their own field; in addition, they were requested to place a check by the names of persons known to them to be outstanding as teachers or lecturers.[13] Since the largest number of returns thus far has been in economics (101 out of 200), it may be of interest to note in Table IX the results for the ten men most frequently mentioned.

TABLE IX

Frequency Ratings for Ten Living American Economists

Individual	Number of times mentioned for distinction in research	Number of times mentioned for distinction in teaching
A	75	17
B	58	10
C	56	9
D	52	1
E	50	12
F	50	10
G	47	23
H	32	11
I	30	6
J *	23	1

* Individual J was the only economist in the group not in the employ of a university, and therefore not engaged in teaching.

Although teaching appears to be a more important factor in the reputations of men in the liberal arts than in the sciences (judging from returns not shown here), research is given much the greater weight as a basis for professional prestige in every field. Some individual comments from respondents may throw further light on the lesser importance of teaching. The following remarks are not representative of all respondents, since those who checked for teaching or lecturing ability refrained, for the most part, from making comments,

[13] This inquiry, which is being made in connection with another monograph, is still in the data-gathering stage. Special mention is made of the economists, since this is the only group that is as yet adequately represented.

but the remarks do reveal reasons for skepticism on the part of many.

I doubt whether any professional recognition, either within or without one's own campus, comes through classroom ability. Perhaps through lecturing ability—if it includes enough strategic addresses during a year—but not classroom or seminar work. I should doubt whether many of your candidates for 'valuable contributions' are listed for inspirational qualities as teachers rather than for authorship of some book or books.
(From a historian)

I must confess that those men whom I considered my most effective classroom teachers—as a graduate student—are not creating such a big ripple in the waters of research and publication . . . They are not totally quiet, but their names are not so well known as those of the persons I have listed.
(From an English teacher)

I give a rating such as you asked for, but without any attempt to decide what the reputation of the men mentioned is in their class-room work. Professors practically never visit each others class-rooms; they knew of their colleagues' work only indirectly—through a kind of academic tittle-tattle which is absolutely without value. I have heard diametrically opposite estimates of William James as a teacher (from friends who studied under him), and from persons whose judgment I valued. All such estimates reveal more about the student than about the professor. Most students have a curious standard of their own concerning what they *ought* to find in the classroom work—often a very unintelligent standard.
(From a philosopher)

I do not know anything about these men as teachers or as lecturers. What do these latter have to do with a person's contributions to chemistry?
(From a chemist)

I know nothing of the undergraduate teaching of these men, except in one case. In this one case the man is ordinarily regarded as a poor teacher since he fails to 'inspire' poor students. He is, however, an excellent teacher in my opinion.
(From a psychologist)

None of the men have been teachers of any class of which I was a member. Hence I am not indicating any opinion of teaching ability.

(From an economist)

The Status of the Teacher

In his recent book, *The Social Role of the Man of Knowledge*, Znaniecki has mentioned that however important teaching may be socially, it is scientifically unproductive, and that for the most part teachers merely imitate the thinking of others and assimilate results as best they can. In many institutions, therefore, this function is entrusted to young scholars or to those who have no hope of ever adding anything significant to scholarly knowledge. This may be an extreme point of view, but it cannot be denied that the over-valuation of research in major universities has as its corollary the under-valuation of teaching as a main measure of worth. As an A.A.U.P. Committee has said, 'It is idle to profess any special solicitude for the good teacher when existing conditions are such that a man's success in research is everywhere rewarded as a matter of course, while success in teaching is not.' The proposition that good teaching should be on a parity with recognized research as a basis for promotion is given more lip-service than actual support by administrators. There is seldom any systematic basis for recognizing good teaching, and even the individual who is quite conscientious in the performance of his teaching function may be loath to exert a great deal of effort toward maximum improvement when such effort often goes unrewarded in leading universities.

Research activity, on the other hand, is bound to be noted, if not rewarded. Publication in book form, in scholarly journals and scientific periodicals, election to learned societies, and numerous other forms of recognition exist for the researcher. It is true that teachers share in these kudos, but not on the basis of their distinction in the field of instruction. The researcher's reputation, no matter how specialized, may be national and international as well as local; the reputation of the good teacher, on the contrary, regardless of merit, is usually confined to his own institution, and even then often to his students rather than known to his colleagues. One can readily cite such exceptions as Shaler, Royce, Agassiz, Sumner, Copeland, Hopkins, and others, but, as a test, the doubter can sit down with a pencil and paper and make two columns for familiar universities other than his own (or perhaps including his own), listing in one column all the outstanding teachers and in the other all the men outstanding for their publications. The average academician can list dozens of outstanding names in his own and related fields, yet in few instances does he know anything about their teaching proficiency.

The chief acclaim of the teacher comes from below, which source is not important as a means of raising one's status. The acclaim from one's peers is frequently of the sort that decries too much attention to teaching, and belittles the popular teacher as a mere showman. Thus, as between the individual who teachers well, gives a great deal of individual attention to students, and donates freely of his energy to other associates, and the individual who gives only the necessary attention to such matters but concentrates upon results that eventuate in publication, the palm is usually to the latter. The whole institutional situation is so defined that he is the first to be promoted to the top rank in his own university or called to a better position in another. There are no starred listings in *American Men of Science* or long entries in *Who's Who* for effective teachers, and, still more relevant, few high berths in major universities if they be not equally distinguished in research.

Certain universities, such as Wesleyan (Connecticut) and the University of Chicago, have adopted the practice of citing outstanding teachers and rewarding them with substantial increases in salary. (In Wesleyan these persons are chosen by polling the faculty and graduates.) The consensus of the

Chicago faculty is that this stimulus has been very effective in the 'development of excellence in collegiate instruction.' At colleges and smaller universities, to be sure, there is a stress upon and recognition of effective teaching, and instances could be cited of faculty members who have been refused partial relief from their teaching duties despite the recognized importance of their research projects.

There is also a wider causal explanation of the higher prestige of the scholar-scientist as over against the teacher. The scholar-scientist is identified in the public mind as one who works with costly and complicated apparatus (e.g. atom smashers), who goes upon hazardous, exciting expeditions into strange places, who effects momentous discoveries that may alter the course of civilization or our knowledge of past civilizations. He is respected because of his potential material value to technology and business. (Conversely, this partially accounts for the decline of the humanities during the past decades.) The researcher has a chance of escape from the campus, which the educator does not have. Private laboratories bid for the scientist and researcher, and a political bureaucracy demands experts and advisers. Such potential or actual outside connections strengthen their prestige on the campus, and explain the better bargaining power of chemists and economists than of teachers of eighteenth-century prose and of medieval history.

In addition, all teaching is subject partly to the control of political power holders, and even the inventor of the 'Socratean method' had to succumb to the politicians. There is always the demand of the citizenry group in power that education should mean training in terms of its own interpretation of citizenship. Whether in Germany, Russia, England, or the United States, the teacher is highly dependent, and there is no further court of appeal; hence, there are definite limitations placed upon the career of the teacher. The scholar-scientist is more independent of these demands, as is witnessed in the relatively privileged position of such men as Planck and Sauerbruch in Nazi Germany; they could have their 'word' when few others could risk it. The scholar belongs primarily to the *universitas litterarum* and has avenues for escape into a wider career closed to the teacher. If his eminence is sufficiently great he has an internationally recognized scarcity, a value that gives him the chance even to be readily accepted in other political communities. The commodity market for teaching skill, on the contrary, has no international currency.

The prestige of the educator is primarily dependent on his students, that of the scholar is independent of his students. The latter performs for an audience of experts, competes with equals, and therefore his prestige and the visibility of his achievement are relatively independent of the institution that supports him. Faithful teaching service may leave its marks upon 'the hearts and minds of men,' receive its local rewards, and be the occasion for expressions of esteem at alumni banquets, but unfortunately these do not form part of the higher specie of the professional trade.

XI. PRESTIGE AND THE RESEARCH FUNCTION

THE meaning of research is so equivocal that almost any sort of investigative enterprise may be connoted, but academic men ordinarily have in mind the kind of inquiry that yields publishable results. As we have already observed, in spite of the constant demands of teaching duties, the real road to distinction lies in another direction. Teachers spend much of their working time in a universe of adolescent personalities, yet only by escaping into the universe of ideas do they attain the most coveted symbols of prestige. Individual amounts of time spent in research range from zero to 100 per cent, with most persons toward the lower end of the scale. Thus, paradoxical as it may seem, professional recognition is achieved through activities engaging a minor portion of the average man's energies.

Because of the great importance of the research function as a medium of personal recognition, our objective in this chapter is to examine sociologically some of the common behavior patterns that occur. Our interest will be in the personal rather than the technical aspects of research, and in the motivations affecting intellectual inquiry.

RESEARCH

A candid summation of the importance of research is found in an address to teachers by President Walter D. Scott, of Northwestern University:

When you consider the value of your personal research, you will without doubt regret that you have not paid more attention to this phase of your activities. You will discover that distinction in a professor is usually founded on successful research; that men for our faculty positions are selected largely on the basis of research ability; that the most essential credential is a research degree; that promotions within the faculty are based very largely on research accomplishments; that the only official record made by the university of the members of this faculty is the record of the publications of each member of the faculty; that the administrative officers scan this list from year to year to see which men are engaged in productive research; that research is looked upon with favor by your associates.[1]

An extensive investigation of policy in a large number of colleges and universities inquired of presidents, 'Is it your view that research is a part of a professor's work in your institution, and a necessary accompaniment of good teaching?' Though the question is worded in such a way as to bias speech reactions (which do not necessarily reflect actual practice), it is interesting to note that except in the case of colleges for women and some smaller institutions, the answer was almost unanimously in the affirmative, and most of the executives added that research is rewarded with promotion and salary increases.[2] A statement of policy by the North Central Association of Colleges and Secondary Schools gives further support to the importance of research in summarizing its bases of accrediting: 'In determining the competence of the faculty, consideration will be given to the amount and kind of education that the individual members have received, to their experience and educational work, and to their scholarship as evidenced by scholarly publication and contact with learned societies.'[3]

In universities where research assumes priority over teaching as far as security and prestige are concerned, the occupational culture exerts definite pressures to overcome individual

[1] 'Occupational Description of our Faculty Positions,' *School and Society*, Vol. 14, 1921, pp. 293-4.
[2] Wilson Gee, *Research in the Social Sciences*, N. Y., The Macmillan Co., 1929, p. 82 ff.
[3] Quoted in *Depression, Recovery and Higher Education*, p. 110.

inertias and deflections. Symbols of recognition are provided, tacit suggestions are given by colleagues and superiors, annual reports to the administration set up invidious comparisons. All of these and many more factors come together to precipitate any research activity of which the academic man is capable.

Because of the individual researcher's necessity for maintaining his status or heightening his visibility in order to enhance chances for horizontal or vertical mobility, intellectual inquiry, unlike the growing of mushrooms, is not carried on in hidden recesses away from the public gaze. There is the necessity for bringing results to light in the form of publication, for in the academic scheme of things results unpublished are little better than those never achieved. The prevailing pragmatism forced upon the academic group is that one must write something and get it into print. Situational imperatives dictate a 'publish or perish' credo within the ranks. Numerous media exist to furnish outlets for the printed results of research and to give recognition to achievements of scholars and scientists (not to mention the disseminative functions of scientific meetings), so that any new formulation or discovery may be added almost immediately to the total sum of knowledge.

PUBLICATION AGENCIES

The three main agencies for publication are journals of the scholarly societies, commercial firms, and university presses. If the result of research never gets beyond the manuscript stage, then from the point of view of the organization sponsoring the project it is largely a fruitless investment, and the individual's ideas remain still-born. When results are publishable, various factors determine the medium to be used. In any case what gets into print is subject to the discretion of an editor or editorial board. This is true alike of society journals, and the publications of private and university presses, so that here is one source in the patterning of research.

The publication agency, however, is also determined by

other considerations. Because of the yardstick test of the scholar's productiveness, a major research project or a lengthy piece of writing is often fractionalized for publication into as many separate articles as feasible, for the sake of adding yardage to the author's bibliography. And too, the only audience for a specialized investigation may well be the group in that field—individuals who can be reached only through mailing lists or through specialized journals which limit the length of articles. In mathematics and the physical sciences, for example, it is possible that not more than a handful of specialists will be concerned by or interested in the work of another specialist; hence a subsidized medium is essential. The scientific and scholarly journals provide an outlet, but in no sense a market, for their authors receive only the satisfaction of seeing their names affixed to their work. Because of the competitive order and academic symbols of prestige, this satisfaction is nonetheless quite sufficient to supply academic journals with more manuscripts than they have space to print, and to delay publication from several months to several years.

Another publication agency that in actuality runs on a non-profit basis is the university press. Leading institutions maintain their own presses for bulletins, series publications, special monographs, and, in many cases, titles of general interest. California, Wisconsin, Minnesota, Colorado, Washington, Michigan, Oklahoma, Louisiana, Yale, North Carolina, Harvard, Columbia, Chicago, and a number of other universities have active presses. The University of Chicago, for example, facilitates faculty publication by sponsoring five journals in the physical and biological sciences, six in the humanities, and five in the social sciences. In 1931-2 its press issued 132 books, a good proportion being written by members of the university staff. Lengthier monographs so specialized as to find no commercial outlet are often published by university presses. Universities thus subsidize the dissemination of much commercially profitless information, and get their returns in prestige for their own staff or in making available the meritorious contributions of outsiders. A complaint of press managers is that scholars often unload their unprofitable writings in this way, while turning their marketable works over to publishers who will make returns in royalties.[4]

Very fortunately, the average academician is not as dependent as the actor or commercial writer upon audience favor, as the general interest of what he does is typically very low or limited. It is true that unless there is some effective demand for his output, he must change his occupation, for he must have a certain public, be it ever so small. Despite the limited appeal of much academic writing, there are a number of college professors who vie with professional authors in the extensity of their reader audiences and the profitableness of their production.[5] Some of these are persons who have already distinguished themselves in research and have turned to textbook and popular writing merely as an avocation or profitable side venture. Perhaps more numerous, though, are the academicians who are likely to think of textbook production and popularization as a full-time activity and form of 'research.' Here the possibilities vary widely from one field to another, so that the bulk of titles in one field may be textbooks, whereas in another, the opportunity in this direction is more circumscribed because of the limited number of potential undergraduate buyers of textbooks and the static nature of the subject matter.

Society generally recognizes that the higher learning, unlike many other occupations, requires a permanent subsidy in order to operate effectively. About 40 per cent of all longer items published, however, apparently offer expectations for profit, for it has been found that of several thousand such titles printed during a given period, 2,056 were by commer-

---

[4] It has been proposed that the university share in the profits as well as the losses of staff writings by taking a portion of textbook royalties, since professors are presumably paid salaries on a full-time basis.

[5] It should be borne in mind that the major universities produce a disproportionate amount of material for the presses turning out scientific and scholarly writing.

cial concerns, 2,069 by colleges and universities, and 1,034 by various associations.[6] Commercial publishers are constantly looking for profitable ventures in the textbook field, and, irrespective of beneficial effects, their competitive activities are in no small part responsible for much waste and duplication of effort by scholars and scientists. Private publishing firms are no more to be blamed, though, than are scholars themselves, as it has been estimated that there are in the world today no fewer than 33,000 different scientific periodicals. (See the *World List of Scientific Periodicals*.) With such a plethora of publication media, the appearance of work of very uneven if not dubious value is to be expected. The excessive number of outlets also raises net publication costs (incidentally burdening individuals and libraries with subscriptions to many worthless journals), and results in the burying of published materials.

Mass Production and Popularization

Though the elite in the academic world scorn the mere textbook writer, there are outstanding scholars who use this means of financing other activities, while incidentally exerting a vast disseminative influence. In his autobiography, *Seventy Years of It*, E. A. Ross states:

Of my *Principles of Sociology*, 42,000 copies have been absorbed; condensed as *Outlines of Sociology*, 23,000. Of my *Civic Sociology*, a high-school text, 90,000 copies have been sold. Altogether the American public has bought upwards of 300,000 copies of my twenty-four books and has paid for them more than two-thirds of a million dollars, of which sixteen per cent got to me. These royalties made possible my costly social explorations.

But in persons of less repute there is often a confusion of notoriety and fame, a feeling that quantity of output is more

[6] See *School and Society*, March 14, 1935.

important than quality, that one's name must be kept constantly in print—hence the common phenomenon of the textbook writer who turns out a volume almost annually. Despite the disseminative utility of an optimum number of good textbooks, the mass production of them tends to substitute lower motives for higher ones and leads to the establishment of rival and unnecessarily bizarre points of view. Collective enthusiasm for the genuine advancement of learning is diminished in the struggle for adoptions. In the intervals between textbook writing and popularizations, research takes on the pattern of short-time *ad hoc* inquiries that are productive of immediate results. Since extended and ambitious research projects frequently require considerable financing, universities themselves lend a hand in promoting intellectual enterprises that are inexpensive, and indirectly the short view prevails over the long one.[7]

Much of the time given to the production of printed matter contributes nothing to knowledge *per se*, and, recognizing this fact, many of the leading universities discourage those who would be prolific without being profound. Too often, though, opportunists are aware that they are judged as much by the number and bulk of their titles as by their merit. Time that could more profitably be devoted to study, reflection, and the free play of the mind in mental or laboratory experimentation is curtailed by the need for 'results.' Especially is this true in the case of young scholars and scientists who must demonstrate their productivity in order to be advanced.

Too much 'pot-boiling,' textbook production, and premature publication of second-rate material may readily bring more disrepute than repute to the author, yet the vast outpour of the presses is not without some benefits to the cause of

[7] The amount of money expended on a research project, to be sure, is no indication of its importance or real significance. Relatively inexpensive enterprises are often of the greatest significance. Likewise, there is the subject-matter variable to be considered. Astronomers and engineers usually require rather expensive equipment; mathematicians ordinarily need only pencil and paper.

learning, for from the tons of wasted pulp come a few ideas of inestimable worth. Though the gross expenditure of energy is prodigious considering the trivial and inconsequential nature of much that is said, the trial and error probabilities for genuine accomplishment are increased. In addition, publication brings before a critical audience the results of a man's work and furnishes a check upon error; as James Harvey Robinson has observed, 'A discovery to which no one listens is obviously of little or no importance.' [8]

Textbook writing is not the only road to a more general renown, for there are other forms of popularization related to the disseminative function of the academic man. Professional ethics hold that the scholar or scientist should first have his results or formulations verified by his fellows, and that his main satisfaction should be in their approval. Disapproval from within the ranks is likely to confront the popularizer, for the esoteric is often more reputable than the popular among academicians, yet the society that supports them is entitled to some understandable interpretation of research activity. Many academicians defend their endeavors in this respect by pointing out that society needs to be protected against ignorant vulgarizations and erroneous journalistic misconceptions.[9] These often arise because of the scientist's complete absorption in his specialized tasks and because of his unwillingness or inability to communicate with the general public. Neilson has cited the examples of Tyndall, Faraday, and Huxley to show that interpretative work of this sort can be done with dignity and no sacrifice of scholarly integrity, and has concluded that the attempt to do so is a 'wholesome and brac-

[8] *The Humanizing of Knowledge*, N. Y., George H. Doran Co., 1923, p. 17. For a publisher's view of part of this whole phenomenon, see Frederick S. Croft's *Textbooks Are Not Absolutely Dead Things*, New York Public Library pamphlet, 1938.

[9] For a lucid and urbane presentation of the disseminative obligations of the scientist, see W. A. Neilson, 'The American Scholar Today,' an address before a meeting of the American Association for the Advancement of Science, 1936.

ing discipline' for the cloistered mentalities of many professors.

It is easy to exaggerate the presumed reluctance of academicians to popularize and publicize their work. In fact, most pressures within the university system today operate in the opposite direction. The university world is hardly less publicity minded than the commercial world, and is not unwilling to discriminate in favor of 'the more advertised or more advertisable' aspects of the higher learning. Low income, democratic values, and the desire of both the institution and the individual to secure public support, sentimental as well as financial, for research, work for rather than against popularization.

Relevant here is the following observation:

The only way to stop the selling of scientific research by public utterances resembling the tooting of a steam calliope is by the vigorous disapproval of scientific men themselves. This is not so easy or as certain of results as its sounds. University trustees have been known to promote the professor who rushes to the public with visions of driving vessels across the ocean by releasing the electronic energy of a thimble full of matter. Just what kind of matter or just how the energy is to be released and applied are, of course, details that are omitted in the rush for publication. So long as trustees desire this type of professor one cannot be surprised if there are a few professors willing to supply the demand. There has been a genuine desire shown by the best of our public press to keep the scientific quack and charlatan out of its columns, but every newspaper loves a sensation and only the best of them hope that the sensations which they print are all true. The American Chemical Society has been holding a series of special summer meetings given over to round-table discussion of research subjects, an altogether pleasant and worthwhile series of meetings. But there is always at least one jack-in-the-box, who must jump up, if only to say something which the late afternoon press will feature with the baseball scores . . .[10]

[10] Benjamin T. Brooks, 'The Interpretation of Research,' *The Scientific Monthly*, Vol. 27, 1928, p. 412.

Popular utterance and frequent utterance are likely to cause strains and distortions upon objectivity while creating notoriety. Granted that extensity of audience and of titles may bring recognition of a sort, quality is still important with the elite. A relatively slight output of highly original work is more valued in certain circles than a large output of mediocre matter. More often than not, however, on the local scene where judgments of most immediate urgency are rendered, a regularity of contributions to journals and other media is considered an index to the amount of work a scholar is doing. Is it small wonder, then, that even able scientists and scholars should turn opportunists, when they are seldom being judged by their peers, much less by an elite group within their speciality?

ATTENTION GETTING TECHNIQUES

More has been said in traditional methodology about the admitted than the hidden premises of research activity. If one were to take these methodological treatises literally, one would presume that intellectual inquiry is carried on by logical machines rather than human beings who possess all the passions of other human beings. One is reminded of certain old-fashioned political theorists who (having forgotten Machiavelli) speak of how states are supposedly governed rather than how they are actually run. Some rather interesting questions arise when tangential but nonetheless important phases of the higher learning are given attention. Aside from the sound methodological merit, significance, and voluminousness of a scholar's work, are there certain approaches or techniques that in themselves are more likely to bring prestige or recognition than others? And this in turn leads to the criteria by which judgments are made. In business, for example, the criteria of success are rather well established, so that it is not difficult to ascertain whether a sales manager is worth $5,000 or $25,000 a year. The sales manager increases his visibility and usefulness by stimulating the sale of goods. What does the scholar or scientist do?

Everywhere science has ceased to be the occupation of intellectually curious individuals supported by wealthy patrons, yet the change from an individualistic to a collective enterprise has not produced equal co-ordination in all spheres. The academic scientist is much more individualistic and is permitted considerably more freedom in his work than is the scientist who finds employment in private enterprise or in government service. Except in the case of the most conscientious individuals, however, this greater freedom is not without its ill effects. Its negative results are seen collectively in duplication of efforts, lack of co-ordination, anarchic organization, and a general lack of integration in the field of research. (Much is said of the tremendous benefits of science, but relatively little attention has been publicly called to the appalling inefficiency with which these benefits are achieved.) The negative results of extensive freedom and its usual corollary, anarchic organization, also appear on the individual level. In contrast to the research worker in federal or industrial employ, where the individual typically contributes anonymously to the collective enterprise, the academic scientist seldom works in co-operative anonymity. There is less limitation upon self-aggrandizement, and a greater tendency to high self-valuation. The academician is placed under the institutional necessity of seeing that his name is attached to his work, and that it get as wide a hearing as possible, since publication rather than some more positive form of action is often the sole and final result of his research.[11] Individualism in academic research

11 'A sample analysis shows that while the number of scientists employed in industry represents some 70 per cent of all qualified scientific workers, the number of papers they contribute to scientific journals is only 2 per cent, and even to technical journals only 36 per cent of the total number of published papers.' (J. D. Bernal, *The Social Function of Science*, p. 55.) The findings mentioned by Bernal are for England; a similar situation probably prevails in this country.

shows itself at best in highly original and significant discoveries of a pioneering sort in pure science, which are much less likely to be made under the more practical exigencies of government or industrial research. At worst, however, the academic situation is productive of individual flamboyancy, self-advertisement, and a mere puttering away at problems.

Irrespective of the kind or amount of work the academician does, he labors under the necessity of some form of self-advertisement, be it ever so indirect. If he is to gain attention there are certain devices more conducive than others to success, and many of his problems are set with this condition in mind. How the competitive milieu often affects scientific work has been mentioned by Hans Zinsser:

It puts a premium upon quantitative productiveness, spectacular achievement and practical success, which will bring administrative applause, often because of its advertising value in institutional competition. These tendencies, to be fair, are in every university known to be resisted by the men who have the determining influence; but the psychology of the situation is too logical to be offset by individual idealism, the natural pressure too strong. In the field of medicine it is already obvious, to those who are willing to see the truth, in a rising spirit of institutional and personal competition in matters of discovery that leads to trivial and premature publication and a desire to dazzle the public with the necromancies of medical progress. Often the first jury that decides upon the validity of a biological announcement of the greatest importance is no longer that of scientific peers, but one composed of administrative spokesmen and the lay public . . . We have seen in this country the expenditure of thousands of dollars in the correction of important errors, which, nevertheless, gave fame and institutional acclaim to those responsible for them. We have at present in the United States two rival causes for important maladies publicly accepted, one east, the other west, of the Mississippi river, a truly geographical division of truth. We have three causes for measles, two for Hodgkins' disease, and the public have passed judgment on the B.C.G. vaccine for tuberculosis and a number of cancer cures long before the informed have had a chance thoroughly to sift the evidence . . .[12]

Elaborating the obvious is just as tedious, and even more wasteful in scientific circles than in the drawing room; thus from the start the researcher's eye must be cocked for the unusual, since the pettiest sort of discovery may be inflated into tremendous publicity values. The pressure toward flamboyancy is situational, in that there seems to be a sort of dialectic at work among those who formulate dialectics, for when an old theory has about run its vogue the time is ripe psychologically as well as sociologically for a new one.

This situation forces the research man in the humanities and in the social sciences to be constantly on the alert for novel ideas, even in familiar material. If such ideas can be substantiated by data and put before a sophisticated public ever-weary of sameness, then a fresh point of view or unique approach is sure to find some acceptance—at least among those who do not have their own vested-interest theories trodden upon. If the new theory is entirely counter to an established standpoint and there is a large amount of relativism in both, there follows the 'battle of books' that is such a familiar literary phenomenon. The resultant conflict serves the very useful and necessary purpose of advancing learning, and the presumption is that the more accurate theory always emerges victorious, but incidentally it furnishes a major indoor sport to some research men in relieving the rather monotonous tedium of laboratory and field work.

System Building

Though small amounts of prestige accrue bit by bit to the scholar who turns out monographs on subjects of no wide interest, the heights are not reached until a man has created a system and formed a school of followers. Numerous scholars rest content upon contributing 'bricks' to the monumental edi-

[12] *In Defense of Scholarship*, Providence, R. I., Brown University Papers, VII, 1929.

fice of learning, and even rationalize their bricks as parts of a hypothetical structure that may or may not be erected by future builders—yet at any rate they justify in this way their prodigious expenditure of labor over trifles.[13] To return to the observation concerning the system builders, one has only to note the activity patterns of well-known figures in such fields as sociology, economics, and psychology, where it is difficult to have penetrative insight without broad interests. Formulating a system does entail, nonetheless, the assumption of one point of view over a long period of time, and most systems are built by what Sorokin calls the 'monogamous' rather than the 'polygynous' theorist, for if his perspective is shifted, as a 'turncoat' he loses in the general esteem, since consistency is psychologically more useful because it is more uniform and more associative. Once such a system is formulated and gains some acceptance, its prestige is inevitably enhanced, as is that of its originator, by the number and the standing of its followers. Likewise, prestige may be inferred to some extent from the number, vigor, and status of its attackers. The academician thus gains attention by riding one idea hard rather than by being eclectic.

CULTISM

If a professor lacks the creativeness to achieve in his 'own right' he may gain minor renown by attaching himself as a satellite to some already established school of thought and filling in the gaps left vacant by the master, or by interpreting and analyzing his views for less specialized audiences, in which latter case he may attain a reputable notoriety. The so-called 'halo effect' not only gives renown to the mediocre works of a great savant, but also sheds some rays upon his followers. (Attaching oneself to a school of thought is often a matter of

[13] For an elaboration of the 'mystical faith in the *brick*,' see Norman Foerster's *The American Scholar*, Chapel Hill, The University of North Carolina Press, 1929.

necessity in a highly ritualized field, however, for the subject matter may be monopolized by networks of 'academic cartels,' similar to the 'Chaucer trust' and others in literary scholarship.) Hence an idea originally effective attracts to it men who are conscious of the power it bestows upon them as a symbol; these late devotees and followers may use it intelligently or unintelligently. As Willard Waller has noted, disciples tend to form a cult, to reduce the doctrines of the founder to an absurdity, so that an original work of genius may well outlive its usefulness and degenerate into dogma. The logic of events in cult formation is such that symbolic aspects are ritualized into unproductiveness in the last generation of members and only a sterile formalism is left.

As long as the cult thrives, particularism flourishes. Members of the in-group are favored by one another in book reviews; complimentary references are made only to the writings of authors with 'approved' points of view. The clique itself may be sufficiently well established to keep all but the elect in subordinate positions, and to exercise a potent influence in retarding the advancement of learning. How a cult operates may be ascertained from parallel developments in Germany, as described in the two following paragraphs.[14]

In the Germanistic sciences performance and result ceased to be of importance, but only method for its own sake was pursued. By means of the method a single professor ruled over a group of individuals dependent upon him, and they could achieve favored positions only if they were loyal to him and his method. The method created the 'school,' and party was more important than science. Scientific mediocrities anxiously read off from the mouth of the master what they themselves would say.

The case of the school of Scherer [a professor of Germanistic at Berlin, 1877-86] is given as an example of a trend of

---

[14] The paragraphs given are a free translation and condensation from Albert M. Wagner's article, 'Die Deutsche Universität und die Deutsche Germanistik,' *Mass und Wert*, November-December 1938, p. 244 ff.

thought that stamped all German philology. So powerful was the *schul tyrannie* that when a contribution did not fit in with Scherer's views, it was doomed to oblivion. In the instance of one of Dilthey's essays, publication was delayed for forty years. Another victim was Friedrich von der Leyen, who wrote an adversely critical essay about Germanistic, and had his book on Gothic grammar throttled. In such an atmosphere opportunism reigned everywhere, and the universities became mere welfare agencies. The master was succeeded by an understudy or assistant: Scherer was followed by Roethe, Roethe by Petersen, and so on, until the ingrown tendencies became so debilitating as to result in immanent degeneration. Such cults of higher learning are means primarily of advancing the status of members rather than that of higher learning. Adherence becomes obsessive to the point that it ceases even to be rationalized, and activities originally instrumental become ends in themselves.

Miscellaneous Techniques

Aside from cult membership, another mode of securing recognition in the academic world is to take a theory or point of view long since forgotten, and bring it out in new dress, or with a little more ingenuity, apply a formulation from some other field to the writer's own. Or if the academician merely wishes to add items to his bibliographical entry for the annual report to the university president, he can resort to what William H. George [15] calls 'pump handle,' 'safety-first,' and 'pot-boiling research.' These terms are explained by George in reference to Hopkins' experiments that demonstrated the marked effects upon health of the addition of a small quantity of milk to a basic diet. Following upon the remarkable results of Hopkins' original experiments, it was inevitable that

---

[15] See his book, *The Scientist in Action*, London, Williams & Norgate, Ltd., 1936.

lesser researchers should have repeated his basic technique hundreds of times using various substances. In the social sciences there are innumerable stereotyped varieties of studies to be unimaginatively duplicated *ad infinitum,* or proved formulations to be applied repeatedly to demonstrate what has long since been generally known and accepted. It is difficult, when acknowledgments are not made, to ascertain where unconscious borrowing leaves off and plagiarism begins. Both conscious and unconscious procedures of a legitimate sort have, of course, the stamp of usefulness, for synthesis, analysis, and re-interpretation are themselves involved in discovery. Verification is just as important as original insight, likewise, and it is not to be inferred that such measures are invariably the resort of second-rate mentalities. Notwithstanding, it is undoubtedly true that academicians spend a good deal of time assaulting hypothetical fortresses that have long since surrendered.

Still another mode of achieving prestige is through criticism of an adverse type. Severely critical scholars exert a healthful influence upon their brasher fellows who are prone to rush into print upon any and every excuse, and it may also be added that in the absence of positive standards of evaluation, one enhances one's own position by depreciating the work of others. Here the iconoclastic perspective brings recognition if it is maintained with sufficient cleverness, for there is frequently a more articulate audience for disproof than for confirmation. The academic mind tends to be skeptical and hence is conditioned to consider criticism 'sounder' if praise is more than balanced by fault finding, as it is in the nature of finished scientific work more difficult for the critic to find wherein it is wrong that in what respects it is right. Disagreement gives one a chance to assert one's own point of view, whereas agreement means subscribing to someone else's—unless the two happen to coincide, in which latter instance the critic may readily find merit in a point of view which strengthens his own stand.

With advancing status, the scholar usually undergoes a transition in the modes of gaining or attempting to gain prestige, and what is appropriate for one stage is not sanctioned for another. Outside the physical sciences, where a rich life experience is not so necessary and intellectual maturity often comes early, the young researcher is usually in no position to establish a school or create a *magnum opus;* hence he has to attach himself as a satellite, look for every chance to discredit the work of his predecessors, or else scurry about for previously unexplored fragments of knowledge and content himself with minor renown for monographic merit in some very limited field.[16] But the mature individual who is still turning out 'pump handle' research or commentaries of a very secondary nature is generally regarded to have outlived any youthful promise he may have had.

The various 'techniques' mentioned may involve any number of activities in a wide range of fields. Whatever the field, though, the researcher's work is likely to conform to the approved dogmatics and rituals. Orthodox literary scholarship, for example, reveals the following:

. . . Collating all existing versions and variants of literary monuments or compositions; 'fixing' the authentic text; making 'standard' editions; ferreting out analogies and parallels and tracing sources; annotating; recovering writing lost or missing; excavating literary ruins or fragments; disinterring works and parts of works deservedly buried alive by their authors; dis-

16 As Bernal has mentioned (*The Social Function of Science*, p. 262 ff.), specialization is greater in some fields than in others. He has pointed out that in a science such as chemistry, based on a relatively simple set of ideas and operations, considerable movement inside the field is possible. Great chemists often cover a wide range of topics, and the specialist is at best a minor auxiliary; in biology, on the other hand, where general principles are not so well established, vast experience in a limited field is more necessary. The mycologist and 'drosophilologist' are efficient and valuable because they are specialists. There is the danger, however, that specialization may lead to a loss of general understanding, to 'monopolizing a certain little corner of knowledge,' and to esoteric attitudes that reflect in the scientist's mind 'the pervasive pressure of a society where the ideal is a striving for individual and private enjoyment.'

closing guarded privacies. To be sure, these humble and rather humdrum services lead to important studies, such as comparative and genetic investigations . . . But as a rule scholars content themselves with the mechanical preliminaries.[17]

To obtain prestige, which is the currency of his profession, the scholar or scientist must be skilled in the means, regardless of the ends to which they are fitted. Because of the vogue of scientism as against intellectualism, the academic climber should know the prevailing methodological credo of his field and give at least overt conformity. In the social sciences he should be aware of the prestige of quantitative as distinguished from non-quantitative procedure, of the fact that the development and exercise of techniques may be more important than the results obtained, and that precision often counts for more than significance.

The academic man should also know that the foundations, the academic craft groups, and others have their cherished prerogatives and special problems that they want investigated. In certain branches the worth of a subject is proportional to its difficulty rather than its usefulness, in others proportional to its publicity value, and in a few fields there are esoteric branches where problems are even judged on a futility scale. Particularly if he desires a subsidy, the researcher should bear in mind the acceptability of his problem according to the current vogues, and whether or not it lends itself to approved technical procedures.

Space limitations forbid a delineation of other means and symbols of prestige that pattern activity in a competitive scheme of things. Though the achievement of distinction in the academic world lies chiefly in research, there are obviously other means of reaching the top with a modicum of scholarship or pseudo-scholarship. What has been said is a bald analysis of what in reality is a subtle process, but the mechanisms

[17] Otto Heller, 'The Pseudo-Science of Literature,' *The Association of American Universities*, Proceedings of the Conference, 1936, pp. 87-8.

through which prestige symbols operate under the stress of competition may be found in operation in any major university where staff productiveness is emphasized. The process has been roughly outlined here without introducing the element of moral obligation, and without passing ethical judgment.

PART IV

CONCLUSIONS

XII. CONCLUSIONS

SINCE this study has attempted to define a field rather than to establish or refute preconceived hypotheses, there was nowhere in the line of investigation a deliberate 'forcing' of material to fit a rigid framework. Although social determinism has been stressed as the prime conditioning factor in the behavior of the academic man, his actions should not be thought of as merely a function, with the organization as an independent variable, for there is a mutual relation between the two. Knowing that a given individual is a university professor does not enable one to predict precisely how he will behave, for there are too many factors involved. The university itself is a complex social environment, and different individuals respond to its multiple stimuli in varied ways. Neither economic determinism nor any other single factor theory is an adequate explanation of the way people react to situations. The complexity of our subject does not lend itself to development in terms of a single variable, and no effort has been made to limit the approach in this manner.

SOURCES OF TENSION IN THE UNIVERSITY SYSTEM

To discover the basic problems of the academic profession it was found useful to employ a number of analytical devices. One of these was the scheme of treating the university as a social system designed to achieve certain ends for which various means may be employed. This social system, as we have seen, has both structural and functional aspects: what it is and what it does. In order to throw structural features into bolder outline, contrasting types of university systems were mentioned. For example, the 'club,' bureaucratic, and autocratic types of organization were described, and in addition, occupational organization was contrasted with that in other forms of enterprise. Viewing the system as a whole and in contrast to other social systems has enabled us to see points of confusion and incompatibility between ends and means, and has revealed weaknesses of co-ordination. Such a scheme shows why means often come to take precedence over ends, how the occupational culture is fraught with disunity of methods and purposes, and why technical organization and human organization develop focal points of opposition.

Sources of tension in the whole structure also are brought to light in the contrast often existing between nominal and real means and ends, or professed aims and actual practices. In certain instances this is made verbally explicit in the contradictions of individual and institutional points of view. In others, it is seen in an ideological organization, which may express what the social system should be and represent very unrealistically what it actually is—or which may express values held by only a small section of the total group.

Throughout this study, such contrasts have been stressed and have appeared in all sorts of contexts. For example, academic organization is ideally expressed in the free association of equals, yet everywhere there is a hierarchical arrangement, in which independence is limited by the delegation of functions. Again, in the ideal pattern, final objects may be definite with details kept fluid, whereas the opposite often prevails. Differences between administrators and the staff are supposed to be functional, yet more frequently than not they turn out to be scalar, since upon examination, authority proves to be centralized rather than collective. The net effect of this is to depreciate the independent status of the scholar-scientist.

Contrasts likewise develop between the anticipated and the unanticipated consequences of different schemes of organization. In the recruiting process, scholarships and fellowships began as marks of distinction. They remain such even today, but have also become a highly competitive scheme for filling the graduate school and have resulted in a form of intellectual peonage. The Ph.D. was instigated as a research degree, but for most persons has become simply a license for teaching on the college and university level. Zealous administrators inaugurate measures to stimulate academic productivity in research, and inadvertently cause it to deteriorate in quality by overemphasizing quantity.

Nominal policies come under the influence of pressures that promote institutionalized evasions. We have seen how this happens. Placement, for instance, is ideally according to merit, yet in many places favoritism and nepotism override criteria of competency, and the ideal pattern is lost sight of. Administrations give lip service to teaching excellence, whereas major universities promote staff members primarily on the basis of distinction in research and conspicuousness of publication. Disinterested activity and the slow ripening of long-time projects become well nigh impossible as situational pressures call for quick results.

Treating the university as a social system with incompatibilities between nominal and real ends and means shows sources of dysfunction, and gives a true cause for pathological behavior that can be explained in no other way. One should be cautioned, however, against considering actual practices 'bad' and nominal procedures 'good,' for institutionalized evasions are often realistic adjustments of the human organization to situations not met by the formal structure.

Personnel Problems

Throughout the treatment of forms and functions we have focused attention upon personnel problems. More problems have been raised than answered, since the breadth of our inquiry prevented the definitive treatment of many emergent questions. The issues brought forth suggest, furthermore, that the human problems of the salaried worker, particularly on the professional level, are in need of the same intensive study being given to those of the industrial and commercial worker by leading applied psychologists and sociologists.[1]

Most universities maintain no specialized personnel organization to formulate policies for employee relations or to see that they are carried out. It is true that this is a significant part of the work of deans and presidents, as well as of special faculty committees, so that in many places these matters are carefully treated. Still, little experimental investigation is carried on among most faculties to determine the best working conditions. Personnel problems are typically dealt with by administrators in an *ad hoc* manner. In few universities is there any systematic basis for bringing forward and analyzing staff complaints and suggestions. Little scientific attention is given to the social organization of the university as it affects the faculty. The student body is surrounded with the best environment that local resources can devise, but the faculty is often left to its own devices in a socio-economic environment for which the university assumes little or no responsibility.

Academicians themselves are not well organized for protection against internal indiscretions and outside interferences. There is no organization comparable in scope or influence to the American Bar Association or the American Medical Association. The American Association of University Professors is well regarded, has a substantial membership, and does not hesitate to use such sanctions as it can command. Yet the effectiveness of its sanctions is limited, many of its local chapters are moribund, and those that are not often hesitate to proceed in any way that might offend administrative officers. Local organizations of the American Federation of Teachers are characteristically outspoken in their formulations, but their influence is frequently handicapped by a membership made up

---

[1] For an excellent piece of work of this sort, see F. J. Roethlisberger and William J. Dickson, *Management and the Worker*, Cambridge, Harvard University Press, 1939.

disproportionately of the younger men and the marginal men of the faculty.

Many influences converge to discourage temerity on the part of the individual academician, and the popular view of college and university faculties as 'hotbeds of political and social radicalism' is a gross misconception. It is a rare thing for scholars and scientists to be displaced because of ideological beliefs. When this does happen, however, they are well aware that it may be the 'kiss of death' professionally to have their causes espoused by a protective organization. Such protection as they have is largely a resultant of an informal organization which is not well integrated.

On all sides there is more thought given to technical organization than to human organization, and the fine shadings of social relations and their tremendous importance in making persons willing to co-operate are treated indifferently. The administration on its part adheres rather short-sightedly to the over-simplified logics of cost and efficiency, and the employee group in turn insists too often upon the logics of sentiment. Between the formal and the informal organization are found many incompatibilities, imponderables, and shams.

If the average administration were half as careful in insuring the personal satisfactions of its staff as of its students, it doubtless would be more than repaid even in the logics of cost and efficiency. Narrow attitudes are rarely the result of deliberate discrimination, of course, but a good many university heads inadvertently treat the faculty member as if he were a hired hand rather than a partner in the advancement of learning. A large part of the lay public naively thinks that magnificent plants and ample endowments will automatically insure creative work, irrespective of the social environment.

THE NEED FOR PARTICIPANT-OBSERVER STUDIES

Most astonishing of all, with notable exceptions, is the lack of systematic investigation that professors have made of their own occupational culture. They seem to assume that the main factors affecting scientific and scholarly enterprise are those stated in published methodological prefaces and introductions. They rather ignore the fact that academic men share the basic passions and prejudices of other human beings. Since social scientists are commonly academicians as well, they need to be exceedingly cautious of the subjective element when working in areas intimately bound up with their personal interests, and especially is this the case when they are acting as participant-observers.

Our point of view has been that of the participant-observer, a position that obviously makes impossible a completely detached perspective. On the other hand, it is equally impossible to detect the nuances of a complex social system without knowing its operation from the inside. Those who work in the social sciences form living parts of the social processes they attempt to analyze, but, as Mannheim and others have mentioned, this participation does not adduce bias or error. Rather, it becomes a condition for understanding, and should lend greater significance to the problems uncovered. Considering the importance of knowing the influences that hasten or impede the development of knowledge, and the possibilities of getting at them through the methods of the social sciences, it is indeed strange that greater efforts have not been made in this direction.

There is as yet, however, nothing that could be called a 'science of the sciences.' A comparatively new and somewhat amorphous discipline, the sociology of knowledge, is attempting to establish itself, but is still in a very embryonic stage of development. Much historical and common-sense data have been accumulated about colleges and universities, libraries, museums, and research institutes, yet we have few systematic analyses of their social structures and functions.[2] Moreover, there is little organized information about those persons whose

---

[2] See Louis Wirth's Preface to Karl Mannheim, *Ideology and Utopia*, N. Y., Harcourt, Brace & Co., 1936, pp. xxx-xxxi.

professional function it is to preserve, disseminate, and add to the higher learning. 'The composition of this group, their social derivation and the method by which they are recruited, their organization, their class affiliation, the rewards and prestige they receive, their participation in other spheres of social life, constitute some of the more crucial questions to which the sociology of knowledge seeks answers.'[3] How do all of these factors affect the results of academic enterprise?

The unimaginative may protest that these matters are of no vital import. What difference does it make whether scholars and scientists are of low or high social origin, what kind of neighborhoods they live in, how they spend their Sunday afternoons, and so on? Who cares what goes on behind the scenes or in the private lives of the actors, so long as the main stage performance is satisfactory!

THE HUMAN COEFFICIENT OF INTELLECTUAL ACTIVITY

Our thesis is that the human coefficient of intellectual activity is of the utmost importance. Yet getting at it is not easy. Seldom do teachers, scholars, and scientists write autobiographical documents that are candid statements about themselves as human beings. And when they do write autobiographies, academic men, like most other individuals, tend to give highly rationalized accounts of themselves. By and large, scholars and scientists simply do not write non-technical commentaries on their work. This omission, as Watson asserts, is a fundamental oversight:

Professional scientists tacitly assume that the chief operations by which science is created are those performed before the footlights, in the laboratory or the study, and recorded so impressively in scientific publications . . . what goes on within the personality of the discoverer (often without his knowledge), and in his interaction with his social setting, is just as important—sometimes much more so . . . the passions

[3] Ibid.

and self-deceptions which scientific men share with the rest of mankind are supremely relevant to the real human worth of the 'scientific truth' that they create. Scientific institutions are founded just as much on ambition, hypocrisy, fear of economic penalties, and urbane plagiarism as they are on a love of truth.[4]

Watson goes on to comment that even eminent men of science are often not notably successful in understanding their immediate social and personal surroundings, and hence the human roots of their work. The scientist frequently maintains that teaching and many aspects of research are arts and crafts that defy analysis. This point of view would deny, however, that the involved processes can be observed systematically by psychology and sociology. We shall leave it for psychologists and biographers to get at individual academicians; our interest has been in understanding the social forces that produce, encourage, or oppose them, and transmit or ignore their work. LePlay's remark that the most important thing that comes out of the mine is the miner may be inverted in the case of science to read that the most important thing put into science is the scientist.

It is to be expected that society should show a greater concern for the results of science and scholarship than for the means used to produce those results. Yet the producers are an essential part of the product, and a complex and chaotic world which is going to be increasingly dependent upon professionalized occupations for the solution of its problems cannot afford to be indifferent to the social welfare and organization of professional men. On every side one sees much attention being given to the problems of business and labor groups, but the internal problems of the major professions, as well as their integration with the social order, have been rather neglected. Particularly is this true of the academic profession. Until recently, comparatively little has been known about the social organization of the higher learning, and about the effects of

[4] *Scientists Are Human,* pp. xiii-xiv.

different types of social situations upon the end-results of scientific and scholarly enterprise. The most effective organization possible for the academic profession can hardly be anticipated, therefore, until we know more about its human coefficients. This immense and important task, it appears, is what lies ahead for the sociology of knowledge and the sociology of the professions.

APPENDICES

I. A COMPARISON OF GRADUATE DEPARTMENTS

Rank Order of the 30 Graduate Centers Leading in the Production of Doctorates Between 1929–30 and 1938–39	Number of Doctorates in All Departments During the 10-Year Period	Ratings of Departments, and Number of Doctorates Conferred During 10-Year Period *								
		1. Chemistry (4467)†	2. Education (3018)	3. English (1509)	4. History (1417)	5. Economics (1288)	6. Physics (1271)	7. Zoology (1094)	8. Psychology (1933)	9. Botany (933)
1. Columbia.....	1946	D269	D630	D 65	D114	D131	D48	D36	D121	D36
2. Chicago.......	1684	D240	D 72	D 85	D 88	D 73	D71	D59	D 62	D96
3. Wisconsin.....	1313	D276	A 66	A 54	A 75	D 88	D58	D53	A 23	D83
4. Harvard......	1311	D130	D 22	D142	D150	D143	D48	D62	D 48	D55
5. Cornell.......	1229	D160	A 67	A103	D 41	D 95	D66	A91	D 19	D62
6. Yale.........	1157	D156	D122	D176	D 72	D 25	D48	D45	D 60	A26
7. California.....	985	D131	D 87	D 35	D 87	D 71	D76	D73	D 32	D47
8. Michigan.....	955	D114	D 55	D 39	D 40	D 27	D83	D82	A 37	D44
9. Illinois........	908	D297	A 16	A 42	A 47	A 93	A43	A42	A 14	N27
10. N. Y. U.......	901	A114	A483	A 31	A 11	A 17	A40	A15	N 19	......
11. Ohio.........	885	D212	D125	N 25	A 45	A 42	A37	A48	D 85	A44
12. Iowa.........	829	A141	D126	A 55	A 48	A 41	A31	A26	D130	A18
13. Johns Hopkins	809	D183	A 22	D 50	A 18	A 36	D45	D60	A 30	A12
14. Minnesota....	739	A157	D 47	A 14	A 19	D 35	A29	A28	D 43	D59
15. Pennsylvania..	648	A 49	A 58	A 96	D 60	D 55	A18	D36	A 29	A26
16. Princeton.....	457	D 86	......	D 46	A 16	D 27	D32	D14	D 11	N 2
17. Stanford......	419	D 79	D 54	A 25	A 32	A 34	A14	A25	D 25	A16
18. M. I. T.......	415	D166	......	......	......	......	D60	A 1	......	......
19. Pittsburgh....	413	A 65	A111	N 20	N 8	A 12	A15	A40	A 11	N16
20. Iowa St. College.......	405	A128	......	......	......	N 1	N16	A21	N 1	A32
21. Catholic......	377	N 20	N 45	N 29	A 46	N 4	N 9	N 2	A 16	N11
22. Northwestern..	355	A 76	A 32	A 21	A 22	A 42	A 8	A11	A 19	......
23. Cal. Tech.....	277	D 63	......	......	......	......	D94	D 2	......	N29
24. Texas........	259	N 49	A 40	A 28	A 45	A 16	N13	A15	N 3	A12
25. Fordham......	238	N 23	N 18	N 28	N 23	N 4	N 1	N 5	N 4	N 1
26. North Carolina	226	A 46	A 14	A 36	A 18	N 12	N11	A 5	A 15	A 6
27. Washington (Seattle)....	221	A 42	A 35	A 24	N 4	N 6	N13	N18	A—	A15
28. Virginia.......	218	A 49	N 11	N 21	N 5	A 24	A25	N11	N 8	N17
29. Duke.........	216	A 35	N 37	A 19	A 37	N 9	N13	A23	A 14	A12
30. Southern California......	207	N 10	A 63	N 15	N 29	N 7	N 1	N 5	N 10	N 1

* All qualitative data are from the American Council on Education's *Report of the Committee American Colleges and Universities*, Washington, American Council on Education, 1940, Table with regard to departmental staff and facilities (prior to 1935) for offering the Ph.D.

† Figures in parentheses denote number of doctorates conferred in all universities in 10-year

‡ No departmental ratings are available.

Ratings of Departments, and Number of Doctorates Conferred
During 10-Year Period

10. Mathematics (764)	11. Romance Studies (692)	12. Physiology (604)‡	13. Engineering (576)	14. Religion (562)‡	15. Philosophy (525)	16. Geology (518)	17. Classical Studies (494)	18. Sociology (492)	19. Political Science (478)	20. Agricultural Subjects (451)	Rating Totals Distinguished	Adequate	NotAdequate
D21	D74	22	D25	2	D73	D38	D29	D47	D12	A1	17	1	0
D94	D42	79	.....	129	A30	D38	D66	D61	D43	D—	16	1	0
A30	A52	41	A10	.....	A12	D31	A12	D35	D36	D51	9	9	0
D43	D69	27	D—	9	D59	D56	D30	A24	D53	D1	17	1	0
A37	A22	43	D26	.....	D26	A21	A18	N16	A6	D97	9	8	1
A20	D24	23	A19	76	D20	D23	D38	A33	A13	A10	12	6	0
A27	D31	34	A15	.....	D20	D15	D14	N5	D30	D8	15	2	1
A60	A19	20	D118	1	D11	A22	D15	A19	D8	A3	12	6	0
A54	A28	8	D25	.....	A1	A13	A27	A—	D24	A30	3	14	1
N11	A15	23	N1	5	A7	N6	A12	A14	A9	.....	0	12	4
A29	A12	7	A33	.....	A10	N5	A7	A20	A9	D16	4	12	2
A19	A21	15	A19	6	N6	A19	A7	A15	A35	A—	2	15	1
A18	D43	18	A29	.....	A7	D23	D17	N1	A37	D2	8	9	1
A8	A14	29	A12	.....	A—	D20	.....	D18	A8	D56	7	10	0
A18	A26	13	A2.	3	A30	N3	D19	A19	A20	D—	5	12	1
D37	D21	9	.....	1	D15	D45	D29	N1	D19	.....	12	1	1
A7	A18	7	A15	.....	A2	D18	A3	N4	A17	A—	4	13	1
D27	.....	1	D96	.....	.....	D21	.....	.....	.....	.....	5	1	0
N18	N17	.....	A6	8	N5	N1	N21	A15	A5	.....	0	9	8
N5	.....	11	A22	.....	.....	.....	.....	.....	.....	D43	1	4	4
N15	N18	1	N2	26	A33	N1	A53	A19	N2	.....	0	5	12
N2	A5	37	.....	8	A4	N5	A1	A9	N7	.....	0	12	3
A15	.....	2	D51	.....	.....	D26	.....	.....	.....	.....	5	1	1
A9	A7	.....	N2	1	A—	N2	.....	.....	A2	.....	0	10	5
.....	N19	3	.....	1	N22	.....	N6	N9	N13	.....	0	0	14
N5	A18	.....	N1	.....	N2	N4	A11	D18	A2	.....	1	10	6
N4	N2	.....	.....	.....	N2	N3	.....	A1	N12	.....	0	6	9
N7	N12	3	.....	.....	N11	.....	N1	N5	N1	.....	0	3	12
A7	N2	4	.....	1	N9	.....	N4	A6	N9	.....	0	8	7
.....	N8	4	.....	2	A15	N2	N2	A15	N2	.....	0	3	12

on *Graduate Instruction* (*passim*); all quantitative data are derived from Clarence S. Marsh, XIII, p. 92. The symbol 'D' means distinguished, 'A' means adequate, and 'N' means not adequate

period.

II. FOUNDATIONS AND HIGHER EDUCATION

SINCE this study has been concerned primarily with internal variables in university organization, no attempt is made to analyze the part played in research by foundations. That university policies are bound to be affected by the existence of foundations, however, may be ascertained from the table below.

TABLE VI

The Fifteen Institutions of Higher Learning Receiving the Largest Aggregate Granted from 1923 to 1935, from Four Major Foundations *

Chicago	$ 28,581,442	19.2
Vanderbilt	15,055,575	10.1
Yale	11,866,700	8.0
Columbia	10,193,633	6.8
Cornell	9,628,400	6.5
Harvard	7,806,757	5.2
Johns Hopkins	7,613,027	5.1
Washington U.	4,858,603	3.3
Cal. Inst. Tech.	4,592,416	3.1
Iowa U.	3,642,500	2.4
Princeton	3,555,950	2.4
George Peabody	2,727,500	1.8
Stanford	2,492,100	1.7
Rochester	2,319,743	1.6
Pennsylvania	1,887,534	1.3
Total	$148,839,114	100.0

* Source of data: Dale O. Patterson and Malcolm M. Willey, 'Philanthropic Foundations and Their Grants to Institutions of Higher Education during the Depression Years,' *School and Society,* Vol. 45, 1937, pp. 661-4.

For the most comprehensive and unbiased work on the activity of foundations, the reader should consult Ernest V. Hollis, *Philanthropic Foundations and Higher Education.* For a readable but prejudiced interpretation, see Horace Coon, *Money to Burn,* New York, Longmans, Green & Co., 1938.

III. CODE OF ETHICS

THE following code represents one of the most elaborate statements of rights and duties yet drawn up for the American Association of University Professors (*Bulletin*, XXIII, 1937, pp. 143-8):

'A CODE OF ETHICS FOR TEACHERS IN COLLEGES AND UNIVERSITIES'

I. Relations of the Teacher to His Profession

A. A profession is delimited in part by the necessary training. The minimum training and performance for different levels of teaching are prescribed by law and by regulations of responsible bodies. Moreover, it is the duty of the teacher to secure the best training possible in the mastery of his field of study, in knowledge and understanding of the behavior of his students, and in teaching technique.

B. The teacher should expect to be governed in accordance with a clear formulation of the conditions for appointment and promotion by the authorities of his institution and, in the absence of such formulation, he should press for it.

C. The first duty of the teacher in all circumstances is the discovery and exposition of the truth in his own field of study to the best of his ability. This necessarily involves a clear orientation within the general field of knowledge. Discovery as here used means the thorough, critical, and independent canvass, so far as possible, of available sources of knowledge and the carrying on of original investigation in so far as time, circumstances, and ability permit. Exposition means the conscientious and thought-provoking presentation first of all to his students and secondarily to others with whom he has occasion to deal. So far as this aim is development of skills rather than knowledge and understanding, discovery and exposition have to do with methods of training rather than with content.

D. Every teacher should be ready to assist to a reasonable extent in the administrative work of the institution, when called upon to do so.

E. Reasonable participation in professional societies, including not only those having to do with subject matter, but also those concerned with the interests and normal affiliation of classroom teachers, is a duty resting upon all teachers.

II. Relations of the Teacher to His Students

A. The ethical obligation to give due time and attention to effective teaching requires of the teacher the prompt and regular meeting of his classes, faithfulness of student consultations, and constant refreshment in the daily work of his classroom programs.

B. The teacher should strive for a timely, just, and unprejudiced appraisal of all student work in terms of whatever grading system may be commonly accepted throughout his institution. He owes students the right of review of their work and grades given and, in cases of serious grievance or dispute, the right of appeal to a faculty committee, or similar agency, regularly provided for this purpose. The individual teacher, staffs, and whole faculties should, from time to time, make comparative studies of grades given and of the effectiveness of their appraisal systems in general.

C. The teacher should be actively concerned for the general welfare of his students so far as this has a clearly discernible bearing upon the success of the educational process.

D. The teacher should secure permission and give credit for the use of original student contributions in his lectures or publications, in the same manner and degree as for borrowed materials from other sources. He should not, in any case, use students to their detriment, fostering his own research, publications, or other ventures.

E. The teacher, who rightfully asks academic freedom for himself, should be extremely careful to accord his students a like freedom.

F. The teacher should not tutor students from his own classes for pay, nor those from the classes of colleagues in the same department or elsewhere except under conditions known and approved by responsible authorities.

G. The teacher should be alert and cooperative in the detection and reporting to appropriate disciplinary agencies of all cases of student dishonesty and of other misconduct that is seriously harmful to the objectives and ideals of the department or institution in which he serves. It is his duty, however, to take care that students charged with offenses of this sort have opportunity for a hearing such as to ensure the submission of all relevant facts and a just disposition of their cases.

H. The teacher should treat the ideas, needs, weaknesses, and failures of students in confidence, whether he has gathered his knowledge in the course of routine activities or from personal consultation, and he should not reveal such facts to others except in the line of duty.

III. Relations of the Teacher to His Colleagues

A. The teacher should give his colleagues active cooperation and encouragement in their individual development as teachers and in measures in behalf of the objectives of his department and institution.

B. The teacher should in no case indulge in unfair competition with his colleagues for position, rank, salary, students, or other advantages of any sort.

C. The teacher should avoid indiscriminate disparagement of his colleagues. He owes to his institution and to the profession a reasonable tact, both as to content and place, in the utterance of disparaging facts. This should not restrain him, however, from an honest and timely appraisal of a colleague that is for the betterment of educational service, nor from his duty to submit to appropriate authorities any substantial evidence in his possession concerning the unfitness of a colleague.

D. A teacher should always secure permission and give credit for the use of materials borrowed from colleagues or elsewhere in his own lectures, publications, or other public presentations.

E. A teacher should not sponsor or promote the rendering of services to students for pay by individuals who would not meet with the approval of the department most closely concerned with such services.

F. A teacher should not fail to recommend a colleague for a better position through desire to retain him in his present position, or for any cause other than that of unfitness for the place.

IV. Relations of the Teacher to His Institution and Its Administrators

A. The teacher should at all times insist upon the exercise of his right of untrammeled investigation and exposition of any matter within his own field or specifically germane to it, but he is also morally bound not to take advantage of his position for introducing into his classroom the discussion of subjects not pertinent to his special field.

B. The teacher should maintain his right as a citizen to speak outside his institution on matters of public interest, so far as this does not interfere with proper attention to his educational duties; but he should make clear always that the institution is in no way responsible for his extra-mural utterances, except where he is specifically acting as its agent.

C. It is the duty of the teacher loyally to support the principles of tenure, promotion, demotion, and dismissal adopted by the profession and to press for the formulation and use of such principles where none have been adopted.

D. The teacher should not intrigue with administrative officials to enhance his own position or to injure that of a colleague.

E. The teacher should always recognize his responsibility to administrative officials, unless their acts conflict with a higher loyalty with reference to which he makes his position clear.

V. Relations of the Teacher to the Non-academic World

A. The teacher should maintain and exercise his right as a citizen to take part in community and public affairs, except for such restrictions as are necessary to prevent the neglect of his professional duties.

B. The teacher should make his abilities and influences available for the service of the public relations of his institution. He should not, however, attempt on his own account to initiate or promote any policy relating to his institution, or seek advancement in rank or salary for himself or a colleague, through connivance with or influence upon governing boards or public officials. In case such officials initiate discussions with him concerning matters of this sort he should report the substance of the discussions to the president or appropriate officers of his institution.

C. The teacher should not, during the academic year, undertake for pay extensive activities outside his institution, such as would consume his time and energy, except with the approval of the proper institutional authorities; and he should not, in any case, exploit his teaching position to secure outside income or favors in competition with non-academic colleagues.

D. The teacher should avoid occasioning sensational publicity by unbecoming speech or conduct.

E. A teacher should not accept pay, directly or indirectly, from outside individuals, groups, or agencies of any sort, for the teaching of partisan views or the promotion of partisan projects, either within or outside his institution.

F. The teacher should maintain a non-committal policy in public on all controversial issues arising within the school. He should maintain in strict confidence all department or school matters not intended for dissemination. If any issue or matter is of such public concern that he must, for his own integrity, speak out, he should make this clear to all concerned.

G. A teacher should defend any member of the profession who is unjustly attacked.

IV. ACADEMIC FREEDOM AND TENURE *

[STATEMENT of principles formulated by joint conferences of the Commission on Academic Freedom and Academic Tenure with the officers of the American Association of University Professors and endorsed by the Association of American Colleges at the annual meeting held in Pasadena, January 10, 1941.]

The purpose of this statement is to promote public understanding and support of academic freedom and tenure and agreement upon procedures to assure them in colleges and universities. Institutions of higher education are conducted for the common good and not to further the interest of either the individual teacher † or the institution as a whole. The common good depends upon the free search for truth and its free exposition.

Academic freedom is essential to these purposes and applies to both teaching and research. Freedom in research is fundamental to the advancement of truth. Academic freedom in its teaching aspect is fundamental for the protection of the rights of the teacher in teaching and of the student to freedom in learning. It carries with it duties correlative with rights.

Tenure is a means to certain ends; specifically: (1) Freedom of teaching and research and of extra-mural activities, and (2) a sufficient degree of economic security to make the profession attractive to men and women of ability. Freedom and economic security, hence tenure, are indispensable to the success of an institution in fulfilling its obligations to its students and to society.

* Reprinted from *Association of American Colleges Bulletin*, Vol. XXVII, No. 1, March, 1941, pp. 127-9 and 124-5.

† The word 'teacher' as used in this document is understood to include the investigator who is attached to an academic institution without teaching duties.

Academic Freedom

(a) The teacher is entitled to full freedom in research and in the publication of the results, subject to the adequate performance of his other academic duties; but research for pecuniary return should be based upon an understanding with the authorities of the institution.

(b) The teacher is entitled to freedom in the classroom in discussing his subject, but he should be careful not to introduce into his teaching controversial matter which has no relation to his subject. Limitations of academic freedom because of religious or other aims of the institution should be clearly stated in writing at the time of the appointment.

(c) The college or university teacher is a citizen, a member of a learned profession, and an officer of an educational institution. When he speaks or writes as a citizen, he should be free from institutional censorship or discipline, but his special position in the community imposes special obligations. As a man of learning and an educational officer, he should remember that the public may judge his profession and his institution by his utterances. Hence he should at all times be accurate, should exercise appropriate restraint, should show respect for the opinions of others, and should make every effort to indicate that he is not an institutional spokesman.

Academic Tenure

(a) After the expiration of a probationary period teachers or investigators should have permanent or continuous tenure, and their services should be terminated only for adequate cause, except in the case of retirement for age, or under extraordinary circumstances because of financial exigencies.

In the interpretation of this principle it is understood that the following represents acceptable academic practice:

(1) The precise terms and conditions of every appointment should be stated in writing and be in the possession of both institution and teacher before the appointment is consummated.

(2) Beginning with appointment to the rank of full-time instructor or a higher rank, the probationary period should not exceed seven years, including within this period full-time

service in all institutions of higher education; but subject to the proviso that when, after a term of probationary service of more than three years in one or more institutions, a teacher is called to another institution it may be agreed in writing that his new appointment is for a probationary period of not more than four years, even though thereby the person's total probationary period in the academic profession is extended beyond the normal maximum of seven years. Notice should be given at least one year prior to the expiration of the probationary period, if the teacher is not to be continued in service after the expiration of that period.

(3) During the probationary period a teacher should have the academic freedom that all other members of the faculty have.

(4) Termination for cause of a continuous appointment, or the dismissal for cause of a teacher previous to the expiration of a term appointment, should, if possible, be considered by both a faculty committee and the governing board of the institution. In all cases where the facts are in dispute, the accused teacher should be informed before the hearing in writing of the charges against him and should have the opportunity to be heard in his own defense by all bodies that pass judgment upon his case. He should be permitted to have with him an adviser of his own choosing who may act as counsel. There should be a full stenographic record of the hearing available to the parties concerned. In the hearing of charges of incompetence the testimony should include that of teachers and other scholars, either from his own or from other institutions. Teachers on continuous appointment who are dismissed for reasons not involving moral turpitude should receive their salaries for at least a year from the date of notification of dismissal whether or not they are continued in their duties at the institution.

(5) Termination of a continuous appointment because of financial exigency should be demonstrably bona fide.

Interpretations

The following interpretations concerning the joint statement on academic freedom and tenure were agreed upon:

First: That its operation should not be retroactive.

Second: That all tenure claims of teachers appointed prior to its endorsement should be determined in accordance with the principles set forth in the 1925 statement on academic freedom and tenure.

Third: If the administration of a college or university feels that a teacher has not observed the admonitions of Paragraph (c) of the section on *Academic Freedom* and believes that the extra-mural utterances of the teacher have been such as to raise grave doubts concerning his fitness for his position, it may proceed to file charges under Paragraph (a) (4) of the section on *Academic Tenure.* In pressing such charges the administration should remember that teachers are citizens and should be accorded the freedom of citizens. In such cases the administration must assume full responsibility and the American Association of University Professors and the Association of American Colleges are free to make an investigation.

V. COUNCILS AND ASSOCIATIONS

RESEARCH activity within the American university has been greatly affected by the influence of outside agencies. That these agencies have much to do with setting the problems and determining the directions of research which goes on within universities goes without saying. Indeed, many of the in-group are more concerned with the projects they are conducting on various types of outside group research grants than with their more local functions. This is not to say, however, that there is necessarily any antithesis between the two, for purely local projects may be furthered solely because of aid received from such organizations.

Many university research institutes, for example, could not be supported entirely by institutional funds. Such organizations as the Industrial Relations Section of the Department of Economics at Princeton, the Social Community Research Committee of the University of Chicago, the Bureau of International Research at Harvard, the Institute for Research in the Social Sciences at the University of North Carolina, the Institute of Human Relations of Yale University carry on types of research and under conditions not entirely possible for the university proper.

It is estimated that in the United States there are more than 54,000 associations for social and auxiliary educational purposes, as compared with 24,000 trade and industrial organizations. The majority of the former are not for university purposes, but the university has its share of organizations whose avowed purpose is to co-ordinate, direct, and aid in advancing the higher learning. Foremost among national research bodies (as distinguished from the Rockefeller Foundation, etc.) are: The National Research Council, Social Science Research Council, the American Council on Education, American Council of Learned Societies. The National Research Council includes businessmen as well as pure scientists, and has a membership of 282 persons, chiefly representatives nominated by the 77 scientific and technical member groups. In 1934-5 it spent $226,368.84 for research fellowships and $228,291.97 for projects (see *Biennial Survey*, p. 58). The American Association for the Advancement of Science has a membership of more than 18,000 in the following fields: mathematics, physics, chemistry, astronomy, geology and geography, zoology, botany, anthropology, psychology, 'social and economic' sciences, history, philology, engineering, medicine, agriculture, and education. It makes only very limited grants to students. The American Council of Learned Societies co-ordinates activities in the humanities, has about 300 member organizations, and in 1934 (peak year for grants) made 50 grants in aid, amounting to $22,760. (For further information, see the *Biennial Survey* and *Survey of Activities of American Agencies in Relation to Materials for Research in the Social Sciences and the Humanities*, published in 1932 for the Council.)

The Social Science Research Council originated in the American Political Science Association in 1921, but now includes the American Economic Association, the American Statistical Association, the American Psychological Association, the American Anthropological Association, the American Historical Association, and the American Sociological Society. It has received large grants for surveys, publication of original investigations, and grants in aid to individuals. In 1930-31 it had 36 advisory project committees to set problems and policies, with emphasis on co-operative projects. In 1935 it spent $353,410.18, including 15 research fellowships in universities and 49 grants in aid. The objectives of the Council have been listed as follows:

I. Improvement of research organization; II. Development of research personnel; III. Discovery, enlargement, improvement, and preservation of research materials; IV. Improvement of research methods; V. Improvement of facilities for dissemination of the materials, methods, and results of research investigation; VI. Extension of the bounds of knowledge or direct methods of facilitating the carrying out of specific research projects; VII. Enhancement of public appreciation of the significance of the social sciences. (From *Annual Report*, New York, The Social Science Research Council, 1930-31, p. 62.)

Such in general is the purpose of most of the co-ordinating scientific societies and cultural associations. These organizations have been a great source of aid to all types of academic research; what types of research they have encouraged or opposed is another matter, but unquestionably their policies merit closer investigation than they have received.

Closer to the interests of the average academician are such bodies as the American Philosophical Society, American Philological Society, American Sociological Society. It is in the publications of these societies that his briefer monographs appear, on whose committees he most often functions, and whose offices he is most likely to hold. Their annual meetings furnish a sort of field day for the 'politicians,' readers of papers, job seekers, and convivialists, as well as for those who are genuinely interested in extending their knowledge and acquaintanceship in more scholarly ways. It is generally recognized that the nominal and the real purposes of these meetings are altogether different matters, even though the two may be combined.

INDEX

Academic 'cartels,' 209
Academic freedom, 67, 127 ff.; statement of principles, 236 ff.
Academic mind, marks of, 3
Academic profession compared to other occupations: army, 57; business, 57, 114, 146, 152; civil service, 21, 50, 77; clerical work, 122, 152; dentistry, 145; diplomatic service, 148; engineering, 26, 52, 145; law, 22, 25, 52, 56, 63, 72, 116, 145, 148, 152, 176, 220; medicine, 22, 25, 52, 56, 63, 72, 114, 116, 145, 148, 152, 176, 220; ministry, 52, 57, 145, 146
Administrative statuses, principal, 71 ff.; in lesser institutions, 92 f.
Agassiz, L. J. R., 192
Age, of starting in various professions, 52; in different ranks, 58
Aids to students, 26; see also Fellowships
American Anthropological Association, 241
American Association for the Advancement of Science, 119, 162, 241
American Association of University Professors, 51, 68, 75, 89, 100, 107, 117, 119, 120, 122, 125, 126 ff., 140, 183, 185 f., 191, 220, 231, 236
American Council of Learned Societies, 241
American Council on Education, 160, 228 f., 241
American Economic Association, 172, 241
American Federation of Teachers, 75, 125 ff., 140, 220

American Historical Association, 241
American Men of Science, 161
American Philological Society, 242
American Philosophical Society, 49, 242
American Political Science Association, 241
American Psychological Association, 241
American Sociological Society, 241 f.
American Statistical Association, 241
Anderson, C. A., 59
Annual meetings, 49, 242
Appointments, 89, 127
Arnett, Trevor, 138
Arps, George F., 103
Attention-getting techniques, 204 ff.
Attitudes, instructors', 62 f.; of disinterestedness, 115, 167; toward the professor, 150 ff.; concerning teaching, 183
Association of American Colleges, 179, 236
Association of American Universities, 27, 41 f., 159 f.
Authoritarianism, 72 ff.

Bacon, Francis, 115
Badger, Henry G., 165
Bargaining power, 70, 122 ff.
Beery, G. S., 183
Bernal, J. D., 177, 205, 212
Bowman, Claude, 151
Brigham, Carl C., 28
Brody, Alexander, 121
Brooks, Benjamin T., 202

Bureaucracy, 60 f., 80 ff.
Burgess, E. W., 10

California Institute of Technology, 161, 165, 228 f., 230
California, University of, 6, 29, 40, 159, 160 f., 165, 188, 198, 228 f.
Canby, Henry S., 147
Career decisions, nature of, 21 f.
Cases relating to academic freedom, 129
Catholic University, 165, 228 f.
Cattell, J. McKeen, 27, 85, 122, 130
Chambers, M. M., 121
Chapin, F. S., 101
Chicago, University of, 6, 26, 29, 48, 52, 58 f., 104 ff., 108 f., 159, 161 f., 164 ff., 172, 180, 187, 192, 198, 228 ff., 240
Class, origins of professors, 31; stratification in the faculty, 60; preoccupations, 117; intermediate nature, 121; proletarian aspects, 46; biases, 149 ff.
Cliques, see In-groups
Code of ethics, 231 ff.
Coercive influences, on staff members, 129
Coffman, Lotus D., 175
Cole, Luella, 179
Colorado, University of, 198
Columbia University, 6, 29, 52, 137, 159 ff., 165, 172, 198, 228 ff.
Competence, criteria of, 100 ff.; faculty, by types of institutions, 159
Conant, James B., 51
Conard, Henry S., 117
Conflicts, A.A.U.P. handling of, 128 ff.
Coon, Horace, 230
Copeland, Charles T., 192
Corey, S. M., 183
Cornell University, 26, 48, 159 ff., 165, 228 ff.
Councils and associations, 240 ff.
Counts, George S., 123
Craig, Hardin, 121
Credit toward higher degrees, 40 f.

Crisis situations, 68 ff.
Criteria of appointment, 54
Crofts, Frederick S., 202
Cultism, 208
Cummins, Earl E., 123

Dale, Edgar, 48
Dana, R., 130
Dartmouth College, 121, 159
Davie, Maurice R., 138 f.
Dean, status of, 87 f.
Degrees, see M.A. and Ph.D.
Democracy, in university government, 77
Departmental divisions, subject-matter, 83 f.
Department head, status of, 88 f.
Dialectic process, among dialecticians, 207
Dickson, William J., 220
Dilthey, W., 210
Disinterestedness, see Attitudes
Dismissals, causes for, 100
Doctorates, kinds, 41; number by fields, 228 f.
Dodds, H. W., 84, 186
Duke University, 165, 228 f.

Earnings, supplementary, 138 f.
Educational 'busywork,' 106
Eells, Walter C., 162
Eigenmann, P., 44
Einstein, Albert, 168 f.
Elite, production of, 31; and in-group ideals, 34
Embree, Edwin R., 23, 161
Employment policy, 54
Engineering college government, 77
Esoteric research, 202
Ethics, professional, 115 ff., 168; see also Code of Ethics
Evaluation, enigma of, 99
Examinations, entry, 31; doctoral, 46

Faculty meetings, 76
Faculty ranks, instructor, 61 f.; assistant professor, 64 f.; full professor, 65 f.
Faraday, Michael, 202
Fellowships, 22 ff.

'Firing the faculty,' 67
Flexner, Abraham, 81, 146, 149
Foerster, Norman, 36, 47, 208
Folklore, in prestige ascription, 171
Fordham University, 165, 228 f.
Foreign university procedures: English, 24, 50, 74, 193; French, 31; German, 25, 29, 37, 74, 122, 147, 193, 209 f.; Polish, 148; Russian, 193
Foster, Laurence, 162
Foundation grants to universities, 230
Freedom of teaching and research, 118
Frictions in the faculty, 131
Friedrich, Carl J., 99 f.
Functions, basic, 3; definitions, 11; of examinations, 38; of the A.A.U.P., 119 f.; of state universities, 175

Gambrill, B. L., 150
Gee, Wilson, 142, 196
General Education Board, 138
George, William H., 210
George Peabody College for Teachers, 230
Gerth, Hans, 141
Goodspeed, Edgar J., 152
Graduate assistants, 25
Graduate centers, comparison of, see Rankings of leading universities
Graduates of distinction, by universities, 159
Graduate training, objectives, 33; rigmarole, 35 ff.

Haggerty, Melvin E., 158
Hand, Harold C., 7
Hartshorne, E. Y., 74
Harvard University, 6, 29, 40, 44 f., 48, 51 f., 90, 137, 159 ff., 165 f., 172, 187, 198, 228 ff., 240
Haskins, Charles H., 123
Heller, Otto, 151, 213
Henderson, Yandell, 138 f.
Herzberg, Alexander, 130
Hobson, J. A., 115
Hockema, Frank C., 179

Hollingshead, A. B., 55, 58, 108
Hollis, E. V., 177, 230
Homo academicus, differentiation of, 3
Honors students, recruiting, 18
Hopkins, Mark, 192
Hughes, Everett C., 171
Hume, David, 99
Hutchins, Robert M., 130
Huxley, Thomas H., 202

Ideal type, of faculty, 73
Ideology, and selection processes, 31; of dissertation activity, 44
Illinois, University of, 159, 162, 165, 228 f.
Inbreeding, 53 ff.
Indiana University, 58, 101, 108, 159
Individualism, in research, 205 f.
Inefficiency of science, 205
In-group evaluations, 168, 209 f.
Institutionalized evasions, 219
Institutions of higher learning, relative drawing power, 29; number of, 33; ratings of, 159 ff.
Intellectual activity, human coefficient of, 223 ff.
Intellectual inbreeding, 90 f.
Intellectual labor, demand for, 30; as affected by employee statuses, 120
Inter-university competition, 158 ff.
Invidious comparisons, local uses, 164 ff.
Iowa State College, 165, 228 f.
Iowa, University of, 165, 228 f., 230

James, William, 190
Jernegan, Marcus W., 18, 107
John, Walter C., 33
Johns Hopkins University, 161 f., 165, 183, 228 f., 230
Johnson, Burges, 151
Judgments, of achievement, 109 ff.

Kant, Immanuel, 99
Kempton, Kenneth P., 147
Kilpatrick, William H., 123
Kinder, James S., 83
Kirkpatrick, J. E., 120

Kittredge, George L., 46
Kotschnig, Walter M., 24, 30
Knight, Edgar W., 84, 187
Knight, Frank H., 168 f.
Kunkel, B. W., 19, 159

Larrabee, Harold A., 123
Learned, William S., 17
Legal status, of the university professor, 120 f.
LePlay, P. G. F., 224
Leuba, James M., 153
Linton, Ralph, 10
Living standards, of academicians, 142 ff.
Louisiana State University, 198
Lovejoy, Arthur O., 125
Lowell, A. Lawrence, 79

Machiavelli, N., 204
McNeely, John H., 55
M.A. degree, 38 f.
Mannheim, Karl, 82, 222
Marginal types, in graduate school, 36
Market, for academic work, 31
Marks, Percy, 177
Marsh, Clarence S., 165, 229
Massachusetts Institute of Technology, 161 f., 165, 228 f.
Mass production and popularization, 200 ff.
Mead, G. H., 10
Mechanisms, of prestige, 168
Medieval academicians, 74
Merton, Robert K., 173
Metabolism, 59 ff.
Michigan, University of, 29, 46, 101 f., 159 ff., 165, 179, 186, 198, 228 f.
Migration, student, 29
Minnesota, University of, 101 f., 161 f., 165, 175, 198, 228 f.
Mobility, vertical, 20
Motivations, in choice of profession, 16; of graduate students, 27; in professions generally, 116; of scientists, 169; inadvertent consequences, 174
Murchison, Carl, 91

National Association of State Universities, 159
National Research Council, 162, 241
National Survey of the Education of Teachers, 184
Nearing, S., 130
Nebraska, University of, 48
Negative selection, in recruiting, 16
Neilson, W. A., 202
New York University, 165, 228 f.
Non-conformists, how treated, 91
North Carolina, University of, 48, 165, 198, 228 f., 240
North Central Association of Colleges and Secondary Schools, 142, 196
Northwestern University, 165, 195, 228 f.
Notoriety and fame, 200 f.
Numerus clausus, 30 f.

Objectivity, distortions of, 204
Occupational hierarchy, 53, 57 ff.
Occupational placement, 47 ff.
Occupational prestige, 16
Ohio State University, 47, 162, 165, 228 f.
Oklahoma, University of, 198
Organization, of the university, 82 f.
Organization, professional, 118 ff.

Parker, James R., 147
Park, R. E., 10
Parsons, Talcott, 116
Participant-observer studies, need for, 221 ff.
Pathological behavior, causes, 219
Patterson, Dale O., 230
Pennsylvania, University of, 159, 162, 165, 172, 228 ff.
Personality, social, 19; inadequacies, 20; professorial, 64 f.; of administrators, 92 f.
Personnel problems, 219 ff.
Petersen, N. M., 210
Ph.D., requirements, 28 f.; denotation and connotation, 41 ff.; as a title, 114
Pine, Hester, 147

Pittsburgh, University of, 165, 228 f.

Professional standing, how evaluated, 101 ff.

Professional status, definition of, 113 ff.

Placement, *see* Occupational placement

Planck, Max, 170, 193 f.

Policy making, faculty participation in, 75 ff.

Politicians, academic, 176

'Pot-boiling,' *see* Stereotyped research

Power distribution, 90 ff.

Prentice, D. B., 159

President, status of, 84 ff.

Pressures, toward productivity, 111 ff.; on major institutions, 167

Princeton University, 91, 159, 161 f., 165, 172, 186 f., 228 f., 230, 240

Productivity, how estimated, 107 ff.; the 'yardstick test,' 198; premium on quantity in, 206 f.

Professor, connotation of, 4

Promotion, statistical probabilities, 58; and tenure, 68; systems used, 98; factors in, 176

Prys, E., 24

Publication, of doctoral theses, 45 f.; importance of, 104; agencies, 197 ff.; *see also* Productivity

Publicizing research, 203

Public service, kinds rendered, 101 ff.

Purdue scale, 184

Radicalism, misconceptions of prevalence, 221

Rankings, of occupations in prestige, 16; of leading universities, 160 ff., 228 f.

Ranks, percentage distributions, 57; *see also* Faculty ranks

Ratcliffe, E. B., 23

Rating systems, 100 ff.

Reed, Anna Y., 179

Reeves, Floyd W., 27, 60.

Remuneration, problems of, 135 ff.

Research, directors, 177; importance of, 195 ff.; costs, 201; institutes, 240

Resources, of leading universities, 165

Ritual, in conditioning process, 37 ff.; and office, 171; in scholarly activity, 212 ff.

Rivalry, departmental, 83

Robinson, James H., 202

Rochester, University of, 230

Roethe, 210

Roethlisberger, F. J., 220

Role, generic meaning of, 10

Ross, E. A., 200

Royce, Josiah, 192

Russell, Bertrand, 130

Salaries, by ranks, 143

Sauerbruch, F., 193 f.

Scherer, Wilhelm, 209 f.

Schneider, Franz, 188

Scholarships, 22 ff.

Science, as a collective enterprise, 205

Scientific periodicals, number of, 200; *see also* Publication agencies

Scientism vs. intellectualism, 213

Scientist, connotations of, 4

Scott, Walter D., 195

Self-advertising, 206

Seniority, rules governing, 57; and tenure, 68

Service load, and productivity, 104 ff.

Shaler, N. S., 192

Sifting process, in selection, 16

Slesinger, Donald, 130

Social origins, of academicians, 18 ff.

Social Science Research Council, 28, 162, 241 f.

Sociology of knowledge, 222 ff.

Sociology of the professions, field of, 6; problems of, 225

Sorokin, P. A., 59, 208

Southern California, University of, 165, 228 f.

Specialization, 41

Standards, in graduate work, 36; of licensure, 116

Stanford University, 162, 165, 187, 228 ff.

State universities, governments of, 77

Status, meaning of term, 10; and competition, 57; intermediate grades of, 63 ff.; changes in, 69; of the teacher, 191

Stereotypes, of the professor, 123, 150 ff.; in research topics, 200 ff.

Student competition, 29

Structure, generic meaning, 11; of the university, 70 ff.; capitalistic influences on, 80; strains in, 172.

Style of life, of academicians, 19; competition in, 144

Subordination and superordination, 72, 87

Subsidy, for graduate students, 21 ff.

Sumner, William G., 192

Supply and demand, and selection processes, 30

Symbols, and higher degrees, 38; of éclat, 65; of recognition, 70; attaching to achievement, 98; and income, 141; of scholarly prestige, 160, 168 ff.; limited possibilities of sharing, 173

System building, 207 f.

Taussig, F. W., 123

Teacher, connotations of word, 4; agencies, 50; performance, 178; types, 180; improvement, 183 ff.; status of, 191

Teachers colleges, government, 78

Teaching, role of, 101 f.; as a personal activity, 178; criteria, 180 ff.; and other functions, 186; and research, 189

Ten Hoor, Marten, 148 f.

Tension, sources of, 63, 217 ff.

Tenure and status, problems of, 60 ff.; defects in systems of, 67

Texas, University of, 165, 228 f.

Textbook production, 199 ff.

Theories, vested interests in, 207

Time budgets, 104 ff.

Turnover, see Metabolism

Tyndall, John, 202

Typological concept, meaning of, 7

Unemployed, the learned, 16

Unemployment and underemployment, 30

Universitas litterarum, 194

University, as a social system, 6 f.

University prestige, factors in, 158 ff.

Values and prestige, 173

Vanderbilt University, 230

Veblen, Thorstein, 81 f., 123 f., 169

Virginia, University of, 165, 228 f.

Von der Leyen, Friedrich, 210

Wagner, Albert M., 209

Waller, Willard, 29, 209

Ward, Jesse L., 103

Ward, Paul W., 77

Warren, Howard C., 91

Washington University, 198, 230

Washington, University of, 165, 228 f.

Watkin, Lawrence R., 147

Watson, David L., 124, 223 f.

Watson, J. B., 130

Weber, Max, 82

Wesleyan, 192

Wilkins, Ernest H., 71

Willey, Malcolm M., 23, 230

Williams, John P., 76

Wirth, Louis, 221

Wisconsin, University of, 6, 136, 159 ff., 162, 165, 172, 186, 198, 228 f.

Wishes for security and recognition, 112, 167

Women's colleges, government, 77

Women teachers, 137

Wood, Ben D., 17

Yale University, 6, 30, 130, 138, 159 ff., 162, 165, 172, 187, 198, 228 ff., 240

Zinsser, Hans, 206

Znaniecki, Florian, 136, 148, 191

Zook, George F., 29, 159